PERGAMON INTERNATIONAL LIBRARY
of Science, Technology, Engineering and Social Studies
The 1000-volume original paperback library in aid of education, industrial training and the enjoyment of leisure
Publisher: Robert Maxwell, M.C.

SECOND HOMES
Curse or Blessing?

PERGAMON OXFORD GEOGRAPHIES

General Editor: W. B. FISHER

Other Titles in the Series

CLARKE, J. I.
Population Geography, 2nd Edition

CLARKE, J. I.
Population Geography and the Developing Countries

CLOUT, H. D.
The Geography of Post War France: A Social and Economic Approach

CLOUT, H. D.
Rural Geography

COOKE, R. U. & JOHNSON, J. H.
Trends in Geography — An Introductory Survey

COPPOCK, J. T. & SEWELL, W. R. D.
Spatial Dimensions of Public Policy

DEWDNEY, J. C. A.
A Geography of the Soviet Union, 2nd Edition

GILCHRIST SHIRLAW, D. W.
An Agricultural Geography of Great Britain, 2nd revised impression

JOHNSON, J. H.
Urban Geography, 2nd Edition

KERR, A. J. C.
The Common Market and How It Works

McINTOSH, I. G. & MARSHALL, C. B.
The Face of Scotland, 3rd Edition

O'CONNOR, A. M.
The Geography of Tropical African Development

SUNDERLAND, E.
Elements of Human and Social Geography: Some Anthropological Perspectives

Other Titles of Interest

BLUNDEN, W. R.
The Land Use/Transport System

CHADWICK, G. F.
A Systems View of Planning

COWLING, T. M. & STEELEY, G. C.
Sub-Regional Planning Studies: An Evaluation

FALUDI, A.
A Reader in Planning Theory

Continued at back of book

SECOND HOMES

Curse or Blessing?

Edited by

J. T. COPPOCK

PERGAMON PRESS
OXFORD · NEW YORK · TORONTO · SYDNEY
PARIS · FRANKFURT

U.K.	Pergamon Press Ltd., Headington Hill Hall, Oxford OX3 0BW, England
U.S.A.	Pergamon Press Inc., Maxwell House, Fairview Park, Elmsford, New York 10523, U.S.A.
CANADA	Pergamon of Canada Ltd., 75 The East Mall, Toronto, Ontario, Canada
AUSTRALIA	Pergamon Press (Aust.) Pty. Ltd., 19a Boundary Street, Rushcutters Bay, N.S.W. 2011, Australia
FRANCE	Pergamon Press SARL, 24 Rue des Ecoles, 75240 Paris, Cedex 05, France
WEST GERMANY	Pergamon Press GmbH, 6242 Kronberg-Taunus, Pferdstrasse 1, Frankfurt-am-Main, West Germany

First edition 1977

Library of Congress Cataloging in Publication Data

Main entry under title:

Second homes.

(Pergamon Oxford geography series)
Includes index.
1. Second homes–Addresses, essays, lectures.
I. Coppock, John Terence.
HD7287.5.S37 1977 643 77-4070
ISBN 0-08-021371-5 (Hardcover)
ISBN 0-08-021370-7 (Flexicover)

In order to make this volume available as economically and rapidly as possible the author's typescript has been reproduced in its original form. This method unfortunately has its typographical limitations but it is hoped that they in no way distract the reader.

Printed in Great Britain by Butler & Tanner Ltd, Frome and London

CONTENTS

FIGURES

TABLES

PREFACE

This book arises from the growing concern expressed in many developed countries over the growth in the number of second homes, a concern which is partly due to greater environmental awareness, partly to a widespread trend towards greater social equality and a consequent resentment that some might have two or more homes when others were inadequately housed or had no home at all, and partly to a growing sense of nationalism, especially among smaller nations whose more articulate members at least feel threatened by a dominant, often wealthier culture which expresses itself, among other ways, in the acquisition or construction of second homes. At the same time there are social pressures to acquire a second home which, once the privilege of the very rich and still owned by only a small minority, is now being sought and obtained by a much wider spectrum of society; like the colour television set and the second car, the second home may move from the category of luxury to that of social necessity.

Because, in its modern manifestation, it is generally a fairly recent phenomenon, little is known about and most governments do not collect statistics on second homes, though there may be as many as ten million; understandably, too, owners of second homes tend to be secretive about their properties. At the same time, and partly in consequence, prejudices and myths abound. Scotland, for example, is thought to have been invaded on a large scale by the English middle class, though the available evidence shows that owners of second homes in Scotland are much more likely to be citizens of Edinburgh and Glasgow or elsewhere in the Lowlands, and second homes account for only some 2 per cent of the housing stock in Ross and Cromarty and some 3 per cent in Inverness-shire. Yet the feeling persists and could lead a correspondent to a Glasgow paper to write 'It is not the black, black oil which will destroy the Western Highlands but the white, white settlers'.

While second homes are eagerly sought or bitterly resented, they are not well understood and will require research by workers in many disciplines, including architecture, ecology, economics, geography, planning, psychology and sociology. This volume presents a selection of what is known and, since the contributors are mainly geographers with research interests in the field of outdoor recreation, there is a fairly marked emphasis on the spatial dimension. The book is broadly divided into discussions of second homes in various countries and analyses of specific aspects of second homes, more particularly within a British context. The final chapter is based upon contributions given at a conference on second homes which epitomises the variety of interests and attitudes involved.

ACKNOWLEDGEMENTS

In all edited books the editor is in the hands of his contributors, and I am grateful to mine for keeping to deadlines and responding promptly to queries. Chapter 9 is based on a paper delivered at the ANZAAS Congress in Perth, Australia, in 1973. Chapter 10 is in part based, with permission, on an unpublished paper presented to a symposium on second homes at the annual conference of the Institute of British Geographers in January 1974. Chapter 13 is based in part on an article by Dr. Ragatz which first appeared in Vacation housing and recreation land development, edited by K.L. Bernhardt (Institute of Science and Technology, University of Michigan, 1973), and I am grateful for permission to include this. Chapter 14 is based largely on tape recordings of a conference of the Town Country Planning Association held in Birmingham on 1 May 1974. The recording was made by R.C. Swift of the Department of Geography, University of Birmingham, to whom I am most grateful, as I am to David Hall, Director of the Association, and to the speakers, though the responsibility for interpreting their remarks is wholly mine. Dr. Gardavasky's chapter has been translated from Czech by Frank Carter and Hugh Clout, both of University College, London, to whom special thanks are due. The maps and illustrations have been drawn mainly by Carson Clark, chief cartographer in the Department of Geography, University of Edinburgh, while those in Chapters 4, 5 and 8 have been drawn by Miss C. Hill and K. Wass respectively; many pairs of hands have typed the manuscripts, but the typescript produced in this book is the work of Mrs. Mona Robertson. I am grateful to all of these people. As always, I am indebted to my wife for much reading of drafts and checking of typescripts, and for helping to improve the readability of the text.

Unexpected delays in a period in which publication has become increasingly difficult owing to rapidly rising costs and problems over cash flows have unfortunately increased the inevitable gap between writing and publication, though neither the authors nor the present publishers bear any responsibility; fortunately, changes since have been relatively minor and the general picture of second homes remains much as it was when these contributions were written. Upward trends in Great Britain have been sharply reversed; but, as Michael Dower points out, this situation provides a breathing space for such thinking (p.163).

August, 1976 J.T. Coppock

Chapter 1

SECOND HOMES IN PERSPECTIVE

J. T. Coppock

There is little doubt that the second home, vacation home, summer cottage, *bach*, *whare*, *wochendhaus*, or whatever the local name may be, is an aspect of the leisure/recreation/tourism field which is of growing political and academic importance. Yet a decade ago very few people in the United Kingdom would have recognised the term *second home* and the phenomenon appeared to be of little public significance. Even now, the literature on second homes in the United Kingdom is very scanty, with a handful of academic publications and a growing number of reports produced by local authorities, all dating from 1972 or later.

Elsewhere, as in Scandinavia and North America, there is a much stronger tradition of owning a summer or vacation cottage, and academic studies go back at least to the 1930s. Such residences are accepted as part of the rural scene (see, for example, Black 1950 and Mead 1958). Even in these countries, the literature that is publicly available in printed form is relatively sparse, though it has been growing rapidly, stimulated by the forces that have led to a massive expansion of outdoor recreation generally. Numerous reports by planning and other consultants and by public planning agencies, usually in mimeographed form, deal with the topic to greater or lesser degree: Colin Campbell's 1967 report to ARDA on second homes in the Georgian lowlands of British Columbia and Richard Brown's 1970 study of the economic impact of second-home communities are examples. France (INSEE 1963) and the United States (1969) are among the few countries which collect and publish information on second homes derived from their periodic censuses, though the data must be treated with caution since a great deal depends on the definitions used. Yet even in these countries, the topic has been neglected. For example, the massive reviews of the Outdoor Recreation Resources Review Commission in the United States do not deal with it and second homes are owned by only about 5 per cent of all households in that country (Ragatz 1974, p.34), while in Canada visits to second homes accounted for only some 5 per cent of vacation trips in the late 1960s (Traveldata, quoted in Baker 1973). Nor are there many academic contributions, as Roy Wolfe noted in his review of recreation research (1964).

Nevertheless, there is rapidly growing interest throughout the western world, for which there are three principal reasons. The first derives from the growth in outdoor recreation generally, which seems to have been one of the fastest growing sectors of the economy in many developed countries and of which the increase in numbers of second homes is part. Secondly, the environmental revolution has made both the public and governments more aware of the need for environmental quality and of problems of conservation and pollution, so that aspects of second-home development, such as loss of visual amenity or inadequate waste disposal, which would previously have been passively accepted, now arouse public protest. Thirdly, considerable publicity has been given to dramatised conflicts between owners of second homes and others, especially where the protagonists are (or are thought to be) from different ethnic groups or of different nationalities, as with the Welsh and the English or Canadians and Americans; possibly, too, a greater social awareness of actual or perceived injustices and a willingness to take direct action in protest are important contributory factors.

The Definition of Second Homes

Rational analysis of the problems posed by second homes is hindered by the existence of stereotypes in a field in which definition is difficult and facts scarce. Problems of definition arise primarily from the fact that second homes do not constitute a discrete type, sharply distinguished from other kinds of accommodation, but form a somewhat arbitrarily identified group within a continuum. The dynamic character of the second home, in particular the changing relationship between the first and second home, also makes identification and measurement difficult. At the one extreme is mobile accommodation, the tent and touring caravan or trailer, which are not generally regarded as second homes though they fulfil many of the same functions, and, at the other, the large country house which serves as an occasional residence but is permanently staffed; but there are many other doubtful categories. Some authorities consider static caravans as second homes, but others do not, since they can be, and often are, moved at the end of the season and are not generally regarded as part of the housing stock. On some criteria, the chalet gardens of European cities might be considered as second homes, since 'it is the general practice for the whole family to remain on its chalet garden throughout the summer weekends and often for the duration of the school holidays' (Departmental Committee 1969, p.250); yet they do not appear to be considered as second homes in official figures although there are some 15,000 in Copenhagen alone (p. 242).

Ownership is sometimes implied as a criterion, but although ownership may be the norm, not all functional second homes are owned; in France in 1967, for example, some 16 per cent of second homes were jointly owned and a further 12 per cent were rented (LeRoux 1968, p.5, quoted in Clout 1969, p.440). Second homes may also be used by others, and it is debatable at what point these should more properly be regarded as rented holiday accommodation; in the United States, for example, between a quarter and a third of all second homes are let at some time during the year (Ragatz and Gelb 1970, p.61), and in France about half a million households used the second home of a friend or relative (LeRoux p.5). A further 1.2 million French households use the primary residences of relatives as their second homes (LeRoux p.5), and although these dwellings would presumably not qualify, it is more debatable whether the households would be regarded as occupiers of second homes.

Other debatable categories include holiday homes, hobby farms, retirement homes and recreational holdings. Holiday homes, often at seaside resorts, may be in exclusive use, but more commonly they may be let for varying periods of the year (Barbier 1966). Marsden's study of the Queensland coast illustrates their complexity (1969, pp.57-8). He recognised four categories of holiday home, which he defined as immobile, unserviced supplementary accommodation: (1) private holiday homes, often visited at the weekend and on holidays by the family and non-paying guests; (2) intermittently commercial holiday homes, which are used as (1), but are let at high season to defray costs; (3) intermittently private holiday homes, often purchased for retirement but meanwhile let as (4) apart from occasional family use; and (4) commercial holiday homes, owned as an investment and usually let and managed by an agent. Hobby farms are characteristically located around large cities but also occur in areas of attractive scenery. They may be run by a manager or worked part-time, depending on their size and the inclinations of the owner, and may similarly be a permanent home or a weekend retreat. Some of these might properly be regarded as second homes, and the weekend hobby farms, which are appearing on 50 acre (20 ha) blocks around Australian cities, certainly would (Robertson 1974). Second homes may also be bought with a view to becoming first homes on retirement, perhaps passing through a phase in which the owner is in semi-retirement and the length and frequency of his visits gradually increase until the second home becomes unambiguously the first. Finally, it is open to debate whether the recreational holdings, now a marked feature of both the United States and Australia, should properly be considered as incipient second homes; some 625,000 plots are being sold each year in the United States, about six times the rate of second homes, but in California only 3 per cent of the plots sold in the decade before 1971 had houses built on them and on sample estates in Florida the ratio was 70,000 to 1 (Reilly 1973, p.250). Much of this land is bought as an investment or for speculation, but on other plots the intention of building a second home may have been frustrated by the cost of bringing services.

Clearly the definition adopted will affect the number of second homes identified and, by the inclusion or exclusion of particular classes of accommodation with distinctive spatial distributions, the geography of second homes. The distribution might include many properties on the urban fringe, where they grade into the first homes of commuters; it might include holiday resorts and predominantly holiday accommodation; or it might be confined largely to areas of poor land and scattered population. For present purposes, the definition of second homes in England and Wales used by Peter Downing and Michael Dower (1973), that a second home 'is a property owned or rented on a long lease as the occasional residence of a household that usually lives elsewhere', is sufficiently general to provide a useful starting point.

Non-Recreational Second Homes

Although current interest in second homes is concerned with those used primarily for outdoor recreation, there are other kinds of second homes. The Downing/Dower definition could of course apply to many forms of seasonal housing, such as those associated with transhumance in mountainous regions. Transhumance is now of minor importance in Europe (although the associated seasonal shelters may now serve as second homes), but seasonal movements between homes are still widespread in the tropics, especially in Africa; in southwest Nigeria, for example, many farmers have a town house, where they spend much of the dry season when work is at a minimum on the farms and a good deal of time is spent on social activities, and a house or houses on their farm or farms, which may be as far as 100 miles (160 km) away (Oluwasanmi 1967, pp.30-2). The suitcase farmer of the American wheatlands provides a contemporary example of a similar relationship in the developed world which results from mechanisation and specialisation in farming; for he will possess a farmstead where he spends some time during the preparation of the land, sowing and harvesting, and a town house, some distance away, with perhaps also a vacation home in California or Florida, to which he retreats in winter (Kollmorgen and Jenks 1958).

The urban *pied-à-terre* in the large city shows a similar relationship to a permanent home, except that occupation is weekly rather than seasonal.

Here, as in the agricultural context, it is the *first* home which provides the opportunity for rest and relaxation, the *pied-à-terre* being related primarily to the needs of work and intended to reduce the inconvenience and strain of commuting.

The Antecedents of Modern Second Homes

Although widespread interest in second homes is comparatively recent, they have a long history. A seasonal migration from urban to rural residence has long been a feature of high society, with ritualised movements from one to the other, accompanied by servants and more portable belongings, marking the beginning and end of the *season*. The large country houses of the rich were certainly serving this kind of function in the post-medieval period, particularly in areas within reasonable travelling distance of London and Paris, though which was the first and which the second home is a matter for debate; for those primarily interested in their landed estates, the country house might be the first home, but for those involved in affairs of state, the town house would have had priority.

Of course, second homes for the rich have a much longer ancestry. They were certainly a feature of ancient Egypt and of classical Rome, and wealthy Romans might have as many as fifteen *second* homes or villas, among which they chose the one that was most pleasant at a given time of the year (Friedlaender 1889, vol.2, pp.201-2). Like the second homes of the modern period and unlike those of pre-industrial Europe, where the magnificent country house or chateau was usually associated with a rural estate, many of these villas were sited on the coast or near other bodies of water. Lake Como was ringed with villas, the Tiber was said to be lined with more villas then any other river in the world and, according to Seneca, 'there was no lake on which the roofs of villas of the Roman great were not prominent, no stream that was not bordered by their buildings' (Friedlaender, pp.201-2). Even more popular were the coastal resorts; from the Gulf of Spezia to beyond the Gulf of Salerno the eastern shore of Italy was lined with villas, though the greatest concentration was on the Gulf of Naples (Friedlaender, pp.112, 206).

The immediate predecessor of the modern concept of a second home is probably the shooting box of Victorian Britain and the summer cottage of the Atlantic coast of North America (which in turn had many affinities with the coastal villas of the Romans). The shooting box, associated particularly with the stalking of deer and the shooting of driven grouse, was often a substantial dwelling to which the name *lodge* seems inappropriate, as was that of *cottage* applied to the luxurious mansions of American millionaires at Newport, Rhode Island, and at other points along the Atlantic seaboard. In fact, rich members of society might, like their Roman ancestors, have several *second homes*, each serving a somewhat different function. The British Royal Family, with Buckingham Palace, Windsor Castle, Sandringham and Balmoral Castle, probably provides the best-known British example, and one which largely epitomises the tastes and interests of the nineteenth century; the several houses of ex-President Nixon, ranging from the White House, through Camp David and Key Biscayne, to San Clemente, fulfilled similar functions, but were more typical, in character and location, of modern tastes. The great majority of second homes are, of course, much more modest in concept and have a humbler ancestry which Roy Wolfe describes in a Canadian context in the next chapter (see also Wolfe, 1962).

The Distribution of Second Homes

The second home used for leisure purposes is widely found throughout Europe and the lands of European settlement, though it is not possible to give any firm quantitative estimate, since figures are not available for all countries and those which exist must be interpreted with caution. France was reputed to have the largest number of second homes in Europe, with 1,232,000 in 1968 (Clout 1970, p.108), followed by Sweden with 490,000 in 1971 (Chap. 3); Great Britain had around 200,000 built second homes (Chap. 7 and Aitkin 1974), Norway 170,000 in 1969 and Denmark 140,000 in 1966 (Chap. 3). The major gap was the lack of data on West Germany, but since only 1 per cent of vacation was estimated to have been spent by city dwellers in second homes around 1960 (Clout 1974, p.105), the number is probably not large, although problems of measurement are likely to be difficult: many industrial Germans and other city workers still retain an agricultural base, and chalet gardens are also important. A not implausible guess at a total for Western Europe might be about three million in 1970, though numbers are rising fast.

Second homes do not, at first glance, seem likely to be a significant feature of life in eastern Europe, where levels of car ownership are much lower and there is much public provision for leisure; but there is scattered and often impressionistic evidence that they are widespread, though probably less numerous than in western Europe. As V. Gardavasky (1960) shows in Chapter 5, there are some 166,000 second homes in Czechoslovakia and there were estimated to be about 3,000 in Slovenia and West Istria in 1967 (Jersic 1968, p.67). Inquiries among those who know the countries well suggest that second homes are also common in Hungary, Poland and the Soviet Union. Extrapolation of the Czechoslovakian data to the whole of eastern Europe would give a figure of some three million, but this is probably much too high; second homes were apparently owned by only 0.7 per cent of Slovenian non-peasant households in 1967, and if this ratio was applied to eastern Europe, it would yield a total of about one million (Jersic, p.67).

There are probably more second homes in North America than in Western Europe. The total for the United States in 1970 was estimated at three million, particularly in the states of the north east (Ragatz 1969), thus broadly reflecting the distribution of population, for the proportion of the population owning second homes did not vary greatly from state to state; over half the national total was in ten states, though their distribution is becoming more dispersed (Clout 1972, p.396). In Canada there were probably half a million second homes, again broadly distributed between the provinces in proportion to population, with some three-quarters of all second homes in Ontario and Quebec (Baker, pp.5,7). Residents of North America are also the main customers for second homes in the Caribbean (Chap. 6).

Second homes are certainly a feature of the areas occupied by whites in South Africa and are common in Australia and New Zealand, particularly in coastal areas; they also occur in many if not all the countries of Latin America, though numbers are likely to be small. There are estimated to be some quarter of a million second homes in Australia, owned by a rather larger proportion of households than in the United States (Robertson and Chap. 9); no data have been discovered for New Zealand and white areas of South Africa, but, given their respective populations, the numbers of second homes cannot be large, even on the likely assumption that the proportions of these populations with access to a second home is high.

The importance of second homes elsewhere is largely a matter of speculation. While second homes certainly exist in Japan, they do not appear to be common, and are certainly much less numerous than the Japanese population and its standard of living would suggest. In part this may be due to the rapidity of its recent economic growth and the strong links that still bind present generations to farming communities, so that visits to relatives probably play much the same role. It seems highly unlikely that, except for official residences, second homes are of any importance in China, and while wealthy citizens, politicians and senior officials thoughout the developing world may well have more than one home, the total number must be small. In all, a world total of about 10 million would not be an unreasonable estimate.

Second homes are, of course, not evenly distributed thoughout these countries; the great majority appear to be on the coasts, in the mountains and near large cities. The main controlling factors appear to be: the distance from major centres of population; the quality and character of the landscape; the presence of sea, rivers or lakes; the presence of other recreational resources; the availability of land; and the climates of the importing and exporting region.

While accessibility must depend on levels of car ownership, on the quality of roads and on the density of the road network, the great majority of second homes appear to be within 100-150 miles (160-240 km) of major population centres. Even in the United States, where personal mobility is high, and state and inter-state freeways minimise the frictions of space, two-thirds of second homes were in the same state as the primary home and over half were within 100 miles (160 km) of the first home (Clout 1972, p.397), though there were wide differences around the mean. In Michigan, where 34 per cent of a sample of second homes were within 100 miles of the first home, 36 per cent were 200 or more miles (320 km) away and 6 per cent were 500 or more miles (800 km) from the first home (Tombaugh 1970, p.57). There is also evidence of regional differences, with westerners, who are used to driving long distances, travelling further than easterners (Clout 1972, p.397). In Australia, the distribution of distances resembles that found in Michigan (Chap. 9), but in Europe (and to a certain extent in eastern North America) distances are generally shorter, reflecting in part the high densities of population, the more compact settlements and generally the less developed network of trunk roads. Evidence from Sweden, for example, suggests that some 80-90 per cent of owners live within 60 km (38 miles) of their second homes (Chap. 3).

Scenic quality has been shown to be a factor in several studies (though the classification of scenery is itself a controversial topic) and its importance is emphasised by the fact that nearer, though uninteresting, landscapes are often bypassed in favour of more distant but scenically more attractive ones. Landscape is also closely related to opportunities for those kinds of recreation which require particular natural resources, such as skiing and rock climbing, and many second homes are located in such areas. The sea and bodies of inland water exert a very powerful influence, not only as a very important component of scenery and a necessary ingredient in nearly all landscapes of the highest quality, but also because they are essential for a wide range of recreational activities, especially fishing, one of the most popular of all forms of active recreation. A high proportion of all second homes are either on the coast or around the shores of lakes; the Michigan survey, for example, showed that 89 per cent of all second homes in a sample were within 5 minutes walk of a body of water (Tombaugh, p.56), and over 70 per cent of those in England and Wales were in coastal districts (Bielckus et al. p.32). This, however, is a factor which many developers now realise can be man-made (Clout 1971, p.549), and one development company in North America has specified as a necessary condition a scenically attractive site or one suitable for the construction of a man-made lake of at least 200 acres (80 ha) (Parsons 1972, p.4).

The availability of land is also important. In North America, where population densities are low by European standards, planning controls often weak (especially in the United States) and large areas of land remain that are both undeveloped and undevelopable for any kind of intensive agriculture, land as such does not present an obstacle; indeed, one of the many land-use problems is the scale on which land is being sold as recreational plots (Reilly). In Canada, where much of the undeveloped land is Crown land and there are large areas which have reverted from agriculture, the quantity of suitable land is vast. In Europe, on the other hand, where most land is already occupied and used for agriculture or forestry, population density is high and planning controls often strict, the availability of land on which second homes would be permitted is often a limiting factor; there is much less point in speculation where there is little prospect of land being released (though it is interesting to note that a London property company, which is seeking permission to develop an estate in Caithness as a leisure centre with luxury housing, sold half the one-acre plots within three months (*The Scotsman* 20th August 1974). Attitudes of landowners may also be important; those owning large estates may be unwilling to sell either properties or land for second homes. Much of the land within weekend access of the large cities of Europe is used for intensive agriculture and does not lend itself to the construction of second homes, which can be acquired only by buying existing properties, whether they be surplus to rural needs or bought on the open market in competition with prospective buyers of first homes.

The role of climate in the location of second homes depends in part on the purpose which they are intended to serve and is important chiefly where summer or winter climates are sufficiently unpleasant to provide a strong incentive to escape them. This kind of relationship has already been noted in classical Rome, but the stereotype is perhaps the numerous residences built by European colonisers to escape the humid heat of the tropics, such as the hill stations in India (though these were generally governmental rather than privately owned). In similar fashion the rich citizens of Rio de Janeiro escape to second homes on the hills around, and those from Guayaquil retreat to the foothills of the Andes. The desire to escape the rigours of northern winters has long provided an incentive for the building of second homes along the coasts of California and Florida or along the Côte d' Azur in Mediterranean France. More recently, a growing interest in winter sports has increased the attraction of a second home in areas where the climate would previously have been a marked handicap.

The Characteristics of Second Homes

The generic term *second home* covers a very wide range of types, the limits of which will depend on the definition adopted. If caravans (trailers) are excluded, second homes range from a shack built by the owner on the coast near Auckland though an adapted barn or seter, a well-built farm cottage or steading, a prefabricated house and the palatial mansions of Newport, Rhode Island, to contemporary dwellings indistinguishable in size and appointments from first homes. It might even be a chalet in a chalet garden, costing a few hundred pounds and lacking all services (Departmental Committee pp.249-50). A major distinction can be made between those second homes which are adaptations of pre-existing structures, whether these were residences or not, and those which have been newly built as second homes. In Europe the former predominate, both because agricultural reorganisation and rural depopulation have released large numbers of dwellings, and because the acquisition of an existing property has often been the only way in which a second home of some kind could be obtained or, alternatively, represented the only use to which an uninhabited property could be put. Such properties are often of stone or brick, though there are many wooden ones, particularly in Scandinavia; some examples are shown in the report on Denbighshire (Jacobs). In North America, Australia and generally outside Europe, the great majority of second homes have been constructed for that purpose, whether by the owner to his own design or from prefabricated parts, or erected by a builder or construction firm. Roy Wolfe describes characteristic Ontario summer cottages in Chapter 2, while an indication of the nature of holiday homes on part of Queensland's Sunshine Coast is given by B.J. Tatnell (1967, quoted in Marsden, pp.69-70). Proportions of temporary structures (including shacks and garages) ranged from 22 per cent to nil in different localities, while those of small permanent structures (fewer than four rooms) ranged from 35 per cent to 4 per cent. A majority had walls and roofs of fibro-cement, which was resistant and easily used by amateur builders; more elaborate material was said to invite vandalism. Increasing proportions of new-built second homes are on estates, with electricity, less frequently piped water and much less frequently sewerage (Ragatz and Gelb, p.52). There is, however, some convergence between trends in Europe and North America. In the latter, trends towards both farm enlargement and the abandonment of marginal land have similarly released a stock of existing dwellings for use as second homes, though a study in Ontario showed that about three-quarters of the houses had disappeared by the time of survey (Noble 1962), a reflection presumably of their size, construction and condition. In Europe, on the other hand, a decline in the supply of suitable buildings, together with a burgeoning demand, has led to an increased demand for built second homes.

Availability is not, of course, the only consideration. Many rural residences are not of a kind which makes them attractive to potential purchasers, either because they are too small or too poorly constructed or because they are in the wrong place; thus, in South America, where the market for second homes has been primarily among the rich and upper middle class, the quality of surplus rural dwellings has generally been too poor for them to be used as second homes. Similarly, while tight planning control has generally made any kind of property acceptable in the United Kingdom, there is surplus rural housing which is not greatly sought after, as in the arable areas of eastern Scotland where it consists of blocks of cottages adjacent to a farmstead. In other places, even ruins have been sought, though it is a matter of dispute whether there is any entitlement to re-erect a dwelling on the site of a derelict house; the Ulster Countryside Committee (1972, pp.23-4) has suggested guidelines to local authorities for applications to replace or reconstruct an existing dwelling.

The Function of Second Homes

Relatively little is known, other than by inference, of the reasons why people acquire homes and what they do with them, and finding out may well prove difficult. The reasons are also likely to vary from country to country, though the widespread occurrence of second homes in cultures as diverse as those of the Soviet Union and the United States, and in environments as different as those of Finland and Queensland, suggests that there are also underlying common causes. It seems reasonable to suppose that in countries such as Australia and New Zealand with a climate which, if not always pleasant, is at least tolerable out of doors throughout the year and with a tradition of *the great outdoors*, the acquisition of a second home in locations where such physical activities as swimming and boating could be practised would be a popular use of disposable income. In highly urbanised communities, where a high proportion of the population lives in flats or apartments rather than in houses with spacious gardens, there might also be a strong incentive to acquire a second home, as open space, although Roy Wolfe noted that in Toronto it was those who were most generously provided with greenery and space in the cities who had the highest proportion of summer cottages (Chap. 2). In Sweden, which has the highest incidence of second homes, two-thirds of the owners of such homes live in flats, a form of living which may make a second home not only more desirable but easier to manage (Chap. 3). The quality and quantity of urban open space is also likely to be factor. Nevertheless, whatever the effect of local and regional circumstances or the strength of desire for a second home, there seems to be fairly general agreement that a major motivation in the acquisition of a rural second home is the desire to escape the pressures of city life, a conclusion which is supported by the rise in the proportion of second-home owners with increasing size of settlement (Clout 1969, p.441). In a more local role, in a study of second homes in British Columbia, C.I. Campbell found that 38 per cent of respondents gave *to relax* as their main motive, and 31 per cent *to get away from the city* (1967, Fig. B1). Other major motives are the wish to participate in some activity which demands access to rural resources, a desire to renew or maintain links with a rural area from which the owner or his relatives originated; to provide a place for holidays; as an investment; to confer status; and to provide a place for retirement. Motivations are also likely to change with the life cycle, particularly as between a family with young children, a family with older children, a middle-aged couple without children, and a retired couple; thus, a home which is acquired primarily as a place for holiday may come in time to be regarded as a potential place for retirement.

Two aspects of the use of second homes are particularly relevant: the amount of time occupiers spend in their second homes and the way they use their time. From what has been said about problems of definition, it will be clear that the former will show a wide range of variation, from a few days on one occasion each year, though use for annual holidays and at weekends in summer and regular weekend use throughout the year, to permanent occupation, the cut-off point for the latter being a matter of debate; a great deal will depend on accessibility and the extent to which second homes are let to or used by others apart from the owner and his family. A mean figure of 53 days has been estimated for the United States (Clout 1972, p.395), compared with a value of about 90 days in England and Wales (Bielckus *et al.*, p.55). Values are, however, widely distributed about the mean: 28 per cent of second homes in the United States were occupied for less than 30 days and 6 per cent for 180 days and over, and in England and Wales 12 per cent were used for more than 150 days (Bielckus *et al.*, p.55). Some 79 per cent of second homes in England and Wales (Bielckus *et al.*, p.53) and half of those in Sweden (Chap. 3) were used both at weekends and for holidays; figures in the United States are not strictly comparable, but only 40 per cent were used throughout the year (Clout 1972, p.395). In evaluating these figures, it would be helpful to know their equivalents in visitor days, for accommodation may be used for the same period with varying degrees of intensiveness and this will probably depend on the composition of groups using second homes. In the United States owners of second homes were older on average than the population as a whole, and one-or two-person households formed the principal group at the time of survey, though there is evidence that younger families are acquiring second homes (Clout 1972, p.395). In Australia, Robertson's survey suggests that families with school age or older children predominate (Chap. 9). One notable feature of the occupation of second homes in Canada and Scandinavia is their use by virtually the whole family during the long summer school holiday, with father living in the first house and coming to the second home at weekends. In France, the near universal tradition of a long summer holiday in August for all workers similarly makes for intensive use of second homes.

No comprehensive study has been made of the use made of leisure time spent at second homes, though some information is available from a number of local investigations. For example, in Caernarvonshire, according to information provided by respondents, walking and riding were the most important recreational activities, followed by beach-and boat-based activities and then by sightseeing and touring, with apparently two-fifths of activities taking place in the immediate vicinity of the second home (Pyne, pp.20, 87). In Denbighshire, walking was again the most important activity, followed by car trips, gardening, fishing and relaxing (Jacobs, p.29). In British Columbia, where respondents provided information about their use of time throughout the 24 hours, 11.8 hours were spent inside the cottage, 5.6 hours around the lot, 2.3 hours on the beach, 2.6 hours in or on the water and 1.6 hours on the shore (Campbell, pp.21-2); of the time devoted to recreation, 29.4 per cent was spent swimming, 19.4 per cent boating and 8.6 per cent on the upkeep and improvement of the cottage. No information was collected on activity in Australia, but the great majority of respondents gave water-based activities, such as boating, fishing, swimming and surfing, as their principal recreational reasons for acquiring a second home (Chap. 9).

A great deal is likely to depend on the social, economic and demographic characteristics of the occupants, as well as on the physical features of the area where the second home is located. Those who intend to retire to their second homes, who constitute an appreciable proportion of all respondents in surveys where this information has been sought, will probably devote much of their time to preparing the home and garden (if any), whereas the young are more likely to engage in active recreation. The most striking, though readily appreciated, fact which emerges from surveys is the correlation, generally strong, between ownership of second homes and occupational groups, levels of education and income; thus in France, 41 per cent of second homes in 1964 were owned by employers, professionals and administrators (Clout 1969, p.440), and in the United States in 1967 one half of second homes were owned by households with an income of more than $10,000 (Clout 1972, p.395). Nevertheless, there seems to have been a fairly marked diffusion of ownership among middle- and lower-income groups in the postwar period.

Problems of Second Homes

Increased personal mobility, through higher rates of car ownership, higher disposable real income and greater leisure time have all led to increased demands for second homes. In England and Wales a threefold increase in numbers of built properties by 1985 has been suggested (Chap. 7), numbers are expected to double in the United States by 1980 (Clout 1972, p.400), and even in France, where the proportions are already eight times as high as in Great Britain, numbers are expected to double by the end of the century (Goss 1973, p.45). As the supply of more accessible properties diminishes, prices rise and prospective purchasers look further afield, a trend which often brings them into conflict with others. At the same time, what may have been tolerable on a small scale becomes intolerable when numbers increase sharply, especially when there is a greater awareness of the environmental consequences of such developments. In Europe, in particular, there is concern about the social and, to a lesser extent, about the ecological effects of the growing number of second homes. Planning controls are strongly developed in some countries, such as Denmark, Sweden and the United Kingdom, but even tight planning control cannot avoid the social frictions which acquisitions of existing properties create (the more so as the market for first and second homes cannot easily be separated). Control over new properties is easier and in Sweden, as Chapter 3 shows, development within 300 m (330 yds) of the coast or within one hour's driving of Stockholm has been forbidden and proper waste disposal is demanded. In metropolitan France, on the other hand, competition for second homes has diminished the housing stock available for rent by farm workers, and occupiers of weekend accommodation impose additional costs on local communes in refuse collection and the like without apparently bringing any benefits in return (Clout 1974, pp.119-20). Similar effects on the supply of housing have been alleged in the remoter parts of Great Britain. In the United States, the lack of planning controls, the ease with which zoning ordinances can be altered, the dominant role of speculators and developers, and the predominance of built second homes have placed more emphasis on the environmental effects of second homes and on the disadvantages of widespread recreational subdivision of land. In California, soil erosion and pollution of streams have been attributed to such subdivision; the California Environmental Quality Study Council has estimated that 37 per cent of stream mileage in the Sierra Nevada has been damaged by residential subdivision (Reilly, p.277), which a representative of the Sierra Club has described as the greatest menace to the Sierra Nevada since placer mining (Parsons, p.7). The creation of fenced and guarded recreational communities is also placing obstacles in the way of public access to land (Parsons, p.8, Clout 1974, p.400). Legislation has been introduced in some states and advertising in inter-state commerce is now subject to supervision by the Department of Housing and Urban Development (Reilly, p.270).

This book is primarily about such problems, particularly about those in Europe. While there is an emphasis on Great Britain, an attempt is made to place the British experience in context by examining the situation in other countries. The main objective is to look at the scale of the problem, since probably one of the most urgent needs is for soundly-based facts on which policies can be based.

All the available evidence suggests that the demand for second homes will grow, though in Sweden an apparent flattening in the growth curve and increased use of caravans (Chap. 3) raises the question, explored in Chapter 8, of the extent to which different kinds of holiday accommodation can be substituted for each other. In some countries there is certainly a large unsatisfied demand; a survey in Houston in 1968 showed that, although only 5 per cent of the sample currently owned a second home, as many as 41 per cent would like to, though admittedly half of those thought they had little or no chance of achieving this ambition and only about one-quarter thought their chances fairly good or very good (Ragatz and Gelb, p.61). Nevertheless, the vast gap between the levels of second-home ownership in France and Sweden and those in other countries provides some indication of the potential for growth. At the same time, there appears to be a widespread trend towards self-catering holidays which require accommodation of a second-home type, though not necessarily in sole occupation, and there is some development of such accommodation for short lets only, as in the Forestry Commission's chalets in Perthshire. There also appears to be a trend towards greater use of second homes within easy reach of the cities, a trend which will be strengthened by any shortening of the working week, and hence a diminishing distinction between first and second homes (a problem which Danish and Swedish planners have tried to meet by prohibiting second homes close to cities). Indeed, the task force sponsored by the Rockefeller Brothers Fund, which has considered these questions in a chapter entitled *Subdividing the Great Outdoors*, has recommended that recreational homes should be required to satify the same environmental and land-use standards that are to apply to first homes (Reilly, p.278). There are prospects of almost continuous holiday accommodation and second homes along the Mediterranean coast of Europe (Hall 1973, p.218) and of widely-dispersed cities in North America which would resemble those foreseen more than seventy years ago by H.G. Wells (1902, p.57). Neither need happen, though paradoxically many rich Americans now live at greater densities in expensive recreational communities than they normally experience in their spacious suburban first homes (Clout 1972, p.401). Effective solutions depend on understanding what is happening, on seeing second homes in the wider context of leisure time and the total pattern of living, and on devising effective policies which do not solve one problem only to create others.

REFERENCES

Aitkin, R. (1974) Personal communication

Baker, W.M. (1973) The Nature and Extent of Vacation Home Data Sources and Research in Canada, Statistics Canada, Ottawa.

Barbier, B. (1965) 'Logements de vacances et résidences secondaires dans le Sud-Est méditerranéen', Bulletin de L'Association Géographes Français 344-5, 2-11.

Bielckus, C.L., Rogers, A.W. and Wibberley, G.P. (1972) Second Homes in England and Wales, Studies in Rural Land Use, 11, Wye College (University of London)

Black, J.D. (1950) The Rural Economy of New England, Cambridge, Mass.

Brown, R.N. (1970) Economic Impact of Second Home Communities, Economic Research Service, U.S. Dept. of Agric., Washington, D.C.

Campbell, C.I. (1967) An Analysis of Summer Cottaging in the Georgia Lowland of British Columbia, Report for ARDA, Vancouver B.C.

Carstensen, H. (1965) 'Bau-und planungsrechtliche Probleme zum Wochendhaus: Dargestellt am Beispiel Schleswig-Holstein', Raumforschung und Raumordnung 23, 29-32; see also note in Landscape 15 (1965), p.8.

Clout, H.D. (1969) 'Second homes in France', Journal of the Town Planning Institute, 55, pp.440-3.

Clout, H.D. (1970) 'Social aspects of second-home occupation in the Auvergne', Planning Outlook, 9, pp.33-49.

Clout, H.D. (1971) 'Second homes in the Auvergne' Geographical Review 61, pp.530-33.

Clout, H.D. (1972) 'Second homes in the United States', Tijdschrift voor Economische en Sociale Geografie 63, pp.393-401.

Clout, H.D. (1974) 'The growth of second-home ownership: an example of personal suburbanization', Ch.6 in Johnson, J.H. (ed) Suburban Growth, Wiley, London.

Departmental Committee of Inquiry into Allotments (1969) Report, Cmnd.4166, HMSO, London.

Downing, P. and Dower, M. (1973) Second Homes in England and Wales, Countryside Commission, HMSO, London.

Friedlaender, L. (1889) Darstellung aus Sittengeschichte Roms Vol.2, 6th ed., Leipzig.

Gardavasky, V. (1960) 'Recreational hinterland of a city taking Prague as an example', Acta Universitatis Carolinae: Geographica 1, pp.3-29.

Goss, A. (1973) 'A site for second homes', Built Environment 2, pp.451-3.

Hall, J.M. (1973) 'Europe's seaside: a landscape of leisure', Built Environment 2, pp.215-8.

INSEE, (1963) Recensement de 1962: Population Légale et Statistiques Communales Complémentaires, Institut National de la Statistique et des Études Économiques, Paris.

Jacobs, C.A.J. (1972) Second Homes in Denbighshire, Tourism and Recreation Research Report No. 3, Denbighshire County Council, Ruthin.

Jersic, M. (1968) 'Weekend houses or dwellings in Slovenia and on the West Istrian shore' Geografisk Vestnik 57, p.67.

Kollmorgen, W.M. and Jenks, G.F. (1958) 'Suitcase farming in Sully County, South Dakota', Annals of the Association of American Geographers 58, pp.27-40.

Marsden, B.S. (1969) 'Holiday homescapes of Queensland', Australian Geographical Studies 7, pp.57-73.

Mead, W.R. (1958) An economic geography of the Scandinavian States and Finland, University of London Press, London.

Noble, N.F. (1962) 'Trends in farm abandonment', Canadian Journal of Agricultural Economics 10, pp.69-77.

Oluwasanmi, H.A. (1967) 'The Agricultural environment', in Lloyd, P.C., Mabogunje, A.L. and Awe, B. (eds), The city of Ibadan, Cambridge University Press, Cambridge.

Parsons, J.J. (1972) 'Slicing up the open space: subdivisions without homes in northern California', Erdkunde 26, pp.1-8.

Pyne, C.B. (1973) Second Homes, Caernarvonshire County Planning Department, Caernarvon.

Ragatz, R.L. (1969) The Vacation Home Market: An Unrecognised Factor in Outdoor Recreation and Rural Development, Bulletin No. 4, New York State College of Human Ecology, Cornell University, Ithaca.

Ragatz, R.L. (1970a) 'Vacation homes in the north eastern United States: seasonality in population distribution', Annals of the Association of American Geographers, 60, pp.447-55.

Ragatz, R.L. (1970b) 'Vacation housing: a missing component in urban and regional theory', Land Economics 46, pp.118-26.

Ragatz, R.L. and Gelb, G.M. (1970) 'The quiet boom in the vacation home market', California Management Review 12, pp.57-64.

Ragatz, R.L. Associates Inc. (1974) Recreational Properties, mimeographed, Eugene, Oregon.

Reilly, W.K. (ed) (1973) The Use of Land: A Citizen's Policy Guide to Urban Growth, Crowell, New York.

Robertson, R.W. (1974) Personal communication.

Tombaugh, L.W. (1970) 'Factors influencing vacation - home location', Journal of Leisure Research 2, pp.54-63.

Ulster Countryside Committee (1972) 6th Report, HMSO, Belfast.

United States Bureau of the Census (1969) Second Homes in the United States, Current Housing Reports, Ser. H-121, 16, U.S. Gov. Printing Office, Washington, DC.

Vielzeuf, B. (1969) 'Le tourism balneaire du lac Balaton', Bulletin de la Societe Languedocienne de Géographie 92, pp.115-38.

Wells, H.G. (1902) Anticipations of the reaction of mechanical and scientific progress upon human life and thought, London.

Wolfe, R.I. (1962) 'The summer resorts of Ontario in the nineteenth century', Ontario History 54, pp.149-60.

Wolfe, R.I. (1964) 'Perspective on outdoor recreation : a bibliographical survey', Geographical Review 54, pp.203-38.

Wolfe, R.I. (1967) 'The changing patterns of tourism in Ontario' in Swainson, D. (ed) Profiles of a province, Ontario Historical Society, Toronto.

Chapter 2

SUMMER COTTAGES IN ONTARIO: PURPOSE-BUILT FOR AN INESSENTIAL PURPOSE

R. I. Wolfe

The subtitle of this present chapter is a paraphrase of the title of the book as a whole. Houses that are built specifically to be second homes are, almost by definition, thought to be a blessing by their owners, for why else should anyone want to own one? Yet at the same time it remains true that they are inessential, in that the world would get along perfectly well without them; and to the extent that we can go further and say that many places would be better off without them (because, being inessential, they are almost inevitably parasitic as well), then they will be a curse.

In the 1940s, nobody talked about second homes, purpose-built (Clout 1972, p.102) or otherwise, or of seasonally occupied dwellings, or of country houses, and only F. Scott Fitzgerald, in *The Great Gatsby* (1925), had had the wit, decades earlier, to recognise them as *inessential* houses. To us, the house or shack or mansion or whatever that people moved to for a few days or weeks or months in the summer - and only in the summer - was a *summer cottage*, and it is this we will discuss here.

This chapter is concerned essentially with the setting and character of cottages and cottagers. Most of it was written, in a somewhat different form, almost a quarter of a century ago and only the opening and closing paragraphs have the benefit of hindsight. Yet much of what was written then seems equally appropriate today.

The Meaning of *Cottage*

The practice of summering away from one's winter quarters is far older than civilisation, and the custom, among more fortunate city-dwellers, of spending some part of the year in the country is, we can assume, as old as the city itself. In this chapter, we use as the generic term cottage, and with us in northern lands the cottage (at least until recently) is almost invariably a summer cottage.

The earliest references in Canadian literature are not to cottages, but to gentlemen's country houses, as in the *Coburg Star and Newcastle General Advertiser* of June 23rd, 1858 and to fishing boxes (Scott 1873, p.279). We are familiar, from references in English literature, with the institution of the shooting box in Scotland, to which English gentlemen travelled to hunt deer or grouse, and which may be claimed as a progenitor of the cottage. And while the word *cottage* originally described a humble dwelling, as it still does in one of its definitions, the manner in which the name became firmly attached to summer residences is thus set forth by Cleveland Amory (1952, p.11):

> To the historian of the future, looking back on the great American resort extravaganza, it is quite possible that its most outstanding single feature may be the use of the simple word *cottage*. Through the years this word has been used, with remarkable aplomb, to denote the million-dollar mansions, marble palaces and chateau castles which today, in various stages of destitution and distress, still adorn such streets as Newport's Bellevue Avenue, Bar Harbor's West Street and Palm Beach's Ocean Drive. Always thought provoking - the Henry Sage cottage on Long Island was, for example, called *the peaks and turrets of outrageous fortune* - it is a curious fact that originally, in the early days of resorts, the word *cottage* was used humbly. It was then used in the dictionary definition of *a modest country dwelling* to denote the small buildings which were built around the large hotels to care for the overflow of guests. Soon, because of the extra space and privacy these cottages provided, they became more socially desirable than rooms in the hotel; their patrons became known as the *cottagers* or the *cottage colony*, in any case, the social leaders of the resorts. Then, when these patrons broke away from the hotels entirely and built their own resort homes, they were loth to lose their social eminence and so kept the word, if not the spirit, when they built their mansions, palaces and castles.

Our use of the word *cottage*, then, is a purely American one. So, too, it would appear to be from the definition in the Funk and Wagnalls dictionary (1913 edition):

> cottage: 1. A humble dwelling: small house...
> 2. A suburban house.
> 3. (U.S.) A residence at a watering-place, frequently large and sumptuous; as, a stylish *cottage* at Newport.

The Natural Background of Cottages

Before turning to a consideration of the social background of recreational land use, let us see what attributes of the natural background are found attractive by Ontario cottagers. At the same time we shall glance at the most concrete expression of the attitude of the cottager to his environment - the architecture of the cottage itself.

The records of Crown land sales for summer resort purposes help us to gain an idea of the preferences of cottagers in Ontario. From 1918 to 1942 inclusive, these records, as presented in the annual reports of the Department of Lands and Forests, gave in detail the exact location and size of each plot sold, and, what is most important for our present purpose, they specified whether the lands sold were on islands or on the mainland.

Out of a total of 2,840 sales made in that period, 1,264 or 45 per cent, were on islands (Table 2.1). Of this number fully half were in the Districts of Algoma, Sudbury, Manitoulin and Parry Sound, and almost all the islands sold in these Districts were in the North Channel of Lake Huron and among the 30,000 islands of Georgian Bay (Fig. 2.1). The islands in these locations, as in the Muskoka Lakes and Stony Lake (in the Kawarthas) have been prized since the earliest days of resorting in Ontario. In the inland lakes all possible locations were taken up by the beginning of the century; the islands in Lake Huron and Georgian Bay sold in the 1930s and 1940s were the smaller, less accessible, more exposed, and in all ways less desirable ones. Yet even a less desirable island, apparently, is better than none; for, though

TABLE 2.1. Relation of island sales to total sales of Crown lands for summer resort purposes, 1918-42

Area	Percentage of Total sales made on islands
1. Kenora	24
2. Rainy Lake	34
4. Lakehead	8
5. Algoma	47
6. Sudbury	33
8. Timagami	25
9. Temiskaming	45
Isolated resorts of northern Ontario	61
Division I: North and Northwest Ontario	36
Division II: Huron-Ottawa tract	57
Division III: Frontenac axis	52
The Shield as a whole	45

Source: Ontario Dept of Lands and Forests, Reports.

Cleveland Amory (1952, p.121) may be exaggerating when he writes, of American resorts, that 'from the Thousand Islands up in the St Lawrence River...to the hundreds of Shangri-las off Nassau, the entire history of resorts could be written in the desire of resorters to own their own island', still the lure of the island in Ontario is a strong one.

This lure is not, by any means, universally felt. In the Frontenac Axis, for example, though in the interim years more than half the cottage sites sold were located on islands (Table 2.1), a surveyor in 1926 noted that very few cottages on the Rideau Lakes were so located, vacationers preferring to be able to reach their cottage by car (Ontario Dept. of Lands and Forests 1926, p.68). In Thunder Bay District only 8 per cent of Crown land sales were on islands.

If we could find a virgin lake on the Shield, and trace the emerging pattern of land occupancy upon it, we might learn a good deal about the aesthetic preferences of cottagers in Ontario. Fortunately, we can do just that. Through the annual reports of the Department of Lands and Forests we are able to follow the growth of the summer resort on such a lake through the first seventeen years of its existence.

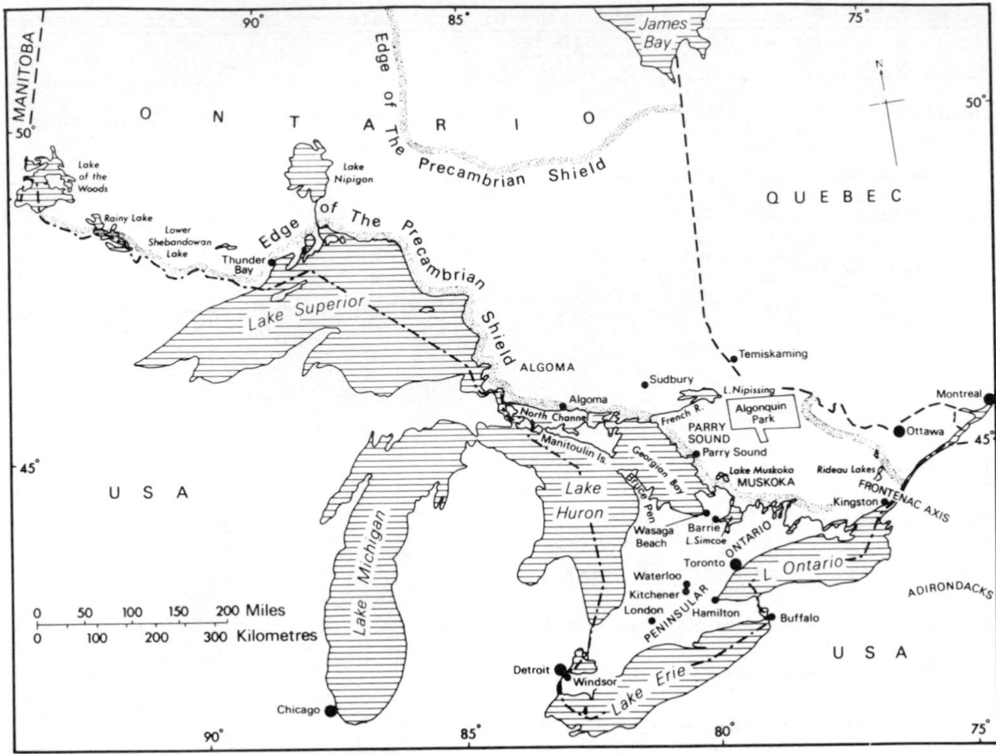

Fig. 2.1. The Province of Ontario

Lower Shebandowan Lake

Lower Shebandowan Lake, on the Dawson road some forty miles (64 km) west of Port Arthur, was surveyed for summer resorts in 1925, and a total of 200 lots, 1½ - 2 acres (0.6-0.8 ha) in area, was laid out (Ontario Dept. of Lands and Forests 1925, p.48). At the time there was only a small settlement on the eastern end of the lake, where the Canadian National Railway line skirted it. The Dawson road, reported the surveyors, was passable by light cars, but would need considerable work for general motor traffic (Ontario Dept. of Lands and Forests 1926, p.65). The best sand beach is on the west side of Castor Island (Fig. 2.2), but there are many small ones on the shores of the lake. It was not possible to get a sand beach at each location; from the surveyor's experience, however, most cottagers were not as anxious for a sand beach as for a good site with a commanding view (Ontario Dept. of Lands and Forests 1926, p.65). As we shall see, they were right.

In the first three years after the lake was opened to settlement, nine cottage sites were taken up (Fig. 2.2). Note how these were distributed in such a way that none could be seen across water from any of the others. While choice still existed, the cottagers chose the illusion of solitude, and an intimate view across a narrow stretch of water. Where both these desiderata could not be had at the same time, the first was chosen.

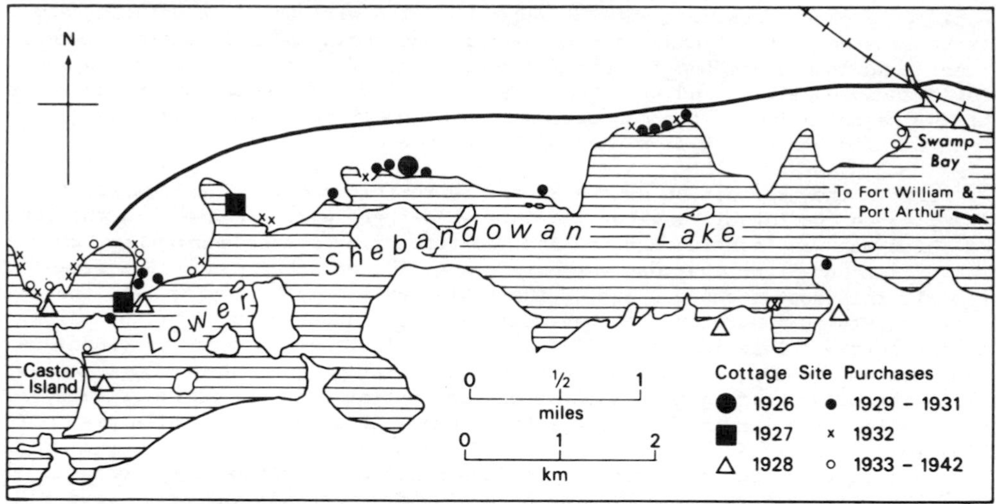

Fig. 2.2. Lower Shebandowan Lake

After 1928, cottages began to appear in clusters, at advantageous locations. The southern shore, which could be reached only by water, and which was at the further disadvantage of having the sun at its back, never attained great popularity. Nor did the eastern end of the lake, the most accessible part. One indication why this is so is given by the surveyors' remark that the water at the eastern end of the lake is dark, whereas it is clear at the other end (Ontario Dept. of Lands and Forests 1926, p.65).

One final point is worth noting: we have seen that the best sand beach was on the western shore of Castor Island. Yet not one cottager has seen fit to take advantage of this beach. There are three cottages on the island, all of them on the eastern shore. Thus, the experience of the surveyors seems to have been borne out and other factors have been weightier than this.

Cottages on the Canadian Shield

The erratic courses of rivers on the Shield, the sinuous shore-lines and many islands of the lakes, imposed upon the low relief, result in enclosed vistas, similar in effect to those in medieval towns. They make excellent retreats and help cottagers on the Crown lands indulge their desire for privacy. The desire for the illusion of solitude seems to oppose Ruskin's frequently quoted dictum to the effect that a landscape, to be pleasant, must have the mark of human occupancy upon it. But there are few cottagers indeed who would prefer the reality of solitude to the illusion; if they do not wish to have a direct view of human works before them, they do like to be able to find it just around the next bend in the shore-line.

Living in the Canadian Shield and travelling across it are entirely different experiences. The Shield is peculiarly unsuited to pleasure travel. The dull rock knobs rolling by, dead and uninteresting where their gleaming colours are not exposed by road cuts; the monotonous forests, too frequently disfigured by the scars left by forest fires; the black, sombre lakes; the unexciting relief; all these weary the traveller who crosses the country rapidly by car or train. But for those who live with the Shield intimately, it becomes beautiful. Examined in detail, the rocks themselves are interesting. No longer are the forests monotonous, for the trees become known and loved individually. And the sombre lakes are enlivened each day by the cries of the parading loons, the manoeuvres of a brood of merganser ducklings, or the flashing arrow-dart of a pair of Canada geese.

Part of the fascination of the Shield is reminiscence. The English, for example, can no longer remember the days when there were frontiers in the land, at which man was fighting nature, and the forbidding forest encroached upon all. For Canadians that day was only yesterday, and they can relive vicariously this most strenuous era of their history simply by moving into the dark forests that stretch, as they well know, for hundreds of unbroken miles to the north. This immanence of the frontier in Canadian folkways cannot be exaggerated. The great out-of-doors is, in Ontario, the out-of-doors against which the pioneers fought. Some of the activities that the pioneers were, often with great hardship, forced into, are now indulged in for pleasure. To live on bare rock can be pleasant only if one is not forced to try to gain one's livelihood from that rock. To live surrounded by the forest entails no hardship when that forest serves as an escape from asphalt and brick, and is not the monotonous year-round dwelling from which there is no escape. Trees are beautiful when they need not be burned down or cut down so that the land under them will be made accessible to the plough. A canoe trip with full pack is exhilarating when we know that the family car is waiting at the end of the last portage, to carry us home again. But to be able to remember, while enjoying the voluntary discomforts of today, that they were the pressing stuff of everyday life to the pioneers of a century ago adds exhilaration to the experiences and, to those who can feel it, the pleasure of helping to make history continuous. Thus, in Ontario the cult of the wilderness is far from being exotic. It takes pleasure in experiences that were recently commonplace and difficult, and are now commonplace and difficult no more.

The nostalgia for pioneer days does not alone account for the cult of the wilderness. Important, too, is the influence of the British nature tradition which has helped to shape our attitudes and has in turn affected the pattern of our recreational use of land. And behind history and tradition there lies a more fundamental aesthetic drive, one that, according to a great many writers, has its foundation in man's biological nature; for there is, these writers maintain, a fundamental, atavistic need in man to return to nature.

An atavistic theory has also been proposed for the love of the seashore, to the effect that primitive man escaped to the seashore from the wild beasts of the forest (Bews 1935, pp.134-6). Whether the reason is atavistic or not, it is undoubtedly true that the presence of a body of water is obligatory at a summer resort in Ontario. This fact was amusingly pointed out by B.K. Sandwell (1946) and in his perceptive words we learn something about the social background of the summer cottage as well:

> Ask any non-seashore-going Canadian where he is going when the summer migration begins, and he will answer without a moment's hesitation: 'To the Lake', or 'To the Beach', or 'To the Bay'...
>
> For the plain fact is that the Canadian will not summer anywhere except beside a lake. It does not matter much how large the lake is, nor how clean, nor what sort of odours emanate from it. A lake is a lake.

> The fish may have all been fished out years and years ago. The water may have gone down and down, as a result of the denudation of the surrounding forest, until acres of ill-smelling morass separate the settlement from its water-frontage.
>
> ... This brings us to another peculiar characteristic of the mind of the Canadian lake-dweller. Merely to dwell alongside a lake is good, but it is not everything. The true ideal of summer residence is to OWN a lake, so that you may dwell by it and nobody else can. This does not imply any selfishness or lack of neighbourliness on the part of the lake-dweller; on the contrary, the man who owns his lake will spend hundreds of dollars of money and months of time taking everybody he knows up to his lake and feeding them every luxury that the express companies will ship to him from the city. It is not that he is unwilling to share the use of his lake, or the fish of his lake... What he wants is to be able to walk all around the blessed thing and say to himself: 'This is mine. If I liked I could drain it dry and nobody could stop me'.

The Architecture of Summer Cottages

As important to scenic beauty as the natural background are the houses that are framed by it. When we see a modest cabin standing upon a rock, beside a lake or river on the Shield, we think it beautiful. That same cabin standing in town or city would be a shack, affronting both aesthetic sense and civic ordinances, but in its environment and with its use understood, it is just right. On the other hand, a marble mansion may serve for ostentation, and may indeed be the only fit dwelling for the economically mighty, but it will never conform with the ideal that ordinary people set up for themselves as to what makes a fit place for summer relaxation; for, as Kant says, 'the beauty of mankind, whether man, woman or child, of a horse and of a building, whether church, palace, arsenal or summer-house, presupposes a purpose which settles what the thing ought to be'. There is, in a word, a fitness in things, and a summer-house should *look* like a summer-house, and invite us to recreate ourselves in an easy, summery way, and then we will find it satisfying to the eye, and call it beautiful. Whoever has lived in a cottage for a week-end or a month or a summer can look at a picture of it only with longing, must feel the slap of water on canoe and the tug on the fishing line, and even smell the burning birch log. Such a house is not simply a house. It is the concrete emblem of a whole class of experiences, experiences that are, at their best, among the most pleasurable and recreative in life.

The architecture of the summer cottage has been one of the few aspects of recreational land use to be given serious consideration in the literature. V.J. Scully, in his historical work on the cottages of Newport (in Downing and Scully 1952, p.121), refers to three early works on the subject (Davis 1837; Downing 1842; and Mason 1875). There is no American writing on modern summer cottages outside architectural and other magazines (an excellent example is the article by G. Nelson (1953), which shows how the southern vacation house has moved northward, and the host of books of the *how to* variety). The neighbourhood public library I frequent has on its shelves close to a dozen such books with such titles as 'How to build your home in the woods' and 'How to plan and build cabins, cottages and summer houses'.

To attempt to discuss the architecture of the summer cottage in Ontario is no small thing. Take any kind of a dwelling that you are likely to find in

Fig. 2.3. Authentic log cabin on a farm near Owen Sound

Fig. 2.4. A cottage built c. 1880 at Grimsby Beach, Lake Ontario

(Figs. 2.3 - 2.6 are all based on photographs provided by the author)

Fig. 2.5 A quintessential cottage on a river in Haliburton

Fig. 2.6 A modern cottage at Wasaga Beach

any city, hamlet or farmstead; add mansions and estates that no city would encompass, and hovels so mean that the worst slum would not tolerate them; there is the range of the architecture of the summer cottage (Figs. 2.3 - 2.6).

Catholic as the conception of the summer cottage is, though, it is possible, in driving through various parts of Ontario, to recognise certain communities as summer resorts, because their houses have certain recognisable characters that set them apart from houses in more utilitarian communities. Yet the range, even in this province and at the present time, is immense. While we have nothing, to be sure, comparable to the *villae rusticae* of the Romans, we do have villas that are impressive enough. There are poor cottages at the other extreme of opulence. One, I remember, was occupied by an impoverished family that refused to allow poverty to keep it in the city during the summer. It was a lean-to standing in the middle of a hay-field; whatever it had leaned against had long since disappeared; it was a mile (1.6 km) from the stony shores and icy waters of Lake Ontario, but only 200-300 feet (60-90 m) from the monoxide fumes of a too-well-travelled highway; water had to be carried from a pump - and the pump was in an orchard a quarter of a mile away (400 m), across the highway. Yet this hovel served its purpose, and the family did have its summer in the country.

Neither places such as this nor the mansions, however, are characteristic of Ontario's cottages, just as their occupants are not characteristic of Ontario's people. The one outstanding character, perhaps, that distinguishes summer cottages from utilitarian houses in Ontario, is this: with few exceptions, the latter are of brick, usually red or buff, while the former are of painted wood. The Ontario summer resort is typically a *strassendorf* or shoe-string village of just such houses, stretching along the shore of lake or river.

This characteristic look of the Canadian summer resort is the most ancient look of the habitations of the white man in Canada. Just as the main street of our non-urbanised summer resort is the lake or river, upon which all houses front, just so the main street of old French Canada was the St. Lawrence. At the time of Confederation, R.B. Small (1867, p.89) described the resulting appearance of the river as follows:

> A peculiar feature of the scenery on the river, the whole way down from Montreal to Quebec, and still further as far as Rivière du Loup, are the numerous white cottages dotting its banks at a few arpents distance from each other (an arpent is about two hundred feet), while behind them in the background the woods and hills stand out in almost their primeval state. These are the dwellings - the little farms of the Canadian *habitant*.

Thus, it is not only their function that gives our summer resorts their distinctive look; for here we have dwellings whose function is as different as can be from that of our inessential houses, yet, since they too are wed to the river, they have a similar look.

Until the Second World War, most Ontario homes were built along traditional, unimaginative lines. They were simple wooden boxes with peaked roofs, and usually a stone or brick fireplace to give the requisite country appearance. After the war, and particularly since 1950, an entirely new, and often exciting, approach has been used. Materials for exteriors have changed little.

There is perhaps a greater use of white frame siding. Window space has been vastly increased, in keeping with the trend of modern architecture, domestic, industrial and commercial. Shapes have become more varied, more individual. But it is in the interior colours that the greatest changes have come. Gliding up the Nottawasaga River, for example, on a dark night, close to shore, one comes upon brilliant flashes of red and green and blue and yellow, strong primary colours - not merely visible, but displayed - through the huge picture windows fronting on the water. Summer clothing has always been boldly colourful; now the housing has become equally so.

The characteristic summer structure of the 1950s was a most recent growth in this country. Yet it had been in existence in the more restricted sphere of Europe for a considerable time. The style is an out-growth of the whole modern trend in architecture, following on the leadership of Gropius, Mies van der Rohe, Frank Lloyd Wright, and others. The summer homes are specifically designed for intermittent use, and therefore differ in detail from the more permanent houses built in the new tradition. They had been in existence in Europe for nearly fifty years and only in the 1950s did they become widespread in Canada.

There is one point of great significance that needs to be stressed. The modern trend has arrived in Canadian architecture in almost all its spheres, but in domestic housing the results are unfortunate. The picture window, in particular, has become a curse, a stereotype lining miles upon miles of uniform suburban streets. The picture window was ostensibly invented to bring the outside inside, to exploit a desirable view; in treeless Suburbia, the view seen from one picture window is the picture window directly across the way. At the summer resort, however, the modern trend, with its low, rangy silhouette and its picture window, makes more sense. The lowness of the building accentuates the perpendicular lines of the surrounding pines; the brilliant colours stand out against the sombreness of the forest; and the picture window gives on just such a view as it was meant for, on the beauty of water and forest. Again, the windows act as a display, showing off to boaters on the water the brilliance of the scenes within. These houses take us back to the very origins of the summer cottage in Ontario, to the miles of cottages among the Thousand Islands of the St. Lawrence. Here the cottages were set among scenic splendours, and their inhabitants enjoyed deeply satisfying views. But beyond this, the inhabitants themselves set about providing satisfying views for the passengers of passing boats, by decorating their cottages to the limits of their purse and their taste, and by nightly setting off fireworks for the enjoyment of themselves and of all neighbours. Here enjoyment was a two-way process, and so it is among the new cottages. This seems a healthy process, for it is evidence of a heightened awareness and an increased involvement of the cottagers with their environment. They enjoy it and they contribute to it, taking satisfaction from increasing the enjoyment of others. It may be ostentation, but it is of a healthy kind, satisfying both the viewers and the viewed.

Modern cottages have used not only new forms of architecture, but new techniques to simulate old forms. The harking back to the frontier may not always be conscious, but it does manifest itself, and often in surprising ways. Perhaps most characteristic of the frontier way of life was the log cabin, and it is becoming increasingly popular at summer resorts (Fig. 2.3). But the logs are prefabricated; they are debarked, shaved down to uniform size, hollowed out, split down the middle, and built into walls that can be erected as units, and coated with an unlovely varnish. Inside, of course, there are usually plastered and papered walls, hot and cold running water, and tiled bathrooms, but it *is*, after a fashion, a log cabin, and the nostalgia for the frontier has been appeased.

One may not entirely approve of this development, yet it is in the right direction. For the log cabin *is* indigenous to the country. It *has* played a critical part in its history, and the observant traveller through the Ontario countryside can find many examples still standing, even still in use. If its reincarnation is synthetic and spurious, that too is part of our civilisation, and if we condemn it we are really condemning an important aspect of the civilisation itself. The reincarnation of the log cabin *can* be beautiful and right, if only intelligent thought is given to it.

The Social Background of Cottaging

Before recreational land use can become important in a society, there must be a significant proportion of the population with the means and leisure to take extended vacations; travel facilities must be sufficiently advanced to make travelling enjoyable and pleasant according to the prevailing standards; and there must be desirable areas of resort to which to travel. As K.M. Mayall (1948) has written:

> If there is one material thing that every Canadian city dweller wants more than anything else, it is a small cottage on a lake or river where he and his family and friends can relax for a few hours or days from the tension and nervous excitement of city life and work.

No feature of present-day society has received more comment than the increase in leisure time we have experienced over the last half a century. Shorter working hours, two- and three-day weekends, and the annual vacation-with-pay have made it possible for more and more people to indulge in leisure activities that, in former times, were restricted to a small leisure class. Never before have most people been able to exercise so much choice in what they do with their time.

The recreational use of land is but one aspect of the larger question of leisure. That it has grown tremendously needs no demonstration. Every summer weekend sees a large part of the population of the United States and Canada on the move, the cities emptying and the resorts filling up. In Canada's larger cities it becomes almost impossible to prosecute any form of business on summer weekends. The summer work-week of adults has been followed by the play-week of children: 'We can only play five days a week', said the head of a juvenile baseball league in Toronto, 'because the kids refuse to play Saturdays anymore. I attribute this to the fact so many more people have summer cottages and the whole family goes away for the weekend' (Toronto Daily Star 4 June 1949).

Perhaps as important a factor as any in the social background of the summer cottage is the public school system of this continent. School children are uniformly given a two-month vacation, in July and August. This extended period of leisure time has made it possible for at least some members of the family to spend most of their summer in the country. This procedure is accepted by most of us as natural and almost inevitable; we would probably resist any attempt to change it, and the summer cottage continues to dominate the pattern of recreational land use in Ontario.

The institution of the summer cottage is a paradox, and the more widely spread its use, the greater the paradox. The holiday impulse has been, for hundreds of years, an impulse to travel. R.S. Lambert (1950, p.10) states a widely held belief when he maintains that man's roving instinct, the nomad instinct, is 'an ineradicable trace of his pastoral ancestry, of the days when he was always on the move'. Vacation time for millions of Americans and Canadians is the time to visit some place new, to move, move fast, and keep on moving. Ownership of a cottage inhibits this mobility. The cottage may be at a greater or a lesser distance from one's city home, but the road travelled is always the same and well known, and the journey, even though it may be through a pleasant countryside, becomes of little more significance than the daily journey to and from work.

Not only does the cottage tie its owner down, but it makes demands on his time, his energy and his pocket. Mother, as newspaper cartoonists annually tell us, works harder at the cottage than she does at home. The rest of the family have duties that may be less rigidly defined, but are to varying degrees arduous, such as varnishing the boat, painting the woodshed or garage, tending the garden or building the stone fireplace. There is always something needed around the cottage.

The financial burden is the heaviest of all. There are the costs of maintaining a separate home, including the original cost of land and dwelling, taxes, electricity and furnishings. There are the extra costs of pleasurable possessions and activities, such as boats and golf equipment. There is the expense of travelling to and from the cottage.

Thus, there are powerful arguments against the ownership of a summer cottage. Yet cottages are nonetheless owned in their hundreds of thousands in Canada alone, and in millions in North America, and their number is increasing more rapidly each year. Evidently the counterbalancing arguments are even more powerful.

Perhaps the greatest paradox has to do with the very reason for the existence of the summer cottage, or at any rate the ostensible reason. The urge to own and spend time at a summer cottage, it is widely assumed, has its origin in the need of city dwellers to return to a closer communion with nature. The cottage is the country home of the city dweller, himself only one or two generations removed from the country, who has otherwise become totally divorced from it. Yet extended observation of summer resorts in Ontario leads to the unmistakable conclusion that it is precisely those whose city environment is greenest, those who live on tree-lined streets and carefully tend their generous gardens, who are most likely to summer in the greenest countryside. In earlier days the city dweller could return to the family farm, or spend the summer with friends who were farmers. But today, unless he himself owns land in the country, in the form of a summer residence, he has no direct personal stake in it, and it becomes nothing more, perhaps, than the object of his casual glance as he drives through it.

Do most cottages now existing in fact bring their owners into a direct relation with nature? We must conclude that they do not. Too many cottages are simply dwellings in a summer city; they are not located in the country at all. One can more easily commune with nature in one's own backyard in the city, and more truly, than in some of our urbanised summer resorts.

The idealised summer cottage does, by definition, function in the way desired, and there are thousands of cottages that meet the ideal more or less closely. Situated on islands, or on reasonably private stretches of beach or rocky shore, they give their inhabitants the illusion, though not, emphatically, the actuality (for that would never do) of isolation from their fellow men. In such locations the activities are those proper to a healthful summer: boating, canoeing, swimming, fishing, sunbathing and plain loafing, in between times when the chores have to be done. And since to get the full benefit of living with nature it is not necessary to make it a twenty four hour-a-day, seven-day-a-week affair, the boat and the car are usefully employed, particularly on a Saturday evening, in travelling to the nearest shopping centre, cinema and dance hall; except for the rare cottage truly isolated in the backwoods, this is not much of a journey - a few hundred yards perhaps.

Ownership of a cottage, then, is for enjoyment. The cottage is a place to have fun, but the fun takes many forms, and the one form that one should expect to be universal, that of getting closer to a state of nature, is far from being so. But there is a form of enjoyment that *is* universal among owners of summer cottages, and that is the enjoyment that comes from *ownership*. The supposedly characteristic American trait of being footloose, of refusing to let one's money and one's sentiment be tied down by a piece of land, is no longer a characteristic of millions of American cottage owners, who are wholeheartedly involved with their bit of land on the lake. More, the cottage frequently becomes the home, the gathering place, to which the far-flung family returns each year, to renew contacts and once again experience the fundamental satisfactions of being part of something, the satisfactions of family. Allied to these satisfactions, frequently, are those of belonging to a cohesive community. The loss of the community spirit in the city is universally deplored; large numbers of city dwellers find it again, as members of cottage associations.

Family and community are but two facets of the enjoyment of ownership. Of some importance, surely, are what R. Weaver (1948, p.131) has called *the last metaphysical right*, the right of property ownership, and the deep satisfactions gained from pottering around one's own house and grounds, mending and creating, and in extreme cases, among thorough-going idealists, building one's own cottage.

But the most important facet of all, and the one prevailing reason for the vast proliferation of the cottage on this continent, is that of status. The ownership of a cottage confers status upon the owner. To be able to say 'My wife is up at the cottage', or 'I'm going up to the cottage for the weekend, as usual; get in a bit of fishing', is to be among the elect. The ability to own and maintain an inessential house is an important index of having arrived. The modest shack crowded among dozens of its kind in some hayfield is the symbol of a very new, and modest, arrival among the elect. Those at the opposite end of the scale can (or at one time they could, for the mode is no longer fashionable) flaunt their unnecessary millions by lavishing splendour on their unnecessary houses. Indeed, for a really good exercise in flaunting, no vehicle ever created has served as well as the summer cottage, right back to Lucullan times.

The key to the American, as to the Canadian, resort is found in de Tocqueville's statement: 'No European is more exclusive in his pleasures'. Since the time when he wrote, the pleasures have become democratised and exclusiveness is hard to come by. It is frequently no longer a matter of excluding the herd, but of *belonging* to the herd. The whole weight of American advertising is exerted to heightening this desire to belong. Yet belonging can give little satisfaction unless some people, however few, are excluded, or the illusion can be maintained that others are excluded. In cosmopolitan Toronto, even the illusion has become hard to maintain.

Fundamentally, summering at the cottage is a symbolic act. It is *not* for amusement; it is *not* an escape from the city, though that is what it seems to be more than any other; it is not even primarily for recreation, though that is its ostensible purpose. It symbolised, in former times, the exclusion by the elect of those not fortunate enough to own the *inessential houses*; today, it symbolises, in its democratised form, the sense of belonging which all of us feel the need to demonstrate in one way or another.

In passing, we may note that because the recreational use of land has for so long been a symbol of privilege, Europe's revolutionary regimes, and their Asian counterparts, have made great propaganda play with their *summer resorts for workers*. Appropriately, from their point of view, they have used the summer palaces of the dead or exiled sovereigns and nobility for this purpose. In the early, idealistic days, no book on Soviet Russia could miss stressing the workers' summer resorts on the Black Sea; propaganda from Soviet China places a similar emphasis on this new privilege of the workers.

Not the nature cult, not the need for leisure, not the wish for amusement, is fundamental to the *ownership* of a cottage. Fundamental is the symbol. In recreational land use as a whole, though, the symbol is less operative. Here the other social factors take on greater importance. Their interplay is most clearly shown in the urbanisation of the summer resort. In the summer city the theoretical needs that recreational land use is thought to satisfy go so obviously unsatisfied and are, indeed, so obviously not recognised by those who frequent them that the investigator is led to re-examine all the premises he finds in the literature on leisure (Wolfe 1952).

Conclusion

Much of this chapter describes the situation that existed a quarter of a century ago. Today it would no longer be possible to write about the summer cottage in so single-minded a way. For one thing, many a summer cottage is no longer such because it has been *winterised* and is now used throughout the year, especially in areas where skiing or snowmobiling is popular. For another, inflation is more than ordinarily virulent here, and the very same cottage that could be bought for \$500 in the 1930s and \$3,000 in the 1950s is now unobtainable for \$12,000, while the cottage built ten years ago for \$20,000 now sells for \$80,000 (and rents for the two summer months for \$6,500). It is all unbelievable, and what it means is that it is simply uneconomic to invest in a place which will be used for only a few weeks in the year; as a result, people are more and more likely to travel to their cottages in all seasons, and even more to move into them permanently when they retire.

The greatest change of all has been the growth in the number of second homes that are not purpose-built. It is astonishing how many working farms have been abandoned throughout Ontario, so that they are no longer *working*, and how many of the original farm houses, which once served an essential purpose, are now serving the inessential purpose of being a second home. These farmhouses can scarcely be called summer cottages: they do not *look* like summer cottages, as did those a quarter century ago when I first began to study this phenomenon. It is now possible to travel through bucolic parts of Ontario, as one can travel through Sussex in England or the Beauce in France, and pass hundreds of recreational homes that are not recognisable as recreational homes at all, except by the expert. Things are not as simple as they were, in recreational housing as in everything else.

REFERENCES

Amory, C. (1952) The Last Resorts, Harper, New York.

Bews, J.W. (1935) Human Ecology, Oxford.

Clout, H.D. (1972) 'Two homes, one away', Geographical Journal, 44, pp.98-102.

Davis, A.J. (1837) Rural Residences, mentioned in Downing and Scully, p.121.

Downing, A.J. (1842) Cottage Residences, mentioned in Downing and Scully, p.121.

Downing, A.F. and Scully, V.J. Jr. (1952) The Architectural Heritage of Newport, Rhode Island, 1840-1915, Harvard.

Lambert, R.S. (1950) The Fortunate Traveller, Melrose, London.

Mason, G.C. (1875) Newport and its Cottages, mentioned in Downing and Scully, p.121.

Mayall, K.M. (1948) 'Recreation on the Humber', in Ontario Department of Planning and Development, Conservation in South Central Ontario.

Nelson, G. (1953) 'The house in the desert', Holiday, 13: 3 March, pp.60-3, 135-6.

Ontario Department of Lands and Forests (1925) Report.

Ontario Department of Lands and Forests (1926) Report.

Sandwell, B.K. (1946) 'Us amphibious Canadians', in J.D. Robins (ed) A Pocketful of Canada, Collins, Toronto.

Scott, G.C. (1873) Fishing in American Waters, Harper, New York.

Small, R.B. (1867) The Canadian Handbook and Tourist Guide, Montreal.

Weaver, R. (1948) Ideas Have Consequences, University of Chicago Press.

Wolfe, R.I. (1952) 'Leisure: the element of choice', Journal of Human Ecology, 2:6, p.12.

Chapter 3

SECOND HOMES IN SCANDINAVIA

C. L. Bielckus

The almost simultaneous development of second homes in quite different parts of the world exhibits both contrasts and parallels. In North America the second home market has been very commercially oriented from the outset, more so than in European countries where rural properties left vacant by migrants from agricultural areas have been taken over as second homes. Only as stocks of former agricultural housing have diminished in recent years has this sector of recreational demand been met by the provision of purpose-built second homes. During the period before the Second World War, when only a very small proportion of the population could afford second homes, this form of land use had little impact. The increase in personal mobility and wealth since the 1950s, however, and a corresponding reduction in working hours for many people, has created a leisure boom and the number of second homes has soared in many countries. In Scandinavia the stage has long since been reached at which protective measures became necessary to safeguard the countryside whilst continuing to meet this demand. Thus a new sector in recreational planning has been created. In its examination of second homes in Scandinavia, this chapter places emphasis upon the situation in Sweden which has received the most detailed documentation. Investigations in both Denmark and Norway have drawn extensively on Swedish sources as a guide to the trends which are increasingly affecting these countries.

Some background statistics are presented in Table 3.1 which allow comparisons to be made between the three Scandinavian countries under consideration. In view of the very high percentage of its population which is urban, Denmark at first glance appears to have more in common with Sweden than does Norway. In both economic and physical terms, however, Denmark is very different from the other two countries and the demand for second homes has understandably been expressed in a rather different way. Developments have been almost exclusively coastal and thus essentially purpose-built. The greater availability of space for outdoor recreation in the forested and mountainous areas of Norway and Sweden has given scope for a range of types of second home, both adapted and purpose-built.

Even in Scandinavia, where second homes are a long-established form of recreational land use, it would seem that in order to merit serious study some threat to nature conservation in general must arise, or local economic or environmental problems be created on a sufficient scale to cause concern. Although both Norway and Denmark lag behind Sweden in their investigations of second homes, the consequences of the rapid growth of second homes have been considered and some national figures are available (see Table 3.1). In many instances some interest has arisen from the reduction of access to outdoor areas by the general public, rather than direct damage to the landscape.

TABLE 3.1. Population, land area and second homes in Scandinavia, c.1970

	Population (000s)	Percentage of urban population	Land area (000s ha)	No. of second homes (000s)
Denmark	4,976	77.2	4,237	140-145[a]
Norway	3,918	57.5	30,833	170[b]
Sweden	8,115	81.4	41,140	490[c]

Sources: a - Landsplanudsvalgets Sekretariat 1966
b - Ouren 1969
c - Lantmäteristyrelsen 1971
All other figures from Nordisk statistisk arsbok 1972

Denmark

In Denmark, coastal studies show that the private parcelling of land for second homes has prevented public access to many good quality beaches. Over half the second homes are situated in Zealand, where the enormous demand from Copenhagen has been concentrated on the north coast (Landplanudsvalgets Sekretariat 1966; A. Wolstad 1968). Since the main study of second homes in Denmark has been essentially concerned with the quality of the coast, most is known about these seaside developments. Until recently the demand was almost entirely coastal and only a small number of inland districts could be identified, most of them concentrated near the larger lakes.

Examination of the distance from permanent homes in all parts of the country has suggested that 80-90 per cent of owners live within 60 km (37.5 miles) of their second homes. The newest second home areas, however, suggest that greater distances have become more acceptable as mobility has increased and suitable sites near to the larger towns have become scarce. Nevertheless, the tendency towards use throughout the year is growing. At present the market is dominated by standardised and partly prefabricated dwellings, not so different in technical quality and design from permanent homes in urban areas.

Future planning aims at more concentrated development of settlements, in groups of as many as 200 second homes, in an attempt to preserve as much of the natural landscape as possible and to make provision of services for second home areas economically viable. Problems exist in former areas of second homes near urban centres where residential areas of an inferior quality have developed as the role of the dwellings has changed. To prevent future developments of this kind legislation now prevents the building of second homes within a specified distance of urban centres. Second homes may be developed only within the framework of regional plans and it is the responsibility of local authorities to ensure that no planning permission is granted without an approved scheme for water supply and sewage disposal. An attempt has thus been made to ensure that the inherent qualities of an area which attract such development in the first place are not lost through bad planning (Statens Byggeforskningsinstitut 1970).

There is growing recognition in national planning in Denmark that recreational homes constitute a settlement type in their own right and should therefore be located, planned for and maintained on the basis of their specific requirements. Prevention of any kind of invasion by permanent dwellings which might threaten to change the settlement structure has been found necessary, an interesting contrast with other parts of Europe where concern surrounds community imbalance resulting from infiltration of second homes into permanent residential areas.

Norway

Less can be said about the situation in Norway where second homes are not readily separable as such. Accommodation in *hytter* - translated simply as *huts* - can range from a simple cabin in the mountains to a small hotel. A tourist organisation owns a network of huts in the mountains which provide shelter for summer walkers or spring skiers who choose to leave the roads and villages behind them. Others are owned by farmers or hoteliers and are hired out for periods of days or weeks to people wanting a holiday base in a particular area.

> ... Norwegians are owners of summer huts. Most of the huts are situated conveniently near the surroundings of towns, even away from the sea, if that is the only solution for getting there by cheap transport. Some of the huts are fine aesthetically, some are hideous, but nearly all are touching in their indications of happy family life and efforts to make something with your hands just for the fun of it, and to escape urban uniformity and monotonous civilised comforts. Huts and associated fenced properties have become so common that other people thereby have been deprived of their old rights to go everywhere freely (Sund 1960).

It can be seen that the second home is not a clearly defined concept in Norway. All these forms of accommodation occur throughout the country and are a clear expression of the desire of a northern people to enjoy the light summer months. Development is scattered and has taken place with little planning or control in the past. For economic reasons farmers were formerly encouraged to build huts for tourists on their own initiative, and a very dispersed pattern has resulted.

It has been suggested that quite different problems are created by second homes in coastal, forest and mountain areas and, in practice, each planning authority must make its own regulations to safeguard the scenic attractions of the area (Anker 1967). In Hallingdål, for example, a two-year ban on hut building was enforced while investigations on how best to cluster development took place. Regulations have been of a general nature and are not geared specifically to meet or curb the demand for second homes.

Second homes receive attention only as part of the general demand for recreation and are covered in tourist studies of particular areas. Background information for local reports and planning studies throughout the country includes details of second homes, but a specific national inventory has not been made. In an article concerned primarily with nature conservation Langdalen suggests that there were 170,000 second homes in Norway in 1969 (see T. Ouren 1969) and estimated the annual rate of growth to be 10,000. In the same volume an area near the Swedish border where second homes have had some local impact is discussed by L.H. Hertzberg, illustrating the local nature of such studies.

Sweden

It is in Sweden that second homes have received the most detailed attention. The character, spatial distribution and changing location of second homes were first analysed in 1938 in a pioneer study of the Stockholm region (Ljungdahl 1938), but such early documentation is not the only indication that second homes are not new to the Swedish way of life. The semi-nomadic tradition of Swedish farmers, shifting with their herds to summer pastures away from the villages, has its modern counterpart in weekend and summer migrations to the holiday cottage. The modern tendency for urban life to be spent in flats accentuates, both here and in other European countries, the need for a periodic change to a more spacious environment.

Numbers and Distribution

Two-thirds of Swedish second homes are owned by people who live permanently in blocks of flats (Larsson 1969) and so it is not surprising that the second home is idealised, and in some areas typified, by the simple accommodation formerly used in conjunction with summer grazing lands in the Swedish forests. In the late 1960s movement away from the land freed 10,000 farms a year, so that about thirty farmhouses became available for the second home market each day. Nevertheless, this met the demand only to a limited extent, and during the last three years of the decade alone a total of 55,000 plots were parcelled out for recreational accommodation (Lantmäteristyrelsen 1971). In the Dalarna region of central Sweden, however, the traditional style of red wooden crofter cottages, dating from the eighteenth and nineteenth centuries, has been in great demand as holiday accommodation; they have been so popular that such properties are not uncommonly seen nearer urban centres, having been bought, dismantled and moved to the site of the owner's choice. Former agricultural cottages, particularly those of the periodically used *fäbod* settlements (more commonly known as *seters* in other parts of Sweden, and throughout Norway), are perhaps the most coveted form of recreational accommodation.

Yet the supply of rural dwellings is by no means unlimited, and not every would-be owner of a second home can hope for an isolated cottage with access to lake and forest and commanding a spectacular view. Individual aspirations and the needs of the community are not always compatible, and the maintenance of public access to the countryside is a major objective in Sweden's planning for leisure. In a recent survey of second-home owners, almost half of the respondents would have preferred an isolated croft or former farmhouse had they been able to choose their second home again (Larsson 1969). This ideal is clearly not in keeping with realistic long-term planning in a country where, despite private ownership of large areas, legislation aims to maximise public access to all land. Increasing pressures on land resources for outdoor recreation near the larger cities and the rapid increase in numbers of second homes led the government to appoint in 1962 a review commission on outdoor recreation which paid considerable attention to second homes. The survey established that 45 per cent of second homes were at that time within statutory planned areas, 27 per cent were in other forms of concentrated development and only 28 per cent were scattered about the countryside. In broad terms, 85 per cent of second homes were found to be situated in central and southern Sweden (Statens Offentliga Utredningar 1964; see also C-E. Norrbom 1966).

An investigation in 1968 by the National Swedish Land Survey Board estimated that there were over 420,000 second homes throughout Sweden and predicted a rapid increase to over half a million, i.e., one second home for every five households (Lantmäteristyrelsen 1968). The main concentrations were found to be around the urban centres, and one-third of all second homes in Sweden were within 20 km (12.5 miles) of built-up areas with populations over 25,000. Development was particularly concentrated in the coastal zone. Densities were highest in the southern uplands. A follow-up survey in 1970 found that the number of second homes had increased to 490,000 (Lantmäteristyrelsen 1971). As in the earlier survey, statistics were made available for both counties and municipalities and the distribution of second homes was mapped on a 25 km square grid.

Figure 3.1 shows the distribution of second homes, on a county basis, as revealed by the above surveys. The characteristics of the distribution are by no means unique, but illustrate the capacity of the Swedish countryside to meet demands for second homes in coastal or lakeshore locations and at manageable distances from the main centres of population. With only about one per cent of its land area under urban use, a fairly widely dispersed population, and with ready access to rural areas, the whole Swedish countryside has enormous potential for such recreational development (see also Lantmäteristyrelsen 1969). Figure 3.2, showing distribution by 10 km squares, emphasises the importance of the coast and of areas within easy motoring of the major cities.

Where the permanent population is declining there has been some incorporation of second homes into primary residential areas. Thus, on the west coast of Sweden, where there has been a considerable decrease in the permanent population of the fishing villages since the mid-1930s, many additional properties have come onto the market for second homes. A recent survey of land use in some of these villages found that not only were 50 per cent of the dwellings used as recreational residences but that there was complete spatial integration with permanent homes (Swedish Urban Planning Board 1970). The new residential function was not segregated and has been superimposed on the old built-up area as the dwellings have gradually changed their role. Because these cottages are former permanent homes, their conversion to second home use lacks the problems of service provision which beset the establishment of new communities.

Academic studies

In Sweden, second homes as a form of recreational land use have received academic recognition as well as coverage by statistical reports both specific to second homes and on leisure in general. Studies of second homes have been the basis of investigations into the spatial differentiation of settlement patterns and the factors and processes which control them. Basing work on his own inventory of summer houses in the Dalarna region of central Sweden which he made in 1965, H. Aldskogius (1968) has analysed the spatial variations and has made a largely classificatory description of second homes in terms of settlement types, age and rateable value of buildings, and travel distances involved. The spatial pattern of the development of summer houses in an area comprising five local authorities around Lake Siljan was examined within the framework of a multiple regression model, which specified the relationship between the distribution of vacation homes and a set of variables related to spatial variations in recreational place utility. These included rateable values, age of building as a recreational dwelling, and owner's place of

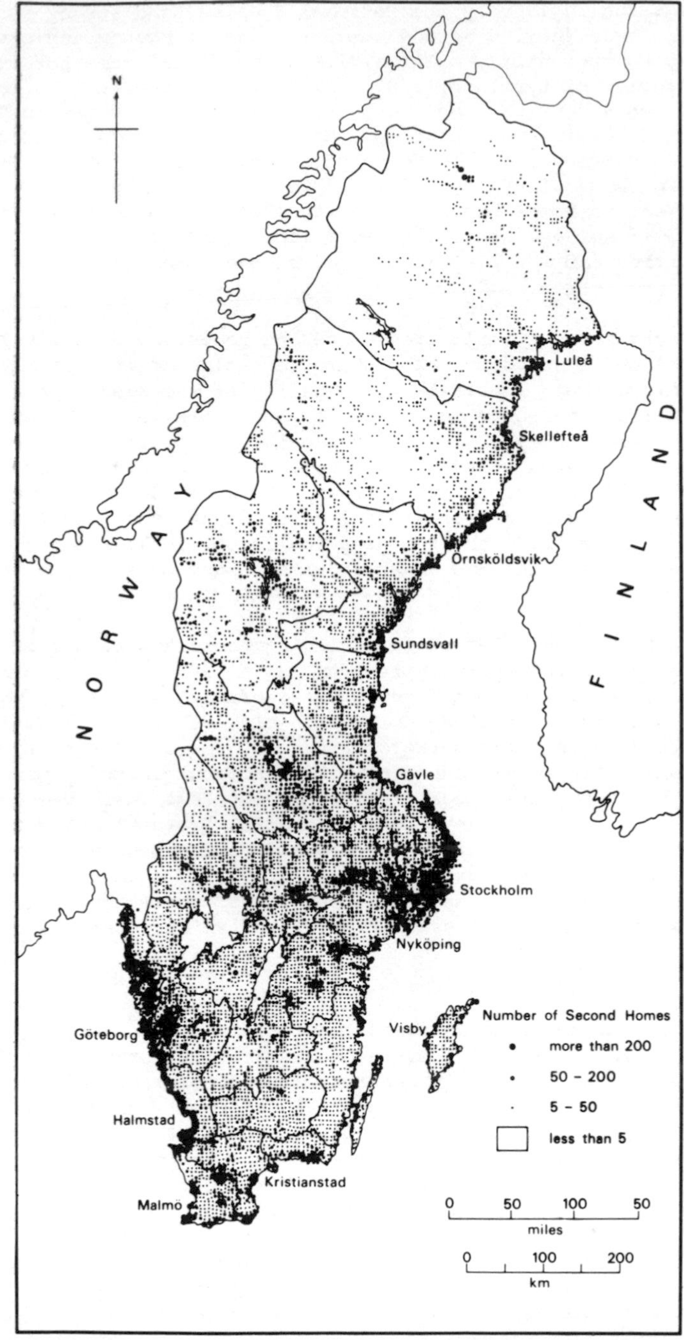

Fig. 3.1. Distribution of second homes in Sweden, by counties, 1970

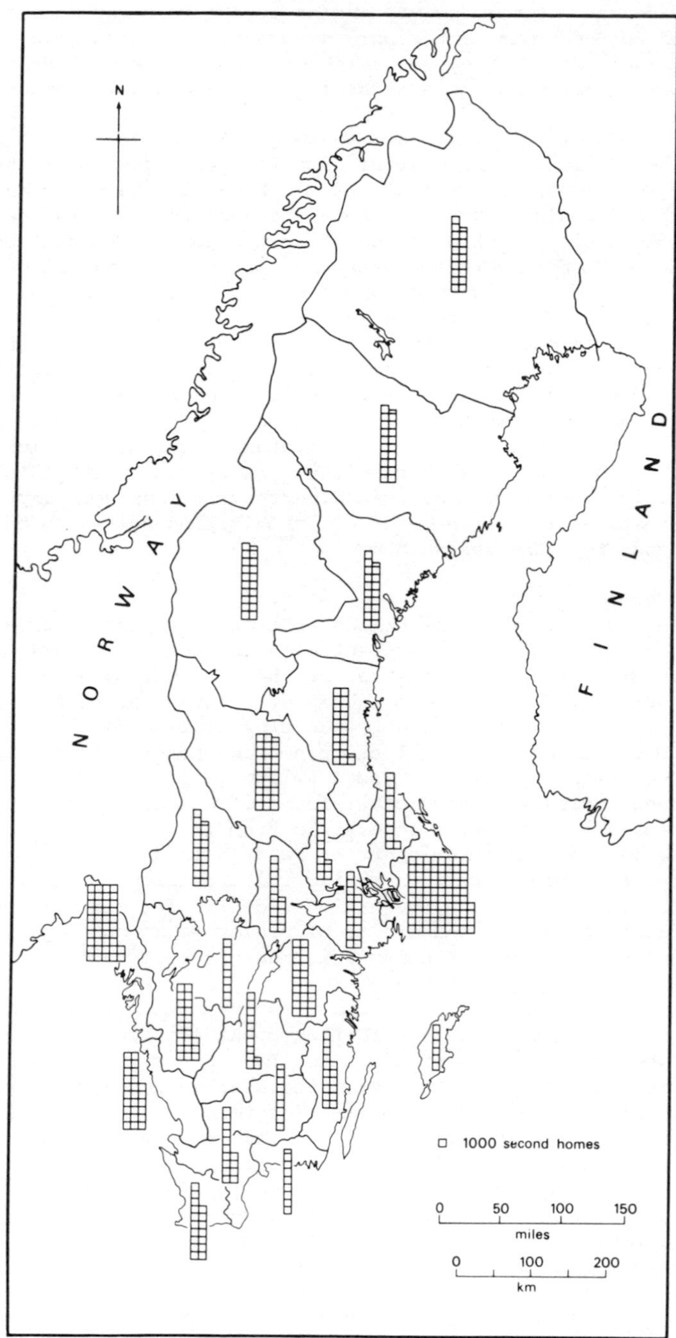

Fig. 3.2. Distribution of second homes in Sweden, by 10 km squares

permanent residence. Contrasts within the region revealed some differential development of second homes, more rapid growth having taken place in the most recently colonized area. The proportion of owners from outside the region is increasing, particularly in these areas of more recent development.

In later exploratory work, Aldskogius sought to illustrate the problems involved in the application of quadrat sampling techniques on a series of maps recording the spatial distribution of second homes in the same area between 1925 and 1945 (Aldskogius 1969). Problems associated with the construction of models of the evolution of patterns of second home settlement were also examined. A useful framework for detailed work of this nature was provided by the Land Survey Board which had mapped second homes to the nearest ten units in each grid square (Lantmäteristyrelsen 1968; see also Fig. 3.1). The distribution of those characteristics on the landscape and other circumstances which influence the location of second homes should not be forgotten. In the Siljan region hotels and pensions were important early centres, and on the Swedish coasts the development of second homes was first encouraged by the location of landing stages and later restricted by the acquisition of the best access points. In the Swedish archipelagos it is not uncommon to find that developments which occurred before planning restrictions were imposed have occupied the best landing places, thereby prohibiting access to otherwise potentially good areas for second homes.

Planning and second homes

Despite the high proportion of holiday cottages in planned areas, planning for second homes is comparatively recent even in Sweden. Nearly all of the plans have appeared since 1960 and most of those in existence at the beginning of the 1970s were made between 1965 and 1967. In 75 per cent of the cases studied, the planning was initiated by municipalities and, although county proposals have great influence on local planning, permission to build must be sought at local authority level. The development of summer and weekend cottages in Sweden vies with many other forms of outdoor recreation for attractive areas that are easily accessible from the principal urban centres. At present the main aim in this aspect of Swedish land use planning is to achieve a balance between vacation housing and provision for active outdoor pursuits. If, in keeping with the national desire for maximum access to the countryside, large areas of land are to be preserved as open space, then conservation for social as well as scientific reasons must have precedence over the development of holiday cottages.

Pressure on the coastline merits further consideration. In the 45 per cent of the Swedish coast classified by the Land Survey Board as the most suitable for recreation, there was twice the average density of second homes in the coastal strip as a whole (Lantmäteristyrelsen 1968). Much of this past development occupies the coast and has reduced the area of immediate access for day recreation. Moreover, the persistence of the old patterns of land holding is an additional obstacle, since in areas where agriculture was formerly important there often remains a retired land-owning population which is prepared to part with land only by small amounts at a time. The fear of large-scale development which might alter the immediate environment is the cause of small-scale, but far more damaging, piecemeal development. The undesirability in the long term of such encroachment is perhaps not fully realised by those who own the land. The larger the parcels of land sold, the greater the scope for efficient plans which will minimise danger to the attractive areas concerned and allow the greatest possible freedom of access to rural areas.

Around Lake Siljan in Dalarna a complex pattern of tightly clustered groups of wooden houses, central to the farming areas around them, survives. Land ownership in this area is characterised by extreme fragmentation of holdings since this area was largely unaffected by *laga skifte* operations. This early nineteenth century system of land enclosure was the first such redistribution to be carried out over the whole of Sweden, and led to the break-up of many villages by moving farm buildings out from the settlements to the new allotments of land. The greatest effects of this process were felt by the nucleated villages in the plains. Woodland areas were less severely affected, and, as one of the last areas to adopt this third major land redistribution in Sweden, the Siljan area was little altered (Nordell and Rydberg 1959; Aldskogius 1960 and 1969). Subdivisions of land in Dalarna were often unrecorded at that time and there is now a confused situation of very small properties with very jumbled patterns of ownership. This structure hinders the buying of appropriate plots of land for second homes but has so far provided many coveted traditional dwellings for conversion to use as second homes by the new owner.

Under the 1966 regional plan for the Stockholm area, in the year 2000 the development of holiday cottages was not to be allowed within a zone which could be reached in under one hour's drive from the city centre. In this way the authorities hope to preserve a zone between permanent residential areas and holiday cottages, in which access to open space and facilities for day recreation can be made available for residents of Stockholm. There is already one area of inner Stockholm where former second homes now serve as poor quality permanent residences and where, because of the former seasonal nature of their use, these properties are not well provided with facilities for waste disposal. Confining future developments of second homes to beyond a certain distance from the city will prevent further occurrences of this kind.

In the past, holiday settlements spread with little regard for their effect on the landscape and no consideration of their role within a general plan for the area involved. Preservation of the countryside for use by the population in nearby urban centres has been overlooked. New legislation, however, regulates even the building of single cottages in the countryside. Planning for holiday cottages in the Stockholm area took place as early as the 1930s but the standards of that time would be totally unacceptable today. Many examples remain to illustrate the shortsightedness of such planning, and extensive stretches of shoreline are almost completely occupied by second homes constructed in this period.

In recent developments, plots are rarely permitted within 300 m (330 yds) of the shoreline, and in the mountain areas there are to be no more buildings above the treeline. Natural woodland in Sweden affords excellent cover for second homes, maximising privacy whilst maintaining the amenity value of the landscape. Because of the private nature of much of the development of second homes, strict planning measures are essential to ensure that certain uniform standards are met. Each plan undergoes rigorous examination before it is approved and the buildings finally erected. The provision of roads, water supply and waste disposal must be adequate before a plan can become a reality. Sites for 50 or fewer second homes are quite common, though sites are often planned for between 100 and 200 cottages. A larger settlement allows economies to be made in the provision of communal facilities, but the larger the development the more it comes to resemble the sort of urban environment to which holiday cottages are intended to provide a welcome alternative. The question of scale is therefore an important consideration and sites are rarely planned with over 200 plots.

There is, however, some indication that the demand for second homes may be levelling off. However traditional this way of recreation may now be in some areas, alternative forms of holiday accommodation are of growing importance. Caravans are increasing in popularity. Improved camping sites exist for both caravans and tents, providing a high standard of facilities and allowing the same access to outdoor life as would a fixed second home. Perhaps these facilities only cater for one section of the demand, for it has been established that 48 per cent of Swedish second homes are used as permanent residences by the wives and children of the families concerned during the school summer break which lasts from mid-June until late August. In addition, in both Sweden and Norway, vacation villages providing chalets and cottages for hire are increasing in both number and standard. In the Sälen area of central Sweden, for example, many new chalets have been built to meet the growing demand for access to the fine natural sports facilities of the area. The newest chalets, whilst built in the traditional style and blending well with the forested surroundings, provide the skier with every modern convenience. If the chalets are filled to capacity then they provide a much cheaper stay in the mountains than other accommodation of comparable comfort.

Strict measures now ensure that future developments avoid shorelines and open mountain areas, though compensation can be sought by would-be developers whose land falls into such protected areas. Planning restrictions within the sites are intended to ensure that in an area of settlement for country cottages, only about one-third of the area may be used for actual cottage plots and the remainder must be given over to roads, open space and service provision. Great emphasis is placed on the provision of open space for public enjoyment in and around each settlement, and the shoreline is included in the green belt wherever possible. The aim is to preserve the attractive countryside of Sweden and to incorporate holiday cottages into the existing landscape rather than to allow them to be superimposed upon it. The principal theme is necessarily protection, since the main locational factor for second homes appears to be access to natural scenic beauty, particularly to forests and lakes, which could easily be destroyed by careless development. Maintenance of the amenity value of the landscape is foremost in current planning, and the preservation of as much natural landscape as possible is rated as more important than the development of second homes. In terms of conservation the trend is away from the preservation of nature for scientific reasons and towards the relatively new idea of preserving land as open space for people to be in and enjoy irrespective of its wildlife. This form of social conservation is a new and important aspect of planning for leisure in Sweden and it emphasises the overwhelming desire to compromise between the recreational ideals and aspirations of the individual and the needs of the community at large. This compromise must also be made in Denmark and Norway as second home development is placed under increasing planning control. In Scandinavia second homes have become a sufficiently widespread phenomenon to warrant specific legislation. Particularly in Sweden, the favourable population-land ratio and attempts at an equitable distribution of economic resources create an environment in which the desirability of second homes as a form of land use need not be questioned at the present time.

REFERENCES

Aldskogius, H. (1960) 'Changing land use and settlement development in the Siljan region' Geografiska Annaler, 42(4), pp.250-61.

Aldskogius, H. (1967) 'Vacation home settlement in the Siljan region' Geografiska Annaler, 49(2), pp.69-95.

Aldskogius, H. (1968) 'Studier i Siljansområdets fritidsbyggelse' Geografiska Regionstudier, 4, Kulturgeografiska Institutionen vid Uppsala Universitet.

Aldskogius, H. (1969) 'Modelling the evolution of settlement patterns: two studies of vacation house settlements' Geografiska Regionstudier, 6, Kulturgeografiska Institutionen vid Uppsala Universitet.

Anker, E. (1967) Hytteområder, en veiledning i planleggning, Report No. 6, Kommonal og Arbeidesdepartement, Distriktplanavdelningen og utvalg for byplanforskning.

Landsplanudsvalgets Sekretariet (1966) Strandkvalitet og Fritidsbebyggelse.

Lantmäteristyrelsen (1968) Planmässig bakgrund vid fastighetsbildning för fritidsändamål, Bulletin No. 2.

Lantmäteristyrelsen (1969) Planmässig bakgrund vid fastighetsbildning för fritidsändamål, Bulletin No. 6, Part 2.

Lantmäteristyrelsen (1971) Planmässig bakgrund vid fastighetsbildning för fritidsändamål, Bulletin No. 7, Part 3.

Larsson, G. (1969) Undersökningar rörande fritidsbebyggelse Institutionen för fastighetsteknik, sekt. Lantmäteri, Tekniska högskolan, Stockholm, Bulletin No. 6, Part 4.

Ljungdahl, S. (1938) 'Sommarstockholm' Ymer 58.

Nordell, P.O. and Rydberg, H. (1959) 'From the plains of Middle Sweden to the high mountains', Geografiska Annaler, 41, pp.170-93.

Norrbom, C-E. (1966) 'Outdoor recreation in Sweden' Sociologia Ruralis, VI (I), pp.56-73.

Ouren, T. (ed) (1969) 'Fritid og feriemilj Norwegian Geographical Studies, 8.

Statens Byggeforskningsinstitut (1970) Fritidsområder og sommerbebyggelse Rapport om planlaegningens og udformninens problemer. SBI-Byplanlaegning 13, København.

Statens Offentliga Utredningar 1964:47 Friluftsliver i Sverige, Part I: Utgångsläge och utvecklingstendenser.

Statens Offentliga Utredningar 1973:52 Turism och Rekreation i Sverige.

Sund, T. (1960) in A. Sømme (ed) Geography of Norden, pp.235-92.

Swedish Urban Planning Board (1970) Västkuston Rapport 5, Part 3.

Wolstad, A. (1968) 'L'habitat des loisirs et la protection des sites au Danemark', paper presented to Aménagement et Nature, Royaumont, October 1968.

Chapter 4

RÉSIDENCES SECONDAIRES IN FRANCE

H. D. Clout

The acquisition of second homes for leisure use is a long-established and widespread phenomenon in France, involving 1.5 million properties in 1970 and affecting almost one-fifth of the nation's households. These facts have attracted the attention of census-takers and social scientists in recent years, so that a large quantity of material has become available for analysis and commentary. Most enquiries have concentrated on conditions in the last ten or fifteen years, but there is abundant, if scattered, evidence of the existence of second homes in the past. Many writers noted the ownership of *châteaux* and country parks by members of the nobility and bourgeoisie around Paris and provincial cities in the eighteenth and nineteenth centuries, and Arthur Young provided valuable details in his journal of Travels in France in the 1780s. Analysis of nineteenth-century archival sources revealed that rich provincials owned houses for weekend use up to 60 miles (100 km) from Besançon and similar cities; and a survey of *maisons de campagne* in Seine-et-Marne *département* in 1846-7 revealed that many were owned by doctors, lawyers and merchants not only from Paris but also from smaller towns around the capital (Chatelain 1970-71). In addition, shopkeepers and tradesmen of distinctly modest means were acquiring weekend cottages and small gardens on the outskirts of Paris where they grew fruit and vegetables. Second homes were not the sole preserve of the very rich at this early stage and the same has remained true in recent years.

Post-war censuses have included questions on second home ownership and thus provide useful bodies of source material. *Résidences secondaires* were defined broadly by the census authorities to include '...houses which owners occupy for only a short period of the year, including holiday homes, and furnished flats used for tourist purposes, but excluding hotels'. This official definition covers all types of built holiday homes, but excludes caravans, moored houseboats and the like. Some researchers have attempted to employ their detailed local knowledge to scale down census figures by separating second homes rented out for short periods to tourists from those occupied on a regular and repeated basis by individual families (Barbier 1965). But in spite of obvious shortcomings, such as breadth of definition and errors of enumeration, successive censuses contain numerical information on second homes for a variety of levels of administrative unit in France and represent a source unmatched in other countries where second homes are important. More detailed information may be derived laboriously from cadastral registers (indicating names and addresses of property owners in each *commune*), other taxation documents, and local lists of building permits issued for the construction of new second homes (Bonneau 1973; Clary 1973). Unfortunately such construction lists are often incomplete. Indeed, each of these statistical sources needs to be treated with critical respect. Sample enquiries by the Institut National de la Statistique et des Etudes Economiques (INSEE) provide valuable insights at national and regional levels, but are not appropriate for local use.

Second homes increased from an estimated 320,000 in 1938, a figure roughly equal to the current estimate of built second homes and static caravans in England and Wales (Chap. 7), to 1,232,000 recorded in the 1968 census (Table 4.1). A sample enquiry in 1970 raised the total to 1.5 million. The curve has not been consistently upward in the past thirty years, being reversed for a short while immediately after the Second World War when many second homes were taken over as primary residences in Brittany, Normandy and regions which had been damaged by war, and again after 1962 when 25,000 second homes in southern France were sold or leased as first homes for *pieds noirs* repatriated

TABLE 4.1. Second homes in France

Year	Total (millions)	Year	Total (millions)
1938[a]	0.320	1966[a]	1,100
1946[b]	0.250	1967[a]	1,150
1954[b]	0.447	1968[b]	1,232
1962[b]	0.960	1970[a]	1,500
1964[a]	1,097		

[a]Official estimate

[b]Census

Source: M.A. Brier (1970) p.2.

from Algeria (Brier 1970, p.21). Ninety-three per cent of the 1,150,000 second homes in 1967 were separate houses, and even now probably no more than 10 per cent of the total are apartments (Grault 1970, p.5). Caravans do not qualify as *second homes* in official statistics, and it is not known what proportion are parked permanently for leisure use. However, total numbers of caravans increased rapidly in the past decade, with 220,000 households (1.4%) owning them in 1967 and one-fifth of French long vacations being spent in caravans or tents in 1971.

French second homes vary greatly in structure, size and equipment, from modest cabins and cottages to sumptuous seaside palaces. In 1968 55 per cent of the total comprised buildings that had been constructed prior to 1914 and had been renovated for leisure use (Table 4.2). Half had either two or three rooms, with only 10 per cent having six rooms or more. Only one-eighth of the national total lacked piped water, but there were considerable inter-regional variations, with 32 per cent of second homes in Limousin and 20 per cent in Bretagne relying on traditional sources of water supply. These, of course, are the most rural regions of France, with relatively low rates of service provision. By contrast, only 5 per cent of second homes in the much more *developed* countrysides of the Région Parisienne and Provence were without piped water. Forty-one per cent of all second homes were equipped with baths or showers, but these facilities were particularly rare in the less *developed* Massif Central. Almost all second homes (96%) were supplied with electricity, with over half containing refrigerators and one-third having television sets.

TABLE 4.2. Date of construction of second homes, 1968

Period	Number	Percentage	Period	Number	Percentage
pre - 1871	417,180	33	1949-1953	36,620	3
1871-1914	276,300	22	1954-1961	106,400	8
1915-1948	220,280	18	after 1961	198,580	16

Source: Recensement de 1968, quoted in C. Brisson and R. Bechmann (1972) p.26.

The increasing number of second homes is the result of a complex interplay of gains and losses that was monitored during the calendar years 1963-66. During that period an average of 25,800 second homes were converted into primary residences each year (Table 4.3). Such losses from the stock of

TABLE 4.3. Average annual changes in second homes, 1963-7

Average annual losses to		Average annual gains from	
First homes	25,800	First homes	56,700
Other uses	13,200	Vacant buildings	6,800
Total losses	39,000	Other buildings	1,200
		Total gains	64,700
		Annual net gain in old buildings	25,700
		Annual construction of new second homes	14,700
		Total net gains	40,400

Source: INSEE (1968a), quoted in C. Brisson and R. Bechmann (1972) p.25.

second homes included properties which were used as first homes by families commuting long distances each day, properties that were swallowed up as first homes by the outward spread of suburbia, and other second homes which became the permanent dwellings of retired people. Houses in the final category, of course, might still be used as second homes by children or grandchildren while elderly relatives were on holiday. A further 13,200 second homes were lost annually to other uses, with three-quarters of these being left vacant and the remainder occupied for non-residential purposes or demolished. Approximately

39,000 second homes were lost each year during the middle 1960s, and it is likely that this process will continue to increase in importance since about two-fifths of French second homes are located less than 25 miles (40 km) from their owners' (predominantly urban) first homes, so that there is plenty of scope for functional change from secondary back to primary residences, as has been noted on the margins of Grenoble (Palatin 1969).

By contrast, on average 56,700 first homes were converted to second homes each year during the mid-1960s. Some 6,800 houses that had been vacant previously, and 1,200 other buildings, became second homes, to give an annual absolute increase of 64,700 and an annual net increase of 25,700 second homes from existing housing stock. An average of 14,700 new second homes were built each year during the study period, but it is significant that the actual volume of new constructions more than doubled from under 10,000 in 1963 to over 24,000 in 1966.

The upward trend in the development of second homes continued apace after the mid-1960s. Results of an INSEE enquiry in 1966 indicated that half of the households sampled intended to acquire second homes, with 3 per cent envisaging doing so before 1970 (Brisson and Bechmann 1972, p.12). By that year it was estimated that second homes were increasing at a rate of 80,000 per annum, comprising the conversion of old buildings to provide 50,000 second home units and the construction of 30,000 new ones (Grault 1970, p.5). This figure accords reasonably with the progression of new building noted for the mid-1960s. Two-thirds of the new second homes were being built around the coast, with construction of the remainder being divided almost equally between the mountains and other rural areas.

Occupiers of Second Homes

Many more households have access to second homes than actually own them. In 1967 2.8 million households (18.2% of the total) made use of second homes for holidays and/or weekends as a result of ownership, long-term leasing or borrowing. Less than half of that number (1,188,000) actually owned the second homes they used (Table 4.4). Some 85 per cent of these households

TABLE 4.4. Access to second homes, 1967

Type of access	Numbers and proportions of households with access to second homes	
	Numbers	Percentage
Own second homes	1,188,000	36.0
Rent annually	68,000	2.1
Use second homes owned by relatives	450,000	13.7
Use friends' second homes	148,000	4.5
Use relatives' or friends' first homes	1,440,000	44.7

Source: J. Antoine and J. Aglietta (1969) p.18.

used one second home apiece, with the remainder using two or more on a regular basis. Third homes were certainly not unknown. Understandably, therefore, there is great divergence between figures on the number of second homes and statistics relating to households making use of them. A study of the housing stock of the Paris Basin, outside greater Paris, estimated that there were 1,200,000 first homes that were simply used as primary residences, but in addition there were 527,000 first homes that were sometimes used as second homes by family or friends when the occupants were away, and 207,000 properties that were used only as second homes (Antoine and Aglietta 1969, p.19).

Ownership of second homes, as opposed to use, is most widespread among affluent strata of French society. Only 2.3 per cent of households recorded as earning less than 3,000 francs per annum in 1967 owned second homes, but at the top of the scale 60 per cent of households with annual incomes in excess of 100,000 francs possessed them (Table 4.5). This fact is confirmed by

TABLE 4.5. Ownership of second homes by household income, 1967

Annual income (francs)	Percentage of households owning second homes
Less than 3,000	2.3
3 - 6,000	2.6
6 - 10,000	4.4
10 - 15,000	6.4
15 - 20,000	6.5
20 - 30,000	12.0
30 - 50,000	19.4
50 - 100,000	29.9
Over 100,000	60.0

Source: C. Brisson and R. Bechmann (1972) p.38.

information relating to socio-economic groups. Only 2.8 per cent of farmers and farm workers owned second homes, by contrast with 21.7 per cent of professional families (Table 4.6). The numerical importance of lawyers, doctors and teachers in second-home ownership has emerged from many local studies (Balseinte 1959; Barbier 1968a). However, some French second homes are owned by agricultural workers and other poorly paid families. This may well be accounted for by the fact that property has been inherited from rural relatives and the choice has been made to keep it for leisure use. In such circumstances issues related to the cost of property do not arise.

Over a quarter of the heads of households owning second homes were more than 50 years of age according to the enquiry in 1967, with 15.9 per cent

TABLE 4.6. Ownership of second homes by socio-economic groups, 1967

Socio-economic group	Percentage of households owning second homes
Farmers and agricultural workers	2.8
Industrial employers	14.0
Professional workers	21.7
Middle management	13.8
Service workers	5.8
Clerical workers	8.6
Manual workers	3.5
Others	13.9
Unemployed or retired	5.1

Source: C. Brisson and R. Bechmann 1972, p.39.

being over 60. Availability of capital for investment and acquisition of a house for eventual retirement are certainly important reasons for acquisition of second homes by middle-aged people. But recent though the second homes *explosion* has been, with the national total roughly doubling between 1950 and 1960, and doubling again between 1960 and 1970, many second homes were acquired by their present owners at various stages in the past when their purchasers were younger. Thus the same study undertaken in the Paris Basin in 1968 revealed that 21 per cent of the second homes had been acquired before 1945, 26 per cent between 1945 and 1958, 18 per cent between 1959 and 1962, and 24 per cent after 1962, with no information available for the remaining 11 per cent (Brisson and Bechmann 1972, p.19). Analysis of the age structure of users of second homes, rather than owners, showed there were many younger heads of households (especially 20-29 years), suggesting that young families made use of first and/or second homes owned by parents or relatives at holiday times.

The ownership and use of second homes is largely in the hands of town dwellers. Only 2.5 per cent of French households living in rural *cantons* owned second homes, with proportions rising progressively through the settlement hierarchy to 19.7 per cent for Paris *département* and 10.1 per cent for the rest of the Paris built-up area (Table 4.7). Similarly, access to second homes was most pronounced among Parisians, involving 41.6 per cent of households living in Paris *département*. Deviations from the crude ratio of 1:3 between ownership and access (or use) involved residents of rural *cantons*, who presumably did not want second homes or were unable to afford them, and Parisians, among whom rates of ownership were particularly high. Thus the Région Parisienne contained 20.9 per cent of the total population of the country and 37.9 per cent of second-home owners. In the southern half of

TABLE 4.7. Ownership of and access to second homes by size of settlement

Size of Settlement	Percentage of households owning a second home	with access to a second home
Rural *cantons*	2.5	6.2
Towns with less than 20,000 inhabitants	4.5	13.6
Towns with 20,000-100,000 inhabitants	7.8	22.0
Towns with 100,000-200,000 inhabitants	7.1	21.7
Towns with over 200,000 inhabitants	11.6	26.6
Paris *département*	19.7	41.6
Rest of greater Paris	10.1	28.4

Source: INSEE 1968b, quoted in C. Brisson and R. Bechmann 1972, p.42.

France, ownership (42.5%) was also well ahead of the proportion of population living there (38.5%). Conversely, 40.6 per cent of the national population lived in northern France but only 19.6 per cent of second-home owners came from that part of the country. There is no simple explanation for this contrast, but any attempt would need to take into account climatic differences between north and south, especially with respect to temperature; the degree of rural depopulation and availability of vacant housing in the countryside for conversion; the volume of rural commuting to urban factory work, which helps to stabilise rural population; and variations in the availability of *attractive* landscapes to appeal to potential second-home purchasers.

Patterns of Second Home Development

Major concentrations of second homes in France are found in the Région Parisienne, Rhône-Alpes and Provence-Côte-d'Azur, each containing more than 130,000 in 1968 (Fig. 4.1). These are the most urbanised and affluent parts of France, generating the greatest demand for leisure homes. The two southern regions contain French sections of the Alps and the most developed stretch of French Mediterranean coastline, and thus exercise a nationwide, indeed international, attraction for summer and winter recreation as well as satisfying the regional demands of citizens of Lyon, Marseille and other southern cities for weekend homes.

When distributions are examined in detail, for example from the pages of the various French regional atlases and the *Atlas de la France Rurale* (1968), second homes are confirmed as numerous in coastal and mountain areas, in stretches of peri-urban countryside, but also in some urban settlements. In 1962, 34 per cent of second homes had been located in *rural* areas, but by 1968 this proportion had risen to 40 per cent. In the Région Parisienne, Nord, Provence and three western regions from the Loire to the Spanish border, more than 50 per cent of second homes were located in towns in 1968. The

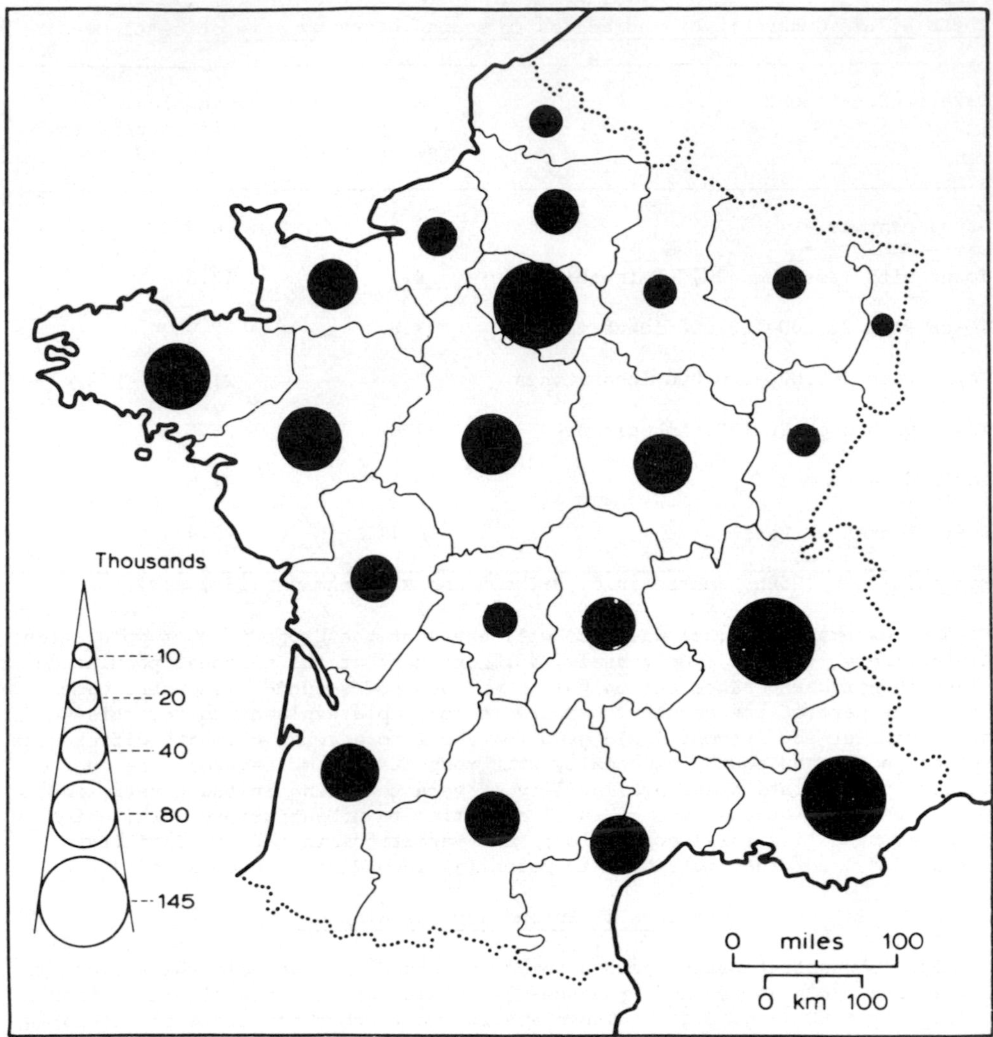

Fig. 4.1 Second homes in France, by regions, 1968

growing importance of *urban* second homes may be elucidated with reference to two facts. First, *pieds-à-terre* in large cities and flats and second houses in seaside resorts have certainly increased in number, with 28,100 being found in Paris in 1968, 8,200 in Nice, 7,860 in Cannes and 5,200 in Marseille (Laborde 1970). But secondly, the official definition of *urban* areas includes *communes* with a minimum population of 2,000 living in their chief nucleation; quite small settlements thus are included in the *urban* category. Such towns normally contain basic services and therefore hold attractions for at least one category of second-home owners, although perhaps not appealing to those who seek solitude.

While the number of second homes in France increased by 30 per cent (262,000) between 1962 and 1968, those in the countryside increased by only 17 per cent (c94,000) and those in rural parts of the Région Parisienne and the Pays de la Loire clearly declined, probably because of the spread of primary suburbanisation. Second homes in urban areas increased by 55.4 per cent (c168,000) over the same six years (Antoine and Aglietta 1969, p.17). Increases in urban second homes of more than 75 per cent between 1962 and 1968 were recorded in regions on the northwestern coast and in Languedoc, where important developments were taking place in seaside resorts, and in Rhône-Alpes, which contains both new and expanded ski centres. The vast majority of urban second homes were located in towns with less than 50,000 inhabitants (30.2 per cent of all second homes), with only 3.9 per cent in the eight *métropoles d'équilibre,* 2.3 per cent in Paris, and 3.6 per cent in other cities with more than 50,000 inhabitants. Rates of urban increase were high in Mediterranean coastal resorts, especially in Gard and Pyrénées-Orientales *départements,* and on the Channel coast (Somme *département*), where large numbers of second-home apartments and new houses, intended as second homes, were constructed.

In the Région Parisienne as a whole, the 130,000 second homes recorded in 1968 made up only 4 per cent of the total housing stock, exactly half the national proportion. But second homes were important in relative terms in the still fairly rural *départements* of Essonne (9.4%) and Seine-et-Marne (17.6%) (Fig. 4.2). *Départements* such as Seine-Saint-Denis (-9.3%) and Val-d'Oise (-1.4%), where suburban development was rapid, experienced reductions in numbers of second homes, but important increases were recorded in the largely built-up *département* of Paris (+22.0%), the inner *département* of Hauts-de-Seine (+28.4%) to the west of the most fashionable *quartiers* in the city centre, and in Seine-et-Marne (+16.4%) which still contains expanses of countryside.

Second-home hinterlands have been identified around French cities, with diameters increasing in relation to city size and consequent volume of demand, and chronologically in response to improvements in transport technology (Cribier 1969). Thus 50 per cent of Parisian owners have their second homes more than 160 km (100 miles) from the city centre, but around major provincial cities the modal split occurs at about 70 km (45 miles) (Brier 1970, p.87). These idealised *rings* of second homes are in fact distorted into sectors along axes of communication, especially motorways, in areas with *landscape* attractions, and in accordance with the social patterning of cities. Thus, second homes are particularly numerous to the west, south and southeast of Paris, but are less so beyond the working-class suburbs of the north and east of the capital (Cribier 1971). Water surfaces, both *natural* and man-made, and sunny microclimates are also important attractors (Beteille 1970). But, in as much as most second homes in France are old farm buildings that have been converted, other explanatory features need to be examined, including existing patterns of settlement, the volume of rural out-migration, availability of vacant housing, existence of social or cultural attractions for particular groups to particular areas, and the role of inheritance in the acquisition of second homes. These and other social parameters are perhaps of limited significance in modelling the development of second homes in New World contexts (cf Chapter 13), where most second homes are newly constructed, but a case must be made for including cultural and historical considerations in studies undertaken in Europe, where social linkages between town and country are long-established and many second homes are old farm buildings. But in both Europe and the New World the spatial impact of planning controls, real-estate development and

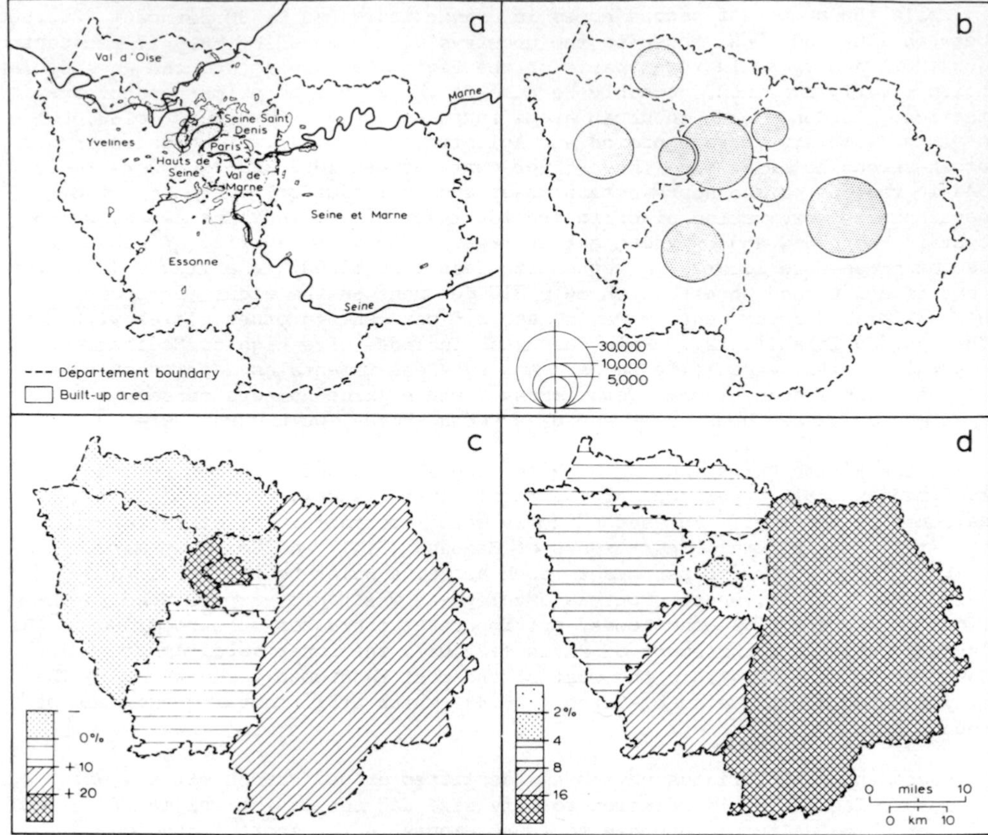

Fig. 4.2 (a) Région Parisienne; (b) Second homes by départements, 1968; (c) Percentage change in numbers of second homes, 1962-8; (d) Second homes as a percentage of first homes, 1968

advertising demands more attention than it has received so far in studies of second homes.

Acquiring a second home

Growing affluence across broader sectors of society has combined with other trends to make the dream of a second home a reality for increasing numbers of French families. The working year for the average salaried employee in France is reported to have dropped from 3,500 hours in 1910 to 2,100 hours in 1960 (Brier 1970, p.6). One month's holiday with pay is now the norm. The number of cars has risen tenfold from 1,300,000 in 1949 to 13,100,000 in 1970, when 58 per cent of households had at least one car apiece, compared with 20 per cent fifteen years earlier.

Four main arguments are frequently advanced to account for the decision to acquire a second home. The first argument interprets the second home as a compensation for city living. In 1968, 70 per cent of the French lived in urban areas, compared with 57 per cent thirty years earlier. Apartment dwelling is, of course, a tradition in cities in Continental Europe, but a recent public opinion poll showed that 82 per cent of the French families interviewed wished to live in detached or semi-detached homes rather than in flats (Brisson and Bechmann 1972, p.12). In France as a whole, 51 per cent of families live in individual houses and in the North the proportion reaches 80 per cent. This point may be of significance in helping to account for the relative sparsity of second homes in northern France. By contrast, four out of five Parisian households live in apartments, compared with only one in seven in rural areas, and two out of every three in cities with 100,000 inhabitants or more. Inner urban development at high densities poses serious environmental irritations of noise, traffic congestion and air pollution. For example, the average Parisian is reported to have 1.8 sq. yds (1.5m^2) of public open space at his disposal in Paris *département*, by comparison with six times that amount in London and thirty times as much in Washington D.C. Almost one-third of French dwellings were classified as *overcrowded* in the 1968 census and in Paris the proportion rose to 38 per cent. Many dwellings lacked basic facilities, with half of all French housing units having neither baths nor showers. There are, undoubtedly, many urban disadvantages from which to escape at weekends. But it is, of course, ironic that city dwellers who endure the worst environmental conditions are least likely to be able to purchase second homes or have access to them.

Buying a country cottage or a leisure apartment is a good capital investment not only for the French, but also for sun-seeking Dutch and Germans on the Languedoc coast, and for the British in the Dordogne, where the proliferation of English language advertisements in estate agents' windows suggests a seasonal reconquest of Perigord by the British each summer (Chadefaud 1973). National statistics show that 46 per cent of French households own their own first homes, 43 per cent rent them, and 11 per cent are housed without charge by employers, relatives and the like. Investment in the purchase of a second home makes a strong appeal to affluent occupants of rented primary accommodation for whom the *résidence secondaire* is both a substitute and a complement to restricted urban housing.

Achievement of short-term leisure objectives undoubtedly motivates many purchasers of second homes. But an important distinction must be drawn between those who try to find a truly isolated country cottage to *get away from it all* and others who wish to indulge in specific recreational activities, such as skiing, sailing or fishing. Some members of this latter group will seek the company of fellow enthusiasts and will, in any case, select sites for second homes only where their particular scarce recreational resources (snow, water surfaces, good fishing streams) are available. The existence of these two types of occupant of second homes, together with the various cultural factors already mentioned, complicates attempts to rationalise the distribution of sites and buildings used as second homes. In addition, expected patterns of use have important implications for the location of second homes. Those used predominantly at weekends are generally closer to first homes than are second homes that are occupied mainly during vacations. Thus the hinterland of weekend cottages around Paris is predominantly less than two hours' driving distance, but the hinterlands of Parisians' vacation homes extends across the whole of France and, indeed, abroad. In practice,

61 per cent of second homes in the Paris Basin are used both for weekends and for holidays, 11 per cent only at weekends and 28 per cent only for vacations (Antoine and Aglietta 1969, p.19).

Finally, the long-term objective of a second home as a place in which to retire may outweight the types of short-term motivation that have been mentioned. Accessibility to services together with other factors relating to future full-time use will be taken into consideration by occupants of second homes who have retirement in mind for the near future.

In the discussion so far, emphasis has been placed on purchase as a means of acquiring second homes, but many urban families in France have parents or grandparents who live in the countryside, and thus inheritance of rural property by city people is not a rare occurrence. This may well also be the case in other European countries where rapid urbanisation has occurred in the twentieth century rather than in the nineteenth. Price, landscape, and the range of other issues to be examined in deciding to *actively acquire* a second home are not relevant to inheritance or *passive acquisition*, where the decision is simply whether to use the property as a second home or to dispose of it in some other way (Soulier 1970).

The importance of inheritance in acquisition of second homes is not known for the whole of France, but regional enquiries provide some insights. A sample investigation in the seven planning regions of the Paris Basin showed that at least 8 per cent of second homes were newly constructed and 76 per cent were old buildings (Table 4.8). The remainder was unspecified. Most

TABLE 4.8. Acquisition of second homes in the Paris Basin

Acquisition category		Percentage distribution by planning region						
		Total Paris Basin	Région Paris-ienne	Norman-die	Cham-pagne	Bour-gogne	Centre	Picar-die
New buildings	purchased	1	1	1	2	0	0	1
	built for/by owners	7	12	7	5	4	5	7
Old buildings	purchased	53	53	53	45	51	51	51
	inherited	24	18	32	41	27	53	21
Not specified		15	12	5	3	17	20	16

Total second homes = 515,282
Source: Commissariat Générale au Tourisme 1968, quoted in C. Brisson and R. Bechmann 1972, p.48.

of the old buildings were purchased for use as second homes (52% of the total sample) but an important proportion was inherited (24% of the sample). Inherited properties used as second homes rose to 27 per cent of the sample in Bourgogne, 32 per cent in Normandie and 41 per cent in Champagne. Thus as many as a quarter of second homes in the Paris Basin were inherited, in areas where commercial pressures were among the strongest in France. One might well expect the role of inheritance to be greater in less-developed countryside, judging from evidence from the uplands of the Hérault (45% inherited), the Chartreuse Iséroise (40%), and parts of the Massif Central (Soulier 1970; David and Geoffroy 1968; Clout 1970 and 1971; Saussol 1965).

In these and comparable rural areas, at least, any attempts to account for the acquisition and subsequent distribution of second homes without reference to out-migration, inheritance and family ties would be inadequate. Of course, there are some areas of France, such as seaside resorts, new ski centres and some stretches of peri-urban countryside, where the acquisition of second homes is largely in the hands of property developers and estate agents rather than family lawyers. A case may be made that this type of transaction will become more important in the future, but there is also evidence for the contrary view. Inheritance may well become even more important in the future, as numbers of second homes grow and these are transmitted to family heirs after the death of initial purchasers. This point will also be relevant to countries in the New World where the majority of second homes are non-agricultural buildings that have been specially constructed for or by their purchasers.

The dispersed distribution of second homes, in the form of either new or converted properties, poses problems of escalating costs of service provision with respect to electricity supply, piped water, road maintenance and garbage collection. Conservation pressure groups express concern about intrusion of second homes built in inappropriate styles into otherwise *unspoiled* landscapes, restoration of old cottages with building materials that disrupt the scene rather than harmonise with it or enhance it, and creation of second-home slums (Lamorisse 1970; Dewailly 1967). Dispersed examples of old and new second homes are numerous in France, but estates of chalets and leisure apartments have been built by real-estate developers to cater for the growing demand in the Alps and other mountain areas and along sections of the coast. The best known example is the Languedoc-Roussillon scheme which involved the creation of six new coastal resorts, each containing specially built second homes (Hall 1973). The scheme has been advertised widely abroad in order to obtain foreign investment. Unfortunately, the sums invested have not been as large as had been hoped, and the scheme has been reduced to three resorts instead of six for a variety of financial reasons. But other important recreation projects involving development of second homes have been started with financial backing from the French government along the coast of Aquitaine, in Corsica, and in a number of mountain areas. In the Alps many sites on lakeshores and near snowslopes have already been developed for second homes. The next stage will introduce development on to intervening slopes (Bonnazi 1970).

Second homes : blessing or curse?

The impact of the development of second homes on rural residents has been the subject of comment by researchers working in many parts of France, but detailed quantitative investigation of economic implications remains to be attempted. Some observers argue that the proliferation of second homes brings economic benefits and social advantages to countryfolk (Barbier 1968b). These would include profits derived from sale of rural property for use as second homes; supply of goods and services to weekenders and holiday residents from local shops, restaurants and garages; generation of employment for local craftsmen in the form of restoring cottages; and collection of additional local taxes from second-home occupants. Cottages that would otherwise be left derelict are restored and lived in, albeit only on a temporary basis, and thus the park-keeping role of second-home residents, with their homes and gardens, provide features of interest in the rural landscape, which might otherwise revert to rough wilderness and be of limited attraction to tourists and weekenders who prefer inhabited landscapes. Country people have the opportunity of broadening their social contacts by the presence of townsfolk in second homes and such people generate inflated seasonal demands for goods which may allow tradesmen to make sufficient profit for their premises to be kept open all year to the benefit of the dwindling permanent population.

Other observers have been more critical, arguing that the proliferation of second homes swamps year-round communities and that the occupation of weekend and holiday cottages cannot bring balanced life back to depopulated and *ruralised* villages (Jung 1971). Inflated property prices and consequent shortages of housing for farmworkers and factory employees who commute to nearby towns form common causes of complaint (Cribier 1966). In some areas growing numbers of second homes have been blamed for accelerating rural out-migration and preventing schemes for plot consolidation and farm enlargement that would benefit permanent residents (David 1966). As in other parts of the western world, evidence may be marshalled to support both arguments and reach either conclusion. One man's blessing can easily be another man's curse.

The establishment of second homes is yet another process whereby the *dispersed city* is invading residual rural space, but this time on a seasonal or temporary basis. Its distinctiveness in France is linked to the following factors (Cribier 1973). Second homes are numerous and widely distributed throughout the country. They display great diversity of size, equipment and house style, reflecting local traditions of vernacular architecture. Most are old farm buildings that have been renovated, with very few being constructed specially for leisure use in recent years. As a result, renovated second homes are often side by side with farm buildings rather than located on special estates. A good proportion have been acquired through family inheritance rather than by purchase. In the wake of the wave of second homes, profound economic, social and visual changes have taken place in many parts of the French countryside and these may be expected to increase in magnitude in future years. In addition, urban *pieds-à-terre* are becoming increasingly popular. The number of second homes will continue to grow and the practice of occupying a second home will become an even more firmly embedded tradition in French life, with cottages and leisure apartments being transmitted from generation to generation. Neither the life styles of city dwellers nor those of countrymen will escape unaltered.

REFERENCES

Antoine, J. and Aglietta J. (1969) La résidence secondaire: phénomène urbain? Revue 2000 2, pp.16-22.

Balseinte, R. (1959) 'Megève: ou la transformation d'une agglomération montagnarde par les sports d'hiver' Revue de Géographie Alpine 47, pp.131-224.

Barbier, B. (1965) 'Méthodes d'étude des résidences secondaires: l'exemple des Basses-Alpes' Meditérranée 1, pp.89-111.

Barbier, B. (1968a) 'Vars: une grande station des Alpes du Sud' Revue de Géographie Alpine 56, pp.265-81.

Barbier, B. (1968b) Villes et Centres des Alpes du Sud, Editions Ophrys, Gap.

Beteille, R. (1970) 'Résidences secondaires en milieu rural: l'exemple du bassin rouergat du Viaur' Revue Géographique des Pyrénées et du Sud-Ouest 41, pp.159-76.

Bonnazi, R. (1970) 'Les résidences secondaires dans le département de la Haute-Savoie' Revue de Géographie Alpine 58, pp.111-34.

Bonneau, M. (1973) 'Résidences secondaires et tourisme en Maine-et-Loire' Bulletin de la Société Languedocienne de Géographie 7, pp.307-20.

Brier, M-A. (1970) Les Résidences Secondaires Dunod, Paris.

Brisson, C. and Bechmann R. (1972) 'Les résidences secondaires en France' Notes et Études Documentaires 3939-40, pp.1-88.

Chadefaud, M. (1973) 'Méthode d'analyse d'une clientèle touristique étrangère dans un espace d'arrivée' Bulletin de la Société Languedocienne de Géographie 7, pp.389-404.

Chatelain, A. (1970-71) 'Les migrations temporaires de détente et de loisirs des Parisiens: XVII-XXe siècles' Études de la Région Parisienne 44, pp.27-32; 45, pp.31-8.

Clary, D. (1973) 'Les résidences secondaires: approche financière du problème. L'exemple de la côte normande' Bulletin de la Société Languedocienne de Géographie 7, pp.321-32.

Clout, H.D. (1970) 'Social aspects of second-home occupation in the Auvergne' Planning Outlook 9, pp.33-49.

Clout, H.D. (1971) 'Second homes in the Auvergne' Geographical Review 61, pp.530-53.

Commissariat Général au Tourisme (1968) 'Les résidences de loisirs dans le bassin parisien' Bulletin Statistique, p.99.

Cribier, F. (1966) '300,000 résidences secondaires' Urbanisme 96-7, pp.97-101.

Cribier, F. (1969) La Grande Migration d'Été des Citadins en France, Centre National de la Recherche Scientifique, Paris.

Cribier, F. (1971) 'Les rapports saisonniers entre la ville et l'espace en Europe occidentale' in I.G.U. Proceedings on Symposium on Population Geography Calcutta, pp.143-48.

Cribier, F. (1973) 'Les résidences secondaires des citadins dans les campagnes françaises' Études Rurales 49-50, pp.181-204.

David J. (1966) 'Résidences secondaires et structures foncières dans le Val du Bourget' Revue de Géographie Alpine 54, pp.489-503.

David J. and Geoffroy, G. (1968) 'Les résidences secondaires en Chartreuse iséroise' Revue de Géographie Alpine 56, pp.65-72.

Dewailly, J. (1967) 'Utilisation du sol et aménagement d'une vallée humide: la vallée de la Sensée' Hommes et Terres du Nord 1, pp.60-75.

Grault, J. (1970) 'Les résidences secondaires ' Tendances 68, pp.5-10.

Hall, J. (1973) 'Europe's seaside: landscape for leisure' Built Environment 2, pp.215-18.

INSEE (1968a) 'Evolution du parc des logements depuis 1962 en France' Études et Conjoncture 9, Institut National de la Statistique et des Études Économiques, Paris.

INSEE (1968b) 'Résidences secondaires des Français en juin 1967' Études et Conjoncture, Supplement 5, Institut National de la Statistique et des Études Économiques, Paris.

Jung, J. (1971) L'Aménagement de L'Espace Rural: une Illusion Écomonique, Editions Calmann Levy, Paris.

Laborde, P. (1970) 'L'appropriation foncière des Parisiens dans une région de villégiature: la côte basque française' Revue Géographique des Pyrénées et du Sud-Ouest 41, pp.29-42.

Lamorisse, R. (1970) 'Economie rurale et démographie dans la Vallée Française' Bulletin de la Société Languedocienne de Géographie 4, pp.341-69.

Palatin, G. (1969) 'Le développement des résidences citadines dans la région grenobloise' Revue de Géographie Alpine 57, pp.747-57.

Saussol, A. (1965) La Vallée Française: décadence et renouveau d'une vallée cévenole Bulletin de la Société Languedocienne de Géographie 36, pp.5-64.

Soulier, A. (1970) 'Tourisme et mutations rurales dans le haut pays héraultais' Bulletin de la Société Languedocienne de Géographie 4, pp.135-64.

Chapter 5

SECOND HOMES IN CZECHOSLOVAKIA

V. Gardavský

An important feature of contemporary society is the existence of migration flows that have concentrated increasing proportions of population in towns and cities. However, rising numbers of city dwellers seek to spend their leisure time in the countryside. Urbanisation in Czechoslovakia has, for several reasons, developed rather more slowly than in some of the other industrial countries of Europe, but since the beginning of the present century, residents of larger towns and cities have made efforts to establish second homes in the countryside. This process became increasingly popular after the Second World War with the mass development of weekend recreation, which was particularly significant among the inhabitants of larger towns and cities. Recreational activities represent a distinctive form of rural-urban interaction with particular implications for the use of land resources. This is the theme of the present discussion.

The economic development of Czechoslovakia, especially between the two world wars, was far from uniform in its spatial impact. Slovakia remained relatively underdeveloped and real progress dates only from the last twenty years, and especially since Czechoslovakia became a federal state (1968). In addition to other factors there are pronounced differences in the volume of demand for weekend recreation and it is therefore appropriate to discuss the two constituent republics separately, namely the Czech Socialist Republic and the Slovakian Socialist Republic. Unfortunately, statistical evidence on short-term recreation in the two republics is both sparse and of limited reliability.

The most characteristic form of weekend recreation in Czechoslovakia involves occupying private chalets or cottages. These types of property vary in several respects, especially in terms of construction. As in other countries opinions are divided as to how second homes should be defined (Bielckus *et al.*1972; Clout 1971; Clout 1974). Many private individuals not only have permanent residences in urban areas but also possess recreation homes that they use at weekends, on free days and during the summer holidays. The proportion of the population that owns recreation homes varies from region to region. In cities of 100,000 or more inhabitants over 30 per cent of families own second homes; another section of the population spends its weekends making use of recreational facilities in their home towns; others visit friends and relatives; and a small number make use of facilities for recreation provided by their factories. Such facilities are mainly in the mountain and foothill regions of the country and are used most intensively during the winter. These various recreational activities are mentioned merely as background information, and are not developed further in this chapter.

Second homes in the Czech Socialist Republic

In 1971 there were 156,402 second homes in the Czech Socialist Republic, of which 24,329 were cottages that had originally been occupied by the rural population. Table 5.1 shows the small size of most of these second homes with more than three-quarters occupying 5o m² or less. Most of these second homes,

TABLE 5.1. Size of second homes in the Czech Socialist Republic by groups

Area	Number
16 m² and less	9,404
17 - 50 m²	109,321
51 - 60 m²	11,561
61 - 100 m²	16,570
over 100 m²	9,546
Total	156,402

86,025 or 55 per cent, were occupied on Saturdays and Sundays throughout the year and during summer holidays (Table 5.2). One-third of the owners (33.3%) used their second homes only during the summer and a further 9.9 per cent used

TABLE 5.2. Structure of second homes in the Czech Socialist Republic by locality and type of use

Locality			Whole year Satur-day and Sunday	Only some weeks of the year	Type of Use In summer	In winter	Irregul-arly
Inner urban wards	Number	38,196	15,967	6,119	9,649	74	5,163
	Percentage		41.8	16.0	25.2	0.2	13.5
Outer urban wards	Number	92,443	38,486	12,877	31,413	204	8,235
	Percentage		41.6	13.9	34.0	0.2	8.9
Forested areas	Number	25,774	10,292	2,284	10,969	51	2,081
	Percentage		39.9	8.9	42.6	0.2	8.1
Total	Number	156,402	64,745	21,280	52,031	329	15,479
	Percentage		41.4	13.6	33.3	0.2	9.1

them very irregularly. In 1971 there were 2,525 second homes (1.6%) that were actually occupied throughout the year. These were mainly former agricultural cottages which were used by retired people, who are given priority for acquiring accommodation outside towns and cities even though they retain their primary residences in the urban areas. A small proportion of families with young children, who lack satisfactory accommodation in the town or city, are willing to live in the countryside for part of the year, with the father joining his family in their second homes at the weekends and perhaps also for a few nights during the working week.

The rising number of second homes in the Czech Socialist Republic is shown in Fig. 5.1. In 1930 there were 22,964 second homes. A further 17,214 were built between 1931 and 1945, and they then increased by 22,309 between 1946 and 1955, by 46,438 between 1956 and 1965, and by 44,548 between 1966 and 1971.

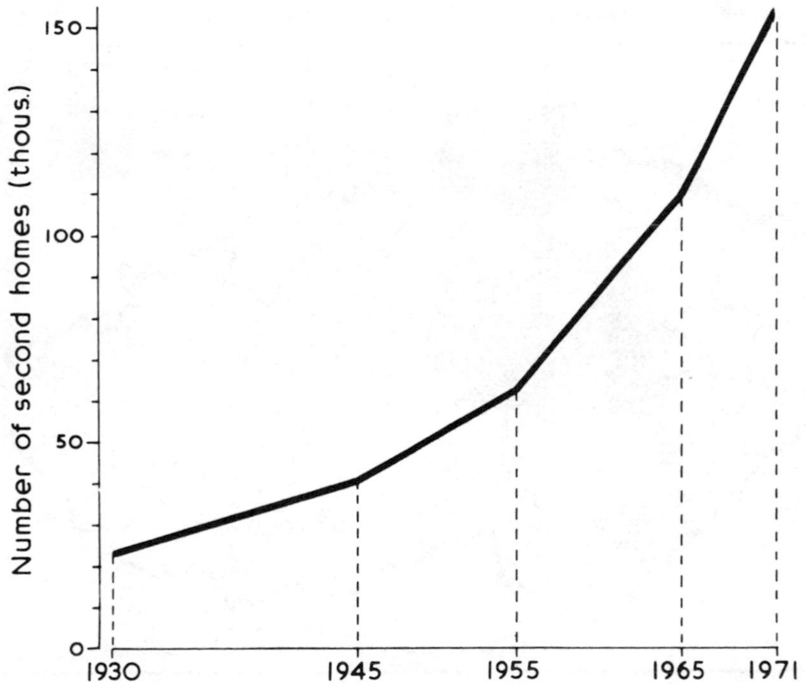

Fig. 5.1 Number of second homes in the Czech Socialist Republic, 1930-71.

During the first stage, prior to 1945, the distribution of second homes displayed two basic features. Many were concentrated in narrow belts around urban areas, where rich city residents constructed villas and *summer seats*. Their function was to demonstrate the material wealth of their owners. A larger group of inhabitants acquired second homes a little further out in the countryside in areas where land prices were lower and communications were good, especially by rail.

After 1945 there was a visible change away from the former ostentatious luxury villas, some of which were built in the peri-urban countryside and some in the internal wards. New buildings were constructed with the help of special loans. Urban inhabitants expanded their interests further into the surrounding countryside, especially into areas with good systems of mass communication. The growth of urban population and increased demand for second homes meant that more distant areas were designated for use for weekend recreation. Important development has occurred in the last ten years, in response to increasing numbers of private vehicles. As a result there is less dependence on public transport and the distribution of second homes is more widely dispersed beyond areas of primary residences. It is not known if second homes were in existence up to 50 km (30 miles) from demand centres in the late 1950s when the speed and frequency of public transport was still of vital importance. Now second homes are found 100 km (60 miles) and more from major cities. Prague, the national capital, with a million inhabitants, commands a very broad recreation hinterland. Figure 5.2 shows the proportion of second homes in individual districts of the Czech Socialist Republic owned

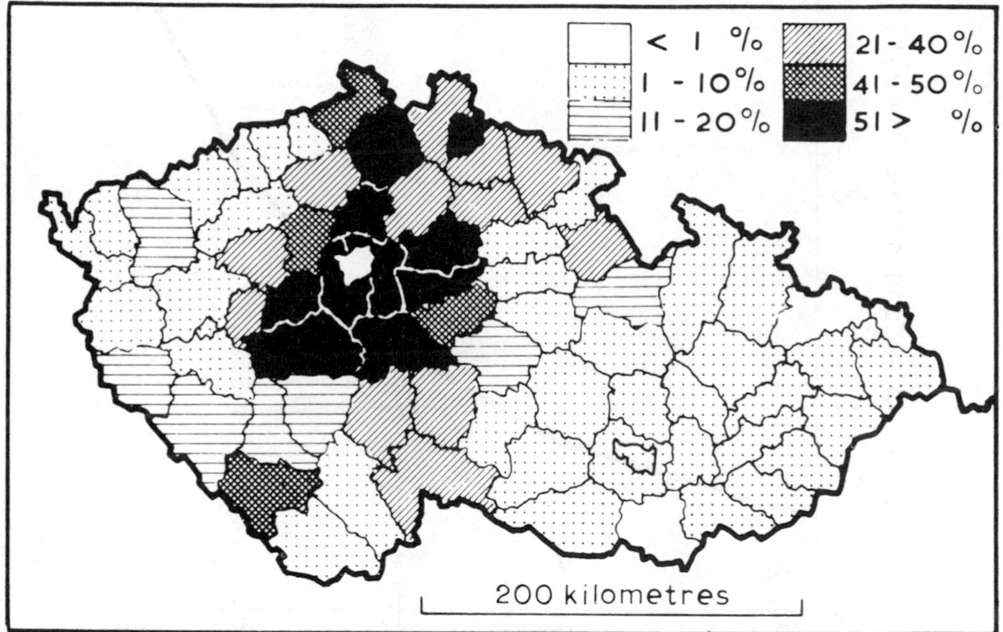

Fig. 5.2 Proportion of second homes owned by Prague residents

by the inhabitants of Prague. Only four of the districts lack second homes owned by Prague people. Three of these districts (Opava, Ostrava and Karviná) are areas of important industrial concentration, especially for production of hard coal, metallurgical goods, heavy engineering products and chemicals, and for this reason such areas have little attraction for recreation.

In order to assess the spatial impact of second homes in the Czech Socialist Republic, further use will be made of information from individual administrative districts. Such units have important limitations, especially in terms of their size, number of permanent residents and variations in density of population. With the exception of Prague districts 1 and 2, which were created from the city's historic core, there are no districts in the Czech Socialist Republic without second homes. A summary of the absolute number of second homes in individual districts is shown in Table 5.3, the largest number of districts (67) contain between 500 and 2,000 second homes. Seven

TABLE 5.3. Number of second homes in the Czech Socialist Republic (by districts)

Number of second homes in district	100-500	501-1,000	1,001-1,500	1,501-2,000	2,001-2,500
Number of districts	7	12	23	12	5
Number of second homes in district	2,501-3,000	3,001-4,000	4,001-6,000	6,001+	
Number of districts	4	4	4	4	

districts contain fewer than 500 second homes, and three of these districts (Ostrava, Karvina and Most) are predominantly industrial. The largest numbers of second homes are found in the districts of Prague-East (10,527) and Prague-West (16,988) where the immediate influence of the city is very pronounced. The origins of the second homes phenomenon in Czechoslovakia occurred in these areas.

For a more meaningful appraisal of the distribution of second homes it is inappropriate to include the total area of each district. Refinements may be made by examining the *potential recreation area* of each district, comprising areas of woodland and water, in addition to orchards, parks, meadows and pastures which contribute to the attractiveness of the environment for recreation. Recreation indices may be calculated by dividing the *potential recreation area* by the number of second homes. Such calculations must take account of the influence of the largest cities of the Czech Socialist Republic (Prague, Brno, Ostrava, Plzeň) over their immediate environs. Short-term recreation hinterlands may be recognised in this way. Second-home hinterlands around these four cities include twenty two administrative districts, and there are a further thirty two more distant districts where additional development of second homes may take place (Table 5.4). These areas include Vsetín, Gottwaldov, Ústí nad Orlicí, Pelhřimov and Bruntál. On the other hand, some industrial districts, such as Sokolov, Karviná and Most, have no future prospects for the development of second homes. This kind of recreation index is of limited value in summarising the geographical character of individual areas, but it does allow a certain measure of precision to be introduced to the discussion and helps the formulation of further enquiries.

TABLE 5.4. Recreation index in the Czech Socialist Republic

Potential recreation area : number of second homes										
1 - 10	11 - 20	21 - 30	31 - 40	41 - 50	51 - 60	61 - 70	71 - 80	81-90	91 - 100	100+
Beroun	Benešov	M.Bolesl.	Č.Buděj.	Písek	K.Vary	Pelhřimov	Č.Krumlov		Klatovy	Prachatice
Kolín	Kladno	Příbram	Tábor	Liberec	Havl.Brod	Strakonice	J.Hradec		Sokolov	Domažlice
Praha-v.	K.Hora	Rokycany	Jičín	Most	Ústí n.O.	Cheb	Tachov		Bruntal	Svitavy
Praha-z.	Mělník	Č.Lípa	Rychnov	Pardubice	Gottwaldov	Vyškov				Břeclav
Plzeň-m.	Nymburk	Děčín	n. Kn.	Trutnov	N.Jičín	Přerov				Karviná
Brno	Rakovník	Chomutov	Kroměříž	Blansko						Šumperk
Brno-v.	Plzeň-j.	Louny	Uh.Hrad.	Hodonín						
	Plzeň-s.	Teplice	Žďár.n.S.	Jihlava						
	Jablonec	Náchod	Olomouc	Třebíč						
	Litoměři-	Semily	Opava	Vsetín						
	ce	Znojmo								
	Ústí n.L.	Ostrava-m.								
	Hradec Kr.									
	Chrudim									
	Prostějov									
	Frýdek-									
	Místek									

The absolute number of second homes, together with the recreation index, are basic pieces of information, but they are insufficient for an appreciation of the importance of recreation in individual regions. In order to provide greater precision, I have utilised the work of P. Déféṙt (1967) who, in his study of the functions of outdoor recreation of towns and cities, believed that an important relationship existed between the number of people visiting places and the size of the permanent population living there. Défert, however, was concerned only with the economic implications of second-home development. In any case, second homes make smaller demands on local employment and services than hotels, guesthouses and other establishments. In addition, I have considered, from a geographical point of view, the significance of including further variables in Déféṙt's formula, namely the *potential recreation area:*

$$Rp_1 = \frac{L \cdot 100}{0} \cdot \frac{1}{R_p}$$

where L = the number of second homes multiplied by four, representing the average number of occupants, 0 = the number of permanent residents in each area surveyed, and R_p = the *potential recreation area* of the area surveyed.

I have included this formula since absolute figures on second homes indicate only one aspect of the development of recreation based on second homes. A second formula might be drawn up relating to the provision of other forms of accommodation for recreation. Only a consideration of both sets of information allows the complete recreational function of the territory to be appreciated. This term, *recreational function*, is used in an economic-geographical, and not in an algebraic, sense in order to state mathematically something about the connection of a place's resident population in relation to the number of people who arrive for weekend recreation. Nevertheless, there are great variations in the number of residents and the number of recreationalists. The *recreational function*, therefore, is the relationship between two socio-geographical elements in each area and there is no clear correlation between them.

Before an appreciation can be made of recreation conditions in the districts of the Czech Socialist Republic, it is necessary to appreciate the range of values, running from 1.2 in Břeclav district to 339.8 in the district of Prague-West. The detailed distribution of these values is shown in Fig. 5.3 which expresses the recreational function for individual parts of the country.

a) Values 1 - 10 cover twenty eight districts and represent the initial stage of short-term recreational development. The term *initial stage* also suggests the possibility of further dynamic development taking place. It is evident that in some areas this stage is almost complete and further development of second homes is not very likely for environmental reasons, for example, in industrial areas such as Karviná, Ostrava and Opava. In the larger districts, however, there is a definite prospect of further development of short-term recreation.

b) Values 11 - 30 involve twenty seven districts and represent the developing stage of short-term recreation. Even so, in some of these districts further development is not likely because of competition from industrial activity, for

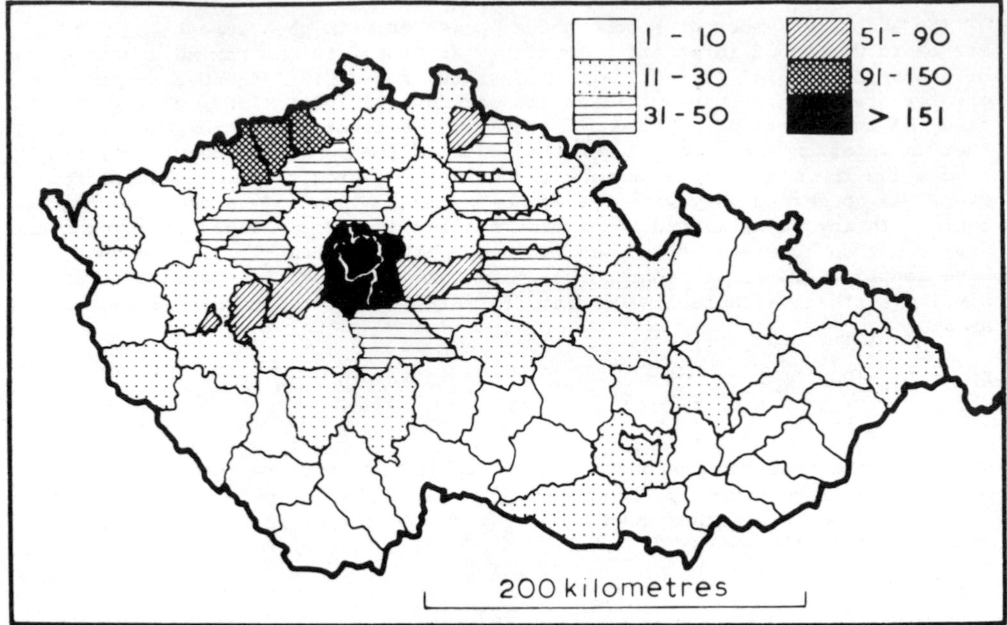

Fig. 5.3 Recreation index in the Czech Socialist Republic

example in the case of Kladno, Sokolov, Chomutov and other districts.

c) Values 31 - 90 involve fifteen districts and represent the culminating stage. Further development of weekend recreation, and especially any further schemes for building second homes, will encounter serious problems and disadvantages, for example, in such areas as the districts of Benešov, Beroun, Mělník, Rokycany and Jablonec. In the past, financial assistance in these areas has gone towards rationalising agricultural production and developing rural service centres/central places rather than for providing recreational facilities. In the future it is to be hoped that aid will become available for recreational purposes.

d) Values 91 - 340 involve five districts and represent the over-developed stage of second-home establishment. These areas contain many examples of land that has been degraded or even devastated for recreational purposes. Such areas are no longer suitable for weekend recreation and it is necessary to make suitable arrangements for dealing with effluent if the quality of their environment is to be preserved.

Second homes in the Slovakian Socialist Republic

The different historical development of the two republics demonstrates itself in various ways, for example, in the differential demand for second homes. The difference in population totals for the two republics (9,341,000 and 4,193,000 in 1970) alone is not enough to explain this, and it is necessary to examine variations in settlement size. In the Czech Republic 47.7 per cent of the population live in settlements of less than 5,000 inhabitants, and in the Slovakian Republic this proportion rises to 63.2 per cent. Settlements with more than 20,000 inhabitants normally demonstrate a demand for second homes. In the Czech Republic 35.7 per cent of the population lives in such settlements, and 18.7 per cent in settlements of more than 100,000. In the Slovakian Republic the respective proportions are 11 per cent and 9.4 per cent. Thus it is clear that there is an important difference in the degree of urbanisation in the two republics and this strongly influences the volume of demand for second homes, which is much smaller in the Slovakian Republic, where there are few districts with 500 or more second homes (Table 5.5).

TABLE 5.5. Number of second homes in the Slovakian Socialist Republic by districts

Number of second homes in district	1-99	100-199	200-299	300-399	400-499	500+
Number of districts	13	7	5	6	3	5

In 1972 the Slovakian Socialist Republic contained 9,844 second homes, of which 217 were former agricultural cottages. Bratislava, the capital of the S.S.R., itself contained 1,005 second homes (10.2%), the Central Slovakian Region had 3,348 (33.7%), the Western Slovakian Region 3,142 (31.9%) and the Eastern Slovakian Region 2,379 (24.2%). In individual districts, especially around Bratislava, the largest number of second homes was in the Bratislava-Rural district (1,292) and Kősice-Rural district (771), followed by Martin (558), and Liptovský Mikuláš (526). If suburban districts around Bratislava and Kősice are added to their inner-urban areas, it is clear that the largest volumes of demand and supply for second homes are located in immediate proximity to the major cities (Fig. 5.4). The development of second homes in Slovakia is largely at the *initial stage*, but as a result of quickening urbanisation it will undoubtedly reach the *developing stage* in the next ten years. One other point needs to be stressed with reference to Slovakia. The republic contains important areas of mountainous terrain that have been equipped with recreational facilities and are within easy access of major cities. As a result, the population of Slovakia may utilise those facilities, especially those provided by factories, during the summer months to a much higher degree than the inhabitants of the Czech Republic. Second-home development in Slovakia confirms our general hypothesis that a close dependence exists between demand for second homes and the size of settlement in which the primary residences are found.

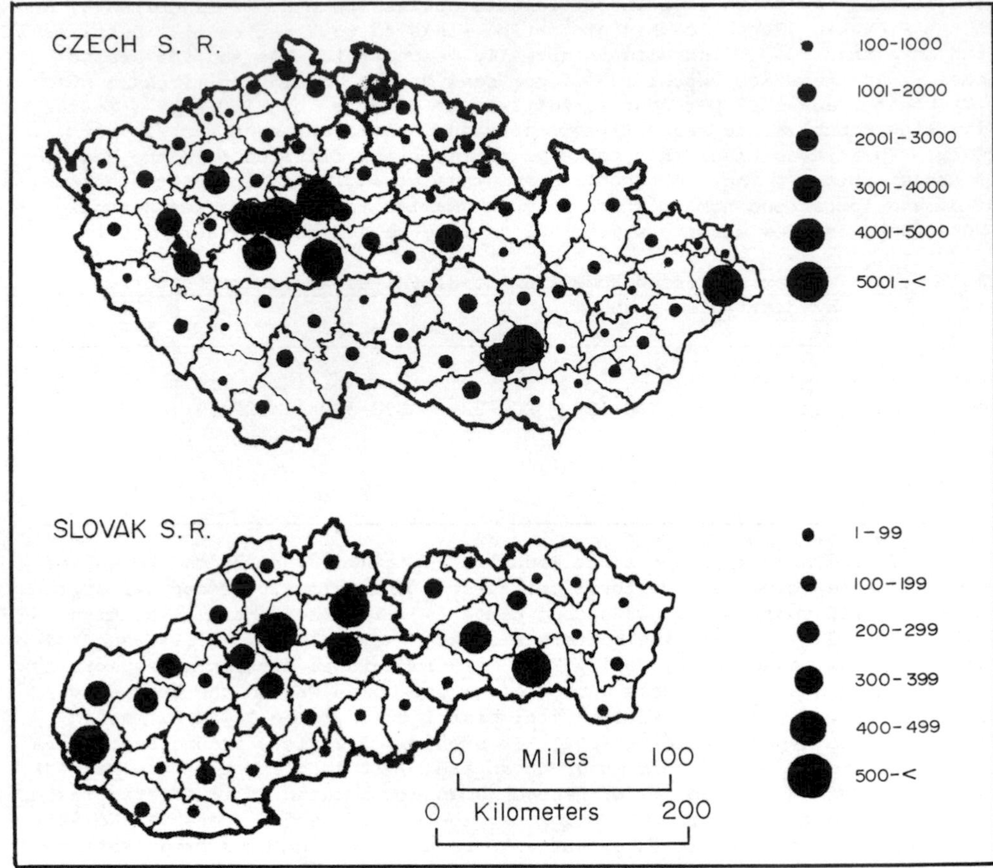

Fig. 5.4 Second homes in the Czech and Slovakian Socialist Republics

Conclusion

Short-term recreation by the population of Czechoslovakia represents a new element in the various flows of human migration. However, the development and distribution of recreation hinterlands has attracted relatively little geographical research. Perhaps more interest will develop in the future when the significance of second homes in modern society is realised and more statistics become available. Land-use planning in both republics is at a fairly basic level but is concerned already with the importance of second-home development. Geographers have a valuable role to play in outlining the range of problems concerned with their development and with other aspects of short-term recreation.

Quantitative information is more abundant for the Czech Republic, but it is also important to stress qualitative aspects of second-home development. In summary, the following points emerge:

1) The development of second homes in Czechoslovakia has occurred rapidly in both the Republics. Extrapolation of past development suggests that there will be further important growth of second homes in the next ten years in those parts of Czechoslovakia that have not so far been affected to any great extent.

2) Growth in private-car ownership has shown a steep rise in Czechoslovakia. Building of express highways and continual improvement of conditions of existing roads has led to a further dispersal of second homes, which in the initial phase were highly concentrated in the immediate hinterlands of towns and cities.

3) With the rapid concentration of agricultural production and its transformation into a large-scale activity, it is likely that funds will become available to aid recreational planning. It is desirable that in territory which is especially attractive for weekend recreation, for example in areas of forest land and with water surfaces, existing cottages which frequently demonstrate vernacular architecture should be used as second homes by urban residents. This would help to preserve existing buildings and also to lessen further intrusion into the environment which the construction of new second homes always involves.

4) Overdeveloped recreation areas, which display high densities of recreational buildings, contain living conditions that are not very different from those found in areas of primary residences. Second homes should not be developed further in such areas. Instead interest should be transferred to more distant areas which offer greater attractions for recreation.

REFERENCES

Anon. Soupis objektů individuální rekreace, in Česká statistika 12, ŽP, Praha 1972.

Anon. Soupis objecktov individuálnej rekreácie v SSSR in Štatistiké informácie, Bratislava, 1974.

Bielckus, C.L., Rogers, A.W. and Wibberley, G.P. (1972) Second homes in England and Wales Studies in Rural Land Use 11, Wye College, University of London.

Clout, H.D. (1971) 'Second homes in the Auvergne' Geographical Review 61, pp.530-53.

Clout, H.D. (1974) 'The growth of second-home ownership: an example of seasonal suburbanisation' in J.H. Johnson (ed) Suburban Growth Wiley, London.

Cribier, F. (1969) La Grande Migration d'Été-des-Citadins en France Centre National de la Recherche Scientifique, Paris.

Défèrt, P. (1967) 'Le taux de fonction touristique' Les Cahiers du Tourisme Université d'Aix-Marseille.

Gardavský, V. (1960) 'Recreational hinterland of a city, taking Prague as an example', Acta Universitatis Carolinae:Geographica 1, pp.3-29, Prague.

Gardavský, V. (1971) K problematice vymezovaní rekreačních zázemí měst, in Problémy geografického výzkumu Bratislava.

Chapter 6

SECOND HOMES IN THE CARIBBEAN

J. D. Henshall

In recent years emphasis has been put on tourism as a means of diversifying the economies of developing nations formerly dependent on a few staple exports. Most of the tourists come from the developed countries and, although in most cases tourism has not yet led to significant *net* flows of foreign exchange from the developed to the developing nations, it seems probable that the Commonwealth Caribbean is one of the few areas of the Third World with an overall surplus on travel account (Bryden 1973, p.65). The number of tourists visiting the Caribbean region has risen from 190,000 in 1938 to 6,650,000 in 1973. Proximity to North America has facilitated this rapid increase, with residents of the United States forming the largest single national group of tourists to each island except to St. Kitts, Montserrat, the Windwards and Trinidad and Tobago, where West Indians are more numerous, and to St. Andres, where Latin Americans predominate. Because of high densities of local population and the fact that most of these tourists are wealthy urbanites, older and generally racially different from the largely poor, young and rural peoples of the Caribbean, the impact of tourists on the region has been very noticeable. Second-home owners form only a small proportion of the total flow of tourists to the Caribbean, but because they make regular visits and stay longer than most tourists their economic and social impact is different from that of the ordinary holidaymaker.

The development of second homes in the Caribbean has passed through three main stages. The first stage was one in which the local elite built second homes in order to escape from the stifling heat of the coastal cities during the hottest months of the year. These homes were usually in hill stations in the Greater Antilles, such as Kenscoff in Haiti and Jaracaboa in the Dominican Republic, and on the cooler, windward coasts of the smaller islands, as at Bathsheba in Barbados. When long-distance travel became easier and faster after the First World War, a second type of vacation home came into existence as the elite of the metropolitan countries sought refuge in their tropical colonies from winters in temperate latitudes. But whether they were local residents or not, these second-home owners were few in number and had only a limited impact on their holiday environment.

Only in the last decade has second-homw ownership become a noticeable element in the region's tourist trade as Caribbean real estate has become an attractive investment to people in North America, Europe and Latin America. In this latest form the definition of second home has perforce to be broadened to encompass the multi-faceted usage of these new buildings, be they villas or condominium apartments, refurbished plantation houses or flats in renovated eighteenth-century barracks. Some, especially in Barbados, are owned by West Indians and rented to visitors from overseas on long- or short-term leases. Some have been bought for retirement in the sun and are permanently occupied by foreigners; others have been acquired with future retirement in mind and are at present occupied only during the winter months by the owner and are left empty or rented for the rest of the year. The pattern of occupancy affects both the social and economic impact of these second homes.

At first these new holiday homes were scattered throughout each territory, but later, as large-scale real estate developments were established, cottage colonies were set up, emphasising the separateness of the second-home owners from the local environment, although only rarely do the visitors go to such lengths as to isolate themselves behind a fence, as at the Mill Reef Club in Antigua. In some cases, as at Holetown in Barbados and Grande Anse Bay in Grenada, cottages are combined with hotels, restaurants and shopping centres to form a tourist enclave within which the visitor can enjoy all the comforts of suburbia.

The spatial relationship between the permanent and temporary residences of these second-home owners cannot be explained in terms of distance, cost and time nor through the application of the concept of *recreational place utility* (Aldskogius 1969). H. Clout (1970, p.33) has shown that these explanations are most satisfactory in the hinterlands of large cities and where second homes are purchased with definite recreational needs in mind. In the Caribbean, virtually all travel to and from the second home is by aeroplane and, since many islands are only a few minutes' flying time apart, accessibility is measured by frequency of flights, the number of changes of plane needed, the convenience of flight connections and the proximity to the holiday house of an airport capable of handling jet aircraft. However, for the true escapist, accessibility has a negative aspect which explains the premium put on sites in some of the smaller islands of the Grenadines or the British Virgin Islands which can be reached only by boat. Air routes often reflect cultural affinities and these reinforce the effects of accessibility. Thus political ties and a common language encourage the French to look to Martinique, the Colombians to San Andres, the Americans to Puerto Rico and the United States Virgin Islands, and the British and Canadians to the territories of the Commonwealth Caribbean for their second homes.

Retirement rather than recreation is generally the reason for investment in a Caribbean second home, and thus it is essentially a southward extension of the Florida pattern rather than the search for recreational space that has occurred around large cities further north. The prospective second-home owner looks to the Caribbean for warmth, clean air and tranquillity, and the recreational possibilities of sea and sand are less important to him than to the average tourist. Consequently, second homes do not compete with the demands of hotels for beach frontages and may utilise inland areas too steep or too dry for agriculture. Differences between territories are perceived in terms not so much of landscape or recreational facilities but rather of the political, fiscal and social advantages of investment in the area, the price of land and the relative efficiency of local construction firms and rental agents. In many instances advertisements put out by estate agents or personal connections may be the deciding factor.

Second-home owners are less fickle than other types of tourist because of their investment in a particular area. This attribute is particularly important at a time when economic problems in North America and Europe have resulted in a slowdown in the growth rate of tourism to the region, and declining hotel occupancy rates are making the profitability of the industry uncertain (West Indies Chronicle 1974, p.355). At the same time, the rapid growth of tourism over the last decade has led to increasing conflict between local residents and tourists, and the unquestioning encouragement of the industry offered by most Caribbean governments is being reconsidered. It is now realised that the relative merits of the various types of tourism, that is, hotel, residential, or cruise ship, must be re-examined in the light of the needs of each host country, although so far little research has been directed to this end and the necessary statistics are only just beginning to be collected (Doxey and Associates 1971, p.9).

In this situation, the vacation cottage has become the fastest-growing element of the tourist industry in many areas, although the relative importance of residential tourism in each area depends largely on local political decisions expressed in terms of the availability of land, fiscal incentives and residence permits for foreigners. In Jamaica in 1969, 19.8 per cent of total visitor-beds were in holiday cottages and apartments, but this figure rose to 22.3 per cent in 1973 (Jamaica Tourist Board 1974). In Barbados in 1957, only 9.5 per cent of visitor-beds were in cottages or apartments, but this proportion had increased to 25.4 per cent by 1967 and reached 39 per cent in 1972 (Pan American World Airways 1959; Barbados Statistical Service 1973). In Montserrat second homes dominate the tourist industry more than in any other Caribbean territory. In 1973 the 246 houses in the residential tourist areas contained 81.5 per cent of the island's total visitor-beds (Momsen 1973, p.46). Hotel occupancy rates in Montserrat are very low, rising from 9 per cent in 1967 to 21 per cent in 1970 when 17 per cent of the island's tourist guest nights were spent in hotels (British Development Division 1971, p.vi), 15 per cent in rented holiday villas and 50 per cent in second homes by owners (Transport and Tourism Technicians Ltd. 1971).

In order to analyse in more detail the social and economic impact of second homes in the Caribbean, a questionnaire survey of occupants of holiday villas and of hotel management, estate agents and market gardeners was carried out in 1973 in Montserrat. This rugged, volcanic island of 40 square miles (100 sq km) lying just 26 miles (42 km) southwest of Antigua, with a population of 11,670 in 1970, was in very severe economic straits a decade ago. Agriculture had been the traditional mainstay of the economy but it had virtually collapsed after the abandonment of the sharecropping system in 1953. In the mid-1950s only 47 per cent of farmland was cultivated and by 1972 this proportion had fallen to a mere 13 per cent, despite short-lived attempts to revive agriculture with such cash crops as bananas, Sea Island cotton and tomatoes. Many of the island's young adults emigrated and the population fell by 25 per cent between 1946 and 1970. Montserrat became a remittance society of grandparents raising the children of migrants, and suffered from a severe shortage of skilled workers (Lowenthal and Comitas 1962). In these circumstances a new source of income was needed. Montserrat could not attract mass tourism because it had few white sand beaches and lay off the main air routes, and its airport could not accommodate jet aeroplanes. However, its peaceful, lush, unspoilt countryside and its political stability as one of the few remaining British colonies made it suitable for the development of residential tourism. The government of Montserrat released almost 1200 acres (485 ha) for purchase by non-Montserratians. The greatest proportion of this land lay on the west coast near the main town, with one piece on the east or windward coast at Spanish Point near the airport (Fig. 6.1). Most of the 2,690 lots, each of between a quarter and half an acre (0.1-0.2 ha) have been sold to approximately 1,600 purchasers, three-fifths of whom bought more than one lot. It was thought that about 30 per cent of the sales were speculative but, according to a 1970 survey, 59 per cent of purchasers plan to build before 1980 and 20 per cent plan to become permanent residents of Montserrat (Momsen 1973, pp.46-7). In order to attain

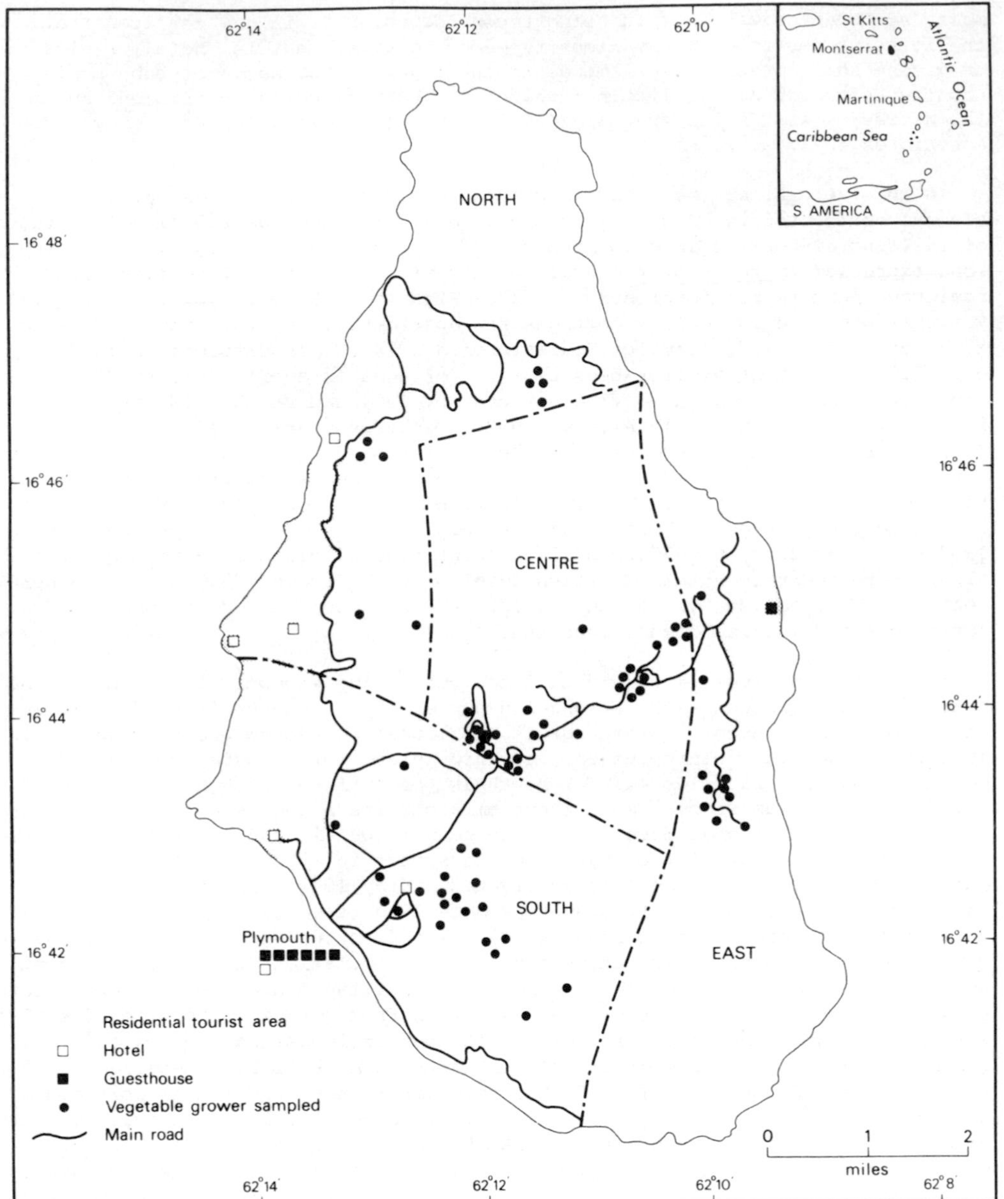

Fig. 6.1 Commercial vegetable production and tourism in Montserrat

this planned level of land development by 1980, an annual average of 97 houses must be built. This construction rate will be hard to reach as the average rate since 1966 has been only 25 houses per year, although development has been faster in some areas than in others (Table 6.1).

TABLE 6.1. Houses built or under construction in residential tourist areas of Montserrat, 1966-72

Area	1966	1967	1968	1969	1970	1971	1972
Olveston/Woodlands/Old Towne	64	75	91	106	114	127	134
Spanish Point	10	13	16	21	25	28	31
Richmond Hill	17	31	36	38	43	49	53
Isles Bay	1	6	6	6	7	8	9
Elberton/Foxes Bay	1	9	9	13	15	16	19
Total	93	134	158	184	204	228	246
Annual increase	-	41	24	26	20	24	18

Sources: Government of Montserrat. First Statistical Digest, Plymouth,1973, and unpublished figures provided by Statistics Officer.

Between 20 and 30 per cent of the houses in these development areas are permanently occupied by their owners, and a further 30 per cent are available for short- or long-term rental (Transport and Tourism Technicians Ltd. 1971). Houses are rented for six to eight weeks per year on average, and non-resident owners of villas spend one to three months per year on the island. Many of the second-home owners had been attracted to Montserrat by real estate advertisements in such widely circulated magazines as *Reader's Digest*, a few had chosen this island after visiting other parts of the Caribbean, whilst some had personal links with Montserrat. Although there were some very wealthy people amongst the villa owners many of the retired occupants of villas were living on quite small pensions. The non-resident owners were mostly North Americans approaching retirement age who planned to settle in Montserrat in a few years' time. They tended to lead a fairly active social life on their frequent visits to the island but, unlike the permanent residents, their social contacts were mainly within the group of villa owners.

There has been some concern as to whether the social effects of residential tourism are greater or less than those of tourism in general. The social impact of tourism in the Caribbean is often described in terms of relative deprivation (Bryden 1973, pp.92-3), feelings of subservience and neo-colonial dependence, and changes in the power structure (Lowenthal 1972, pp.246-7). The extent of this impact is related to the density of tourists, as an indicator of the degree of confrontation, and to the level of expatriate capital and management involved in the industry. In 1973 Montserrat received as many tourists as it had inhabitants, which gave it a confrontation level similar to that of Barbados, but in terms of land area the island had only 123 tourists per square kilometre, half the density of Antigua but thrice that of the neighbouring island of St. Kitts. The level of foreign involvement in the Montserratian tourist industry is remarkably low, with 62 per cent of the hotels and guesthouses (containing 80% of the visitor-beds) being owned by local people and 85 per cent being managed by Montserratians and other West Indians. The real estate subdivisions were in the hands of a North American company but the houses on the sites were largely constructed by Montserratian firms.

Most second-home owners have been eager to contribute to the island and have resented the fact that many of their offers of free assistance, based on their professional expertise or experience, have been refused. Some of the villa owners have been involved in volunteer work, such as setting up village libraries and encouraging local handicrafts. There has been some local resentment of the foreign *takeover* of such charitable bodies as the Red Cross, with many of the Montserratians consequently deciding to opt out of such work in their own society. On the whole, however, the second-home owners keep very much to themselves and rarely stray far from the main roads, so much so that even on an island as small as Montserrat there are communities in the interior to whom the sight of a white person is a strange and unusual occurrence.

The economic impact of tourism is generally seen in terms of employment opportunities, the development of rural areas and the general economic effect of the tourist multiplier (Bryden 1973, p.72). The ratio of staff per guest is usually lower in residential tourism than for hotels. In Montserrat the hotels have an average staffing level of 0.6 employees per bed and 1.2 per room in season and 0.4 and 0.8 respectively out of season, a 36 per cent seasonal decline. There is great variation in the number of domestic servants employed amongst the occupants of second homes depending on personal needs and wishes and the occupancy pattern. Most of the retired permanent residents employ a maid and a gardener for a maximum of two days per week, whilst the non-resident owners employ them for five days a week while they are in Montserrat, reducing this to one day per week during their absence. In addition, the entrepreneurial opportunities offered by the development of residential tourism have attracted some of the most dynamic Montserratians back to the island after many years abroad. Firms specialising in pest control and fumigation, swimming pool maintenance, car hire and repair work, landscaping, house maintenance and rental for absentee owners are all in the hands of Montserratians. In 1973 hotels employed a maximum of 145 persons to deal with their 17 per cent of the island's tourist-nights, whilst the 65 per cent spent in holiday villas directly generated an estimated 250 jobs in the high season. Most of the people employed in the residential tourist areas continued to live in the main town and the economic impact on neighbouring villages has been only slight.

The effect of the tourist-multiplier depends on the type of tourism, the extent of foreign ownership and its effect on leakage from the local economy, and the overall structure of the economy. In general, the tourist multiplier for residential tourism is lower than for hotel tourism, but this is compensated for by the longer length of stay and the greater consistency of visits by second-home owners. However, as Bryden has shown (1973, pp.73-82), the tourist multiplier is difficult to calculate and is often a poor measure of the true economic benefits of tourism.

Costs associated with holiday villas were investigated by means of interviews with the real estate developers and rental agencies, the tourist board and a sample survey of villa residents of all types. Construction costs of houses generally varied between $40,000 and $100,000 and occasionally even higher. (These and all subsequent figures are given in Eastern Caribbean dollars). Almost all the construction materials are imported but labour accounts for half the building costs. Thus construction of second homes provides employment and contributes about $800,000 annually to the local economy. Fixed costs associated with the holiday villas average $2,825 per year, including basic utilities, gardener, and regular fumigation and pool services, plus $40 per month to an agent for caretaker and rental services and about $450 a year for insurance and property tax. Maintenance costs for this type of house in the tropics are especially high, being usually between $1,000 and $3,000 a year. Thus there is an expenditure of approximately $4,000 a year in Montserrat for each of these villas. When the houses are occupied there are additional costs for full utilities, domestic service, food and transport. These costs and their contribution to the local economy depend on the standard of consumption of the occupant's household, whether occupancy is by owners who are permanent or temporary residents or by short- or long-term renters; the proportion of the year the house is occupied and the attitude of the household to the consumption of locally produced goods and services.

Table 6.2 shows the average expenditure patterns for the various types of second-home occupants and compares them with the patterns found for occupants of villas in the Cayman Islands. The proportion of expenditure spent on

TABLE 6.2. Expenditure patterns in Caribbean second homes

	Percentage distribution of expenditure			
	Cayman Islands 1967-9	Montserrat 1973		
	Visitors in cottages	Renters	Non-resident owners	Resident owners
Accommodation - rent - servants and utilities	50.0	39.0 7.0	65.0 5.0	34.0 15.0
Food	22.1	14.0	7.0	17.0
Transport - taxis and hired cars, airport tax	6.7	18.0	13.0	8.0
Entertainment, souvenirs Drinks	11.3 7.6	20.0	9.0	25.0
Gratuities	1.5	2.0	1.0	1.0
Tourist tax	0.7	-	-	-

Sources: Economic survey and projections, Cayman Islands (quoted in Bryden 1973, p.112), and fieldwork in Montserrat

accommodation by non-resident second-home owners has been calculated with the total annual cost of the upkeep of the house allocated to a vacation period of eight weeks. The proportion would be lower if the owners spent longer than average in their Montserrat home each year or if they offset their costs by renting the house out during their absence. The table illustrates the dangers of extrapolating for tourism in general from one type of tourist and from area to area.

In an island the size of Montserrat perhaps the most important economic aspect of tourism is the return per land unit as compared to other uses to which the land might be put. In the case of a land-extensive type of tourism, such as real estate development with a density of perhaps four persons per acre (10 per ha), the spatial element is especially important. On several occasions it has been suggested that real estate development does not optimise the returns from land (e.g., Sargent 1967, pp.131-4; Transport and Tourism Technicians Ltd. 1971). Returns per ha. depend on the number of houses constructed on the 1200 acres (485 ha) alienated for residential tourism. In 1972 there were 246 such houses. By 1980, if construction continues at the present rate, there will be 446 villas. If, however, purchasers of plots carry out their declared intentions then there will be 994 houses built by 1980, which is probably close to the maximum number that the area can support. On this basis, returns per hectare were calculated to be $4,225 in 1972 and $7,743 in 1980 with 446 homes built or $16,388 with 944 houses. The local component of expenditure was reckoned to be 30 per cent. Average returns per hectare from cropland and permanent pasture are $313 and returns from market gardening are generally between $1,250 and $2,500 net per hectare (Sargent 1967, p.132; Momsen 1973, p.53). Thus, even at the present level of development, returns per hectare from residential tourism are comparable to returns from agriculture. If development proceeds as planned, then the contribution to national income per hectare may well be considerably higher than that even from intensive agriculture. Also, once the holiday villa has been built, residential tourism is less susceptible to violent fluctuations than either hotel tourism or agriculture.

The linkages generated by tourism are largely a function of the type of accommodation establishments present and the extent of local involvement in the tourist industry. In Montserrat the number of visitor-beds has grown quite slowly. Hence the rate of increase of generated demand levels has been evolutionary and gradual, allowing the balanced development of backward economic linkages with local producers. However, although the hotels bought almost half of their food requirements from local producers, the second-home owners bought much less local food because of fewer social links with local farmers, less time, inclination or assistance to prepare strange local foodstuffs, and considerable interest in production from their own gardens. They also showed little interest in buying locally produced furniture, clothes or jewellery.

The demonstration effect of the holiday villas and the availability of construction firms and mortgages has led many middle-class Montserratians to build better homes than their counterparts in other Caribbean islands. Whether the architectural extremes of the development areas, where Cape Cod cottages may be found side by side with Chinese pagodas and Arabian palaces, is considered stylistic stimulation or visual pollution is perhaps a matter of opinion. The patterns of consumption of the villa occupants, coupled with higher local incomes - per capita Gross Domestic Product increased from $296 in 1962 to $982 in 1970, have led to an increased marginal propensity to import and to changes in dietary patterns, with imports of traditional staples such as rice and salt fish declining relative to imports of milk and meat over the last decade (Government of Montserrat 1973, Table 41). External economies have also affected the local elite, who have been able to take advantage of improved telephone and aeroplane connections to the outside world, more widely available electricity, better roads and the improved car maintenance facilities which accompanied the increase in the supply of cars for hire, numbers of which rose from 34 in 1964 to 151 in 1971 (Government of Montserrat 1973, Table 27).

The development of second homes in Montserrat has caused remarkably little social disruption. There has been some increase in crime associated with the existence of expensively-equipped houses left empty for long periods. Maids now demand higher pay for shorter hours, much to the annoyance of the Montserratian middle-class housewife, because the elderly vacationer, coming from a largely servant-less society, expected relatively little of his employees. On the whole there is very limited contact between the Montserratians and the tourists or retired people. The occupants of second homes remain generally within the cocktail, bridge and golf circuit of the residential tourist areas. Given the government-imposed restrictions on the expansion of the area available for residential tourism, which limits competition for scarce resources, it seems that this type of tourism has much to recommend it for a small island on which the two societies of visitor and host are so different. However, by 1980, when the residential tourist areas are more fully developed and occupancy rates are higher, increased economic returns may not compensate for greater social confrontation between the two societies nor for the failure of tourism to provide attractive alternative employment as the expansion of the construction industry slows down.

REFERENCES

Aldskogius, H. (1969) 'Modelling the evolution of settlement patterns: two studies of vacation house settlement' Geografiska Regionstudier 6, Uppsala, pp.6-108.

Barbados Statistical Service (1973) A Bednights Survey of Hotels and Guest Houses 1972 Bridgetown.

British Development Division in the Caribbean (1971) Montserrat: Economic Survey and Projections Barbados.

Bryden, J.M. (1973) Tourism and Development Cambridge.

Clout, H.D. (1970) 'Social aspects of second-home occupation in the Auvergne', Planning Outlook 9, pp.33-49.

Doxey, G.V. and Associates (1971) The Tourist Industry in Barbados Kitchener, Ontario.

Government of Montserrat (1973) First Statistical Digest Plymouth.

Jamaica Tourist Board (1974) Travel Statistics 1973 Kingston.

Lowenthal, D. (1972) West Indian Societies Oxford University Press.

Lowenthal, D. and Comitas, L. (1962) 'Emigration and depopulation: some neglected aspects of population geography' Geographical Review 52 (2), pp.195-210.

Momsen, J. Henshall (1973) Report on Food Production and the Tourist Industry in Montserrat Department of Geography, University of Calgary, Mimeo.

Pan American World Airways (1959) Barbados Tourism Potentials and Plans Miami.

Sargent, J.R. (1967) Report of the Tripartite Economic Survey of the Eastern Caribbean HMSO, London, pp.131-4.

Transport and Tourism Technicians Ltd. (1971) Personal communication.

Chapter 7

SECOND HOMES IN ENGLAND AND WALES: A SPATIAL VIEW

A. W. Rogers

Within the last few years the second home as a topic for serious study has reached an importance which is surprising even in such a popular general field as recreation. Yet before about 1968 few people in England and Wales had even heard the term, let alone considered some of the implications of the phenomenon, despite a pioneer article by John Barr in 1967. Within four or five years, however, there has been an upsurge in interest which perhaps belies the true state of information on the subject. The fact remains that we are only marginally better informed now than we were some years ago and we have the disadvantage of a plethora of illfounded opinion and conjecture. It is true that there have been some major studies on the subject, but a *total* view of the situation is still lacking and this will only come when detailed and comprehensive statistics are available, probably through the population census or the general household survey.

To date there has been one major national view of the subject (Bielckus, Rogers and Wibberley 1972) and a number of important reports from county planning departments, notably those for Denbighshire (Jacobs 1972), Caernarvonshire (Pyne 1973) and Merionethshire (Tuck 1973). These and other sources have been conveniently summarised and put in some perspective in a report for the Countryside Commission by the Dartington Amenity Research Trust (Downing and Dower 1973).

Three other sources of information on second homes should be mentioned at this point. First, there are those general surveys of households which have collected data on second homes along with a wide variety of other information. Among these, the most reliable is probably the annual survey of about 35,000 households carried out by the market research firm Audits of Great Britain Ltd., since the sample involved is sufficiently large to be fairly trustworthy. Most other surveys, including the Department of Employment's Family Expenditure Survey and various surveys of housing, contain only partial information which is generally unsuitable for any national figures which might be obtained by grossing up the sample data.

This problem of inaccuracy is also applicable to the only national survey of recreation behaviour which has so far considered levels of second-home ownership. Despite its importance as the first national picture of recreation in this country, the Pilot National Recreation Survey (British Travel Association/University of Keele 1967) is of little value for any consideration of second homes. The relatively small size of the sample (c.3,000) means that a minority interest such as the ownership of a second house or caravan is inaccurately estimated from the survey. The British Tourist Authority (BTA, formerly the British Travel Association), in conjunction with the national tourist boards, has for some time collected details of trips taken to second homes as part of the monthly British Home Tourist Survey, but, while this information enables the proportion of all trips spent in a second home to be calculated, it is not possible, because of the method of survey, to determine the proportion of the population owning or using second homes, or to obtain data on the frequency of use. The British Tourist Authority also operates the annual British National Travel Survey which, though mainly concerned with holidays abroad, collects profile data from a large random sample of the population. Following discussions with the Countryside Commission, Dartington Amenity Research Trust and Wye College, the BTA now include questions in this survey on the use of second homes.

Finally, there is an increasing amount of research and data on second homes coming from academic centres. In some cases this is detailed research work carried out by staff and research students in universities and polytechnics, for example, the study by R.E. Hughes (1973) dealing with second homes in Carmarthenshire. There is also a large number of smaller dissertations being produced by undergraduates in geography, town planning, architecture and other subjects. It should be stressed that, because of the basic nature of raw data on second homes, these studies are inevitably local or at most regional in their context, but they are no less useful for that. If it were possible to collate all the local studies which have been in preparation since about 1970, they would certainly provide an impressive and useful body of knowledge.

Research methods and problems

Perhaps the greatest single problem faced by the researcher interested in second homes concerns the general absence of reliable data. Indeed, this problem is highlighted by the nature of the available information which has just been reviewed. Until such time as the decennial population census contains questions on second-home ownership and use, as is the case in France (Chap. 4), information will have to be based on samples and will consequently be subject to severe drawbacks. It is a pity that the representations of interested parties failed to convince the Office of Population Censuses and Surveys of the importance of such questions for inclusion in the 1971 census. The growing interest and importance of second homes makes it very unlikely that there will be a similar omission in 1981.

As a result of this deficiency, the prime data source remains the rating lists produced each year for all local authorities in this country (Bielckus *et al.* 1972). This source, despite its very high level of accuracy has, of course, to be culled for those properties which seem likely to be second homes; thus it is normal to list those addresses *within* the local authority area for which rate demands are sent *outside* the local authority area. This method must inevitably be haphazard, although experience has shown that this is one case where the local knowledge of the rating officer is invaluable in supplementing the data.

The picture is further complicated by the existence of two main types of second home, the built property and the static caravan. By and large it is fair to say that rating registers provide significantly poorer information on caravans, for although the *site* (but not the caravan itself) is generally rated, it is often impossible to distinguish between caravans used for second homes and those used for other recreational purposes. Indeed, it should be added that this distinction is often not clear even to the caravan owner himself and this inevitably makes for further complications. It has been argued (Bielckus *et al.* 1972) that caravans which serve as second homes need separate consideration, since they clearly bring problems of a rather different nature and also seem to appeal to a different type of person from the conventional second-home owner.

This method of using rating records was first employed by the Wye College team in the preparation of their report for the Countryside Commission, but it has also been used by planning officers in the production of county reports. It should be stressed that this method is deficient in a number of aspects, but it remains nevertheless the best available at the present time. Lists of *potential* second homes gathered from rating registers are probably only about 75 per cent accurate: some addresses where rate demands are sent outside the area refer to landlords or to other members of a family who pay the rates for a relative, while on the other hand there are certainly second-homers who have all correspondence, including the rate demand, sent to the second home itself and who in consequence cannot be identified from the rating lists in the normal way. With the help of local rating officers, however, and the use of electoral registers and some other sources, it is usually possible to produce reasonably accurate lists of second homes, particularly for rural areas where local knowledge is often comprehensive.

The Wye study started with a postal survey of all local authorities in England and Wales outside Greater London, and attempted an appraisal of the accuracy of the sources of data and requested estimates of numbers of second homes. Nearly 250 local authorities were then visited by research staff in the spring of 1969 and a composite list of 20,000 addresses was compiled which was to form the basic sampling frame of the whole study. The plotting of this sample, representing perhaps one-tenth of the estimated number of second homes, together with the original local authority estimates, provides the only available national picture to date of the distribution of second homes in England and Wales.

This basic sample frame was used for two main purposes. First, approximately half the addresses were used for a postal survey to users of second homes to provide the main source of information on second properties, the pattern of use and the social characteristics of second-home users. A proportion of replies to the questionnaire came, as expected, from landlords and others not owning second homes, and, following a reminder, the eventual total of replies suitable for analysis was 2,507, a net response rate (excluding those who were not second-home users) of 25 per cent.

This response rate highlights a further problem with research in this field. The gross response rate (i.e., *including* replies from users and non-users of second homes) was 41 per cent after one reminder, and it was considered that further attempts to improve the rate would not be worth while. Second homes provide a classic instance where there is often a definite reaction against surveys: this is hardly surprising since many people have specifically chosen a rural retreat because of the attractions of isolated living and privacy. On a national survey of this scale, a general response rate of this magnitude was probably quite good. At the local scale, the area studies, which are discussed later, and which depended on interviews rather than postal questionnaires, showed a very much lower rate of refusals.

The basic sampling frame was also used to choose the four study areas which formed an important part of the whole project. There were clearly problems in allocating resources and timing in a situation where second homes were frequently scattered over the countryside, and it was therefore necessary to choose areas where there were concentrations of second homes. The four areas finally chosen were in northeast Essex (Tendring Rural District and Frinton and Walton Urban District), southwest Devon (Kingsbridge Rural District), the southern Lake District (North Lonsdale Rural District) and west-central Wales (Aberystwyth Rural District).

The problems of research on second homes can, therefore, be seen to have three components. In the first place, the source of basic data is subject to several drawbacks which can only partially be offset by checking with other sources. Secondly, there is an inevitable adverse reaction against investigation from the second-home users themselves. Finally, there are logistic problems which impose serious limitations on the resources available for the research.

The number and distribution of second homes

Despite the problems of estimating from samples, there is now general agreement regarding the total number of second homes in England and Wales. As far as built properties are concerned, Audits of Great Britain Ltd. calculated the 1972 total at 161,000, while the Wye study suggested a figure between 180,000 and 200,000 for 1969. Because of some possible under-estimation when rating registers are used, it would seem sensible to put the present total at around 200,000 dwellings.

To this figure there has to be added an estimate for static caravans to cover all types of vacation home. The only trustworthy figure comes from the survey by Audits of Great Britain Ltd. (Downing and Dower 1973) where an estimate for 1972 was 154,000. Together, then, the total figure of second homes of all types is about 350,000.

The fact that all these estimates have to be based on samples taken comparatively recently is again a serious problem when it comes to estimating the past growth in second-home numbers. No time series exist except for some very recent sample figures from market research surveys and for some small county samples, and the pattern of growth has been estimated by a proxy method; respondents to the Wye sample were asked to give the number of years for which they had been using their second home. It will be obvious that this method can take no account of changes from one second home to another, but this method remains the only one available until accurate national statistics are available over a period of time.

Figure 7.1 presents a picture of the estimated growth in the number of built second homes over a period from about 1935 to 1969. Whatever the accuracy of individual totals at specific points in time, the trends portrayed are generally realistic. A major period of growth seems to date from the mid-1950s, when numbers stood at perhaps 40,000, and the average annual growth since then, allowing for some under-estimation, has been of the order of 11,000-12,000 per year. Of course, this average figure hides the exponential nature of the growth curve, and the annual growth during the decade 1960-70 was between 15,000 and 18,000 built properties (Bielckus *et al.* 1972; Downing and Dower 1973). Estimates for caravans are even more dependent upon guesswork and these have been put at c.10,000 per year during the late 1960s.

When the national distribution of second homes is considered, there are major inconsistencies between the two main sources of data, the Wye College

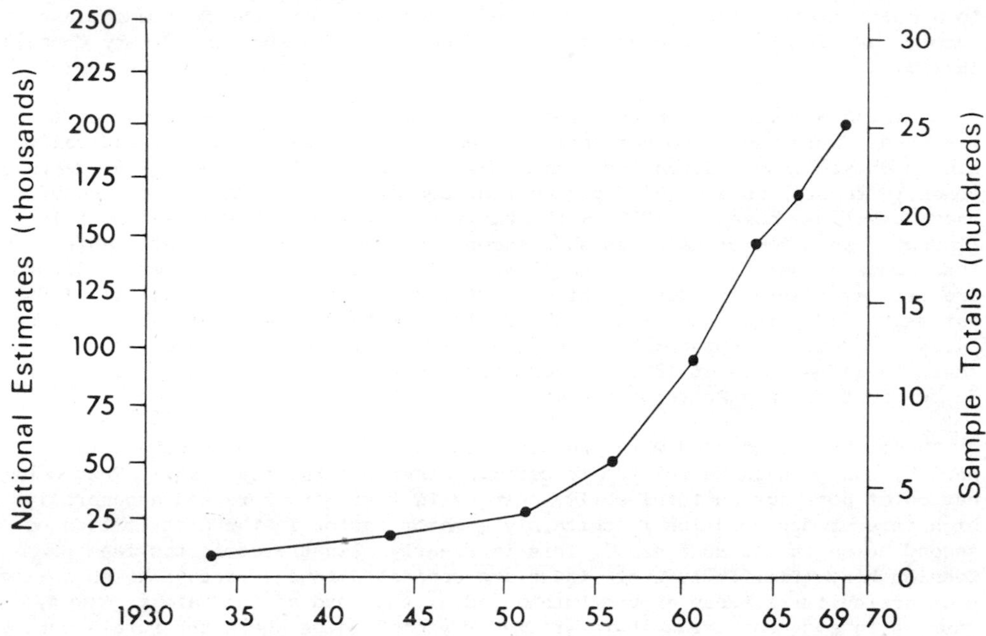

Fig. 7.1 Estimated number of built second homes in England and Wales, 1935 - 69

survey and Audits of Great Britain Ltd. Both are subject to bias of various kinds and both are, of course, dependent upon samples for their estimates, so that only broad indications of the national distribution can be given. Probably between 20 and 30 per cent of all second homes are located in Wales. Although the Wye research generally excluded caravans and concentrated on built properties, there is ample evidence to suggest the importance of caravans in Wales (see, for example, W.T.R. Pryce 1967). Other major concentrations are the southeast, the east coast, the southwest and the Lake District. All but the last of these major regions probably contain more than 25,000 second homes at the present time.

The distribution of second homes is equally important at the local scale, for it is here that the contrasts and conflicts are particularly evident from the viewpoint of both landscape and social contact. Two aspects are of special interest here. One is the location of second homes within each parish in relation to the main nuclei of settlement. Downing and Dower have suggested, on the basis of data from the Denbighshire study and the Wye survey, that there are significant differences between Wales (Denbighshire) and England (Devon). Although it has been suggested (Jacobs 1972) that more isolated locations away from central settlements may be preferred for reasons of privacy, there seems little evidence either way. The reports from Caernarvon (Pyne 1973), Merioneth (Tuck 1973) and Carmarthen (Hughes 1973) confirm this latter view and suggest that there is little regular pattern in the location of second homes other than a possible preference for the smaller settlements in a rural area. Nearly 70 per cent of second homes in the Northumberland sample were located within existing settlements (Northumberland County Council 1971).

A second and more important aspect concerns the ratio of second homes to permanent dwellings. No national figures are available, but some indication can be gained from figures for individual counties. According to the Caernarvonshire report, on average 7 per cent of occupied dwellings in the county were used as holiday homes in 1972, with nearly half the parishes exceeding this figure. In a few cases which show exceptional concentrations the figure rose above 30 per cent (Llanengan, 39%; Betws Garmon, 35%). Average figures are also available for Denbighshire (6.9%), Merioneth (14.2%), Anglesey (10% estimate) and parts of Carmarthenshire (1.9%, with a maximum parish figure of 24.2%). While no comparable figures are available for English counties, there is an estimate of 13.5 per cent for the Lake District with a figure of 33 per cent for the Patterdale area (Capstick 1972).

These ratios, coupled with the distribution of second homes within the parish, can perhaps be related to certain other spatial features. The combination of poor agricultural soils, changes in farm structure and a generally high rate of depopulation is certainly a major factor in the distribution of second homes in inland areas. This is clearly illustrated in the case of Denbighshire (Fig. 7.2), where there are concentrations of second homes in the poor agricultural areas around Ruthin and at the head of the Vale of Clwyd, whereas in adjacent areas there are fewer second homes where the rural economy is more healthy. Secondly, there is the inevitable attraction of coastal sites. Nationally this is important, and 70 per cent of the second homes in the Wye sample were located in coastal parishes. At the county level, this feature is characteristic of Caernarvonshire and Norfolk (Norfolk County Council 1972), but in Denbighshire the coastal areas are dominated by the urban complexes of Colwyn Bay and Abergele which generally seem to have proved unattractive to aspiring owners of second homes (Fig. 7.2), though they have attracted a high proportion of retired people.

Movement to second homes

A major factor which is constantly noted when recreational movements are considered is the importance of the motor car, together with the rapid improvement in recent years in accessibility to remote rural areas owing to the development of motorways and to other improvements in transportation. In many ways, the development of second homes epitomises these trends, for it has so far largely involved that section of the population which, by virtue of its age, family structure, disposable income and general aspirations, has shown the highest potential for mobility. Evidence from all second-home surveys emphasises the fact that movement to second homes is essentially a family-based activity, and as such public transport is largely unsuitable; for the freedom which the second home gives to its owner would inevitably be constrained if he were dependent upon public transport. It is, therefore, not surprising that all surveys so far stress the importance of the car as an essential adjunct to the second home.

Yet despite this dependence on the motor car and the unquestioned freedom of movement which it gives, the pattern of movement from first to second home is still surprisingly local, even at a national scale. Nearly 40 per cent of all second homes in the Wye sample were located in the same BTA region as

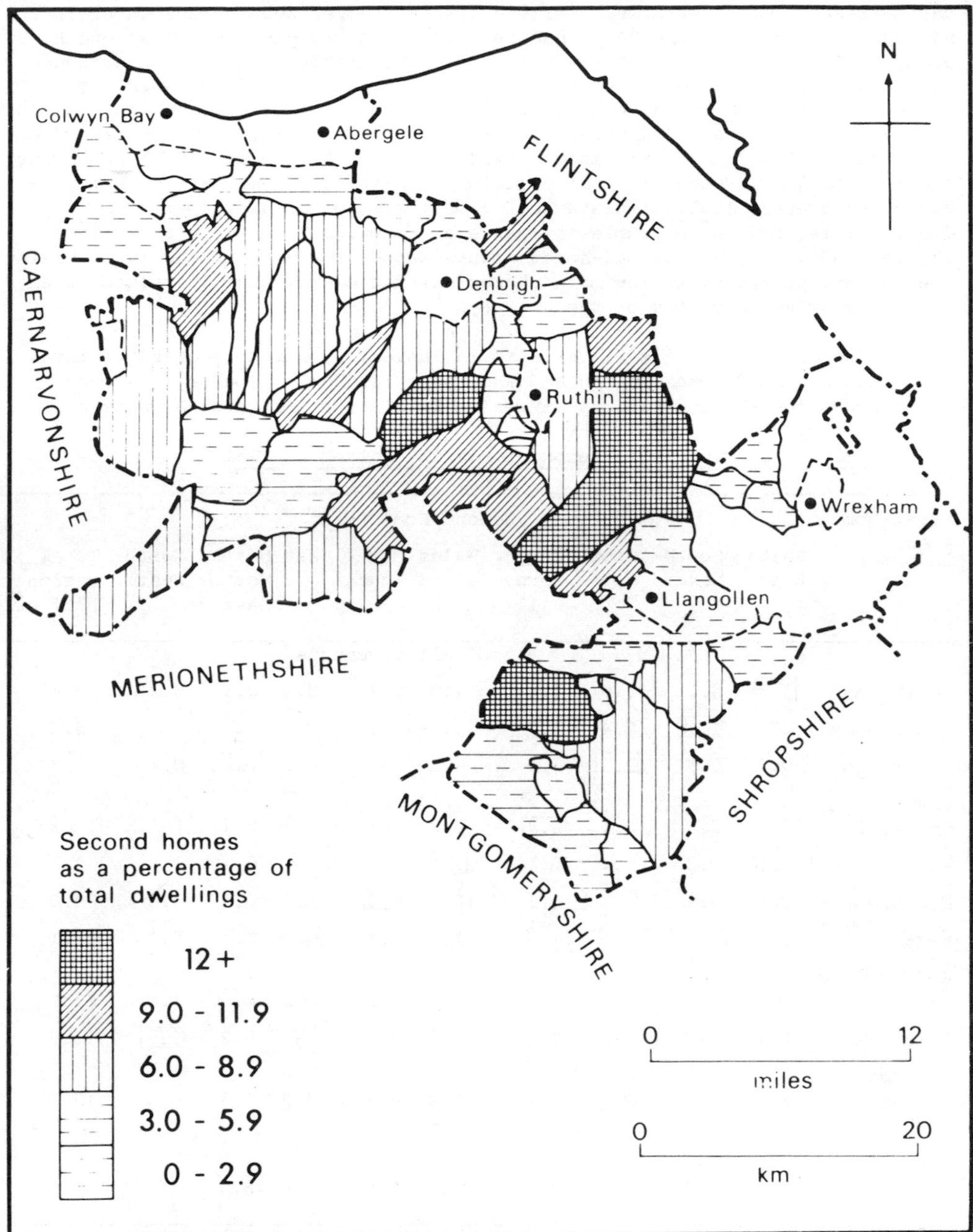

Fig. 7.2 Second-home ownership in Denbighshire, by parishes (Based, by permission of C. A. J. Jacobs, County Planning Officer, on Map 2 in Second Homes in Denbighshire).

the corresponding first homes, while a further 48 per cent were located in the adjacent region. In the Denbighshire study, over 60 per cent of second-home owners lived within 40 miles (64 km) of Ruthin, although in the Carmarthenshire study (Hughes 1973) average distances between first and second homes were rather larger, with 24 per cent travelling over 200 miles (320 km) and only 33 per cent living within 100 miles (160 km). On the whole, evidence from Sweden (Norrbom 1966) and the northeastern states of the USA (Ragatz 1970) bears out these findings and suggests that a radius of perhaps 100 miles (160 km) provides the average limit of distance for most second homes (Chaps. 3 and 13). Clearly this figures is liable to change as technology makes journey times shorter and accessible second-homes areas become crowded, but the fact remains that at the present time the main characteristic of movement to second homes is the relative shortness of the journey.

This general feature is illustrated in Table 7.1, which records the total movement to second homes in England and Wales in 1969. Journeys between first and second-home areas, as expressed in BTA regions, are shown as a

TABLE 7.1. The movement to second homes in England and Wales

First-Home Areas	Second-Home Areas									
	South-East	South-West	South	Devon/ Corn-wall	Wales	Mid-lands	East	North/ North East	North-West	Total regional outflow
	% of all movements									
South East	[3.7]	0.2	1.9	1.4	1.0	0.1	0.8	0.1	0.2	9.4
South West	-	[1.1]	0.4	0.7	0.7	0.1	0.1	0.1	-	3.2
South	0.4	0.3	[2.3]	1.1	1.1	-	0.3	0.2	0.1	5.8
Devon/ Cornwall	-	0.1	0.1	[0.7]	0.2	-	-	0.1	-	1.2
Wales	0.1	0.2	0.1	0.1	[2.6]	-	-	0.1	-	3.2
Midlands	0.1	0.8	0.3	1.1	10.3	[6.3]	1.1	0.5	0.3	20.8
East	0.8	0.1	0.6	1.0	1.2	0.1	[6.1]	0.1	0.1	10.1
North/North East	0.1	0.1	0.1	0.1	0.9	1.3	0.2	[12.0]	1.0	15.8
North West	0.1	-	-	0.1	10.6	0.1	-	0.2	[1.5]	12.8
Greater London	6.7	0.5	2.6	1.2	1.4	0.5	4.3	0.1	0.4	17.7
Total regional inflow	12.0	3.4	8.5	7.5	30.0	8.5	13.0	13.5	3.6	100.0

Journey flows are expressed as a proportion of the total national flow (to nearest 0.1 per cent).
Intra-regional flows are shown in boxes.
Source: C.L. Bielckus *et al*. 1972.

proportion of the total *national* flow. The importance of those movements to second homes which start and end in the same region is clearly seen, notably in the North/Northeast region. Local movements here are particularly important and the Wye survey shows that no less than 75 per cent of second-home owners in this region also had their first homes within the region. The survey of Northumberland (Northumberland County Council 1971) also made this point. Of those with second properties in the rural areas of the county, 34 per cent travelled for under one hour, a further 50 per cent travelled for less than two hours, and only 3 per cent were living at distances greater than four hours' travelling time.

Figures 7.3 and 7.4 use the same data as Table 7.1, except that movements to second homes have been expressed as proportions of the total *regional* movement in each region and not of the total *national* movement. Together they provide complementary illustrations of the national movements of population associated with second homes. Even with the limited amount of evidence available at present, it is clear that there are very definite and individual patterns of movement within the country, related to the disposition of the urban population on the one hand, and suitable areas for second homes on the other.

The contention that most journeys to second homes are comparatively short is well illustrated by these flow maps. Though the maps provide no indication of the proportion of the national total of second homes in particular regions, they do indicate the relative importance of certain areas as *importing* and *exporting* regions. Certain contrasts are very clear. Thus the northeast of England is characterised by a high proportion of internal movements. In contrast the northwest has comparatively little internal movement, with owners of second homes coming particularly from Yorkshire and to a lesser extent from the Midlands and Greater London, while residents of northwest England move out, especially to Wales.

These broad regional movements are naturally crude in their portrayal of more specific locational relationships. Certain links between first-and second-home areas are well known, even though it is not always possible to provide hard evidence for them in the data from the available surveys. For example, within the Midland region (Fig. 7.3) there is a considerable movement eastwards from the main urban centres of the east and west Midlands to the Lincolnshire coast; similarly, within the Northwest region, most internal movement seems to flow northward from the Manchester areas to the Lake District, while the areas in between, particularly the Fylde coast, attract people from west Yorkshire. Some areas receive users of second homes from several parts of the country, while others show a very definite concentration from one or perhaps two regions. Table 7.2 is taken from the Wye report and contrasts two of the four study areas used in this survey, viz., west-central Wales, where the west Midlands is the major source area, and southwest Devon, where the flow is far less concentrated and six other regions each contribute over 10 per cent of the total inflow of users of second homes to the area.

A good example of these specific spatial relationships between first and second homes is provided by Wales. The national picture can be seen from the Wye report (Fig. 7.5) which, although based on sample data, gives a good indication of the general pattern. The northern counties (Anglesey, Caernarvon, Denbigh and Flint) are visited mainly by people from northwest England who in many cases can reach the area in under ninety minutes' driving. The

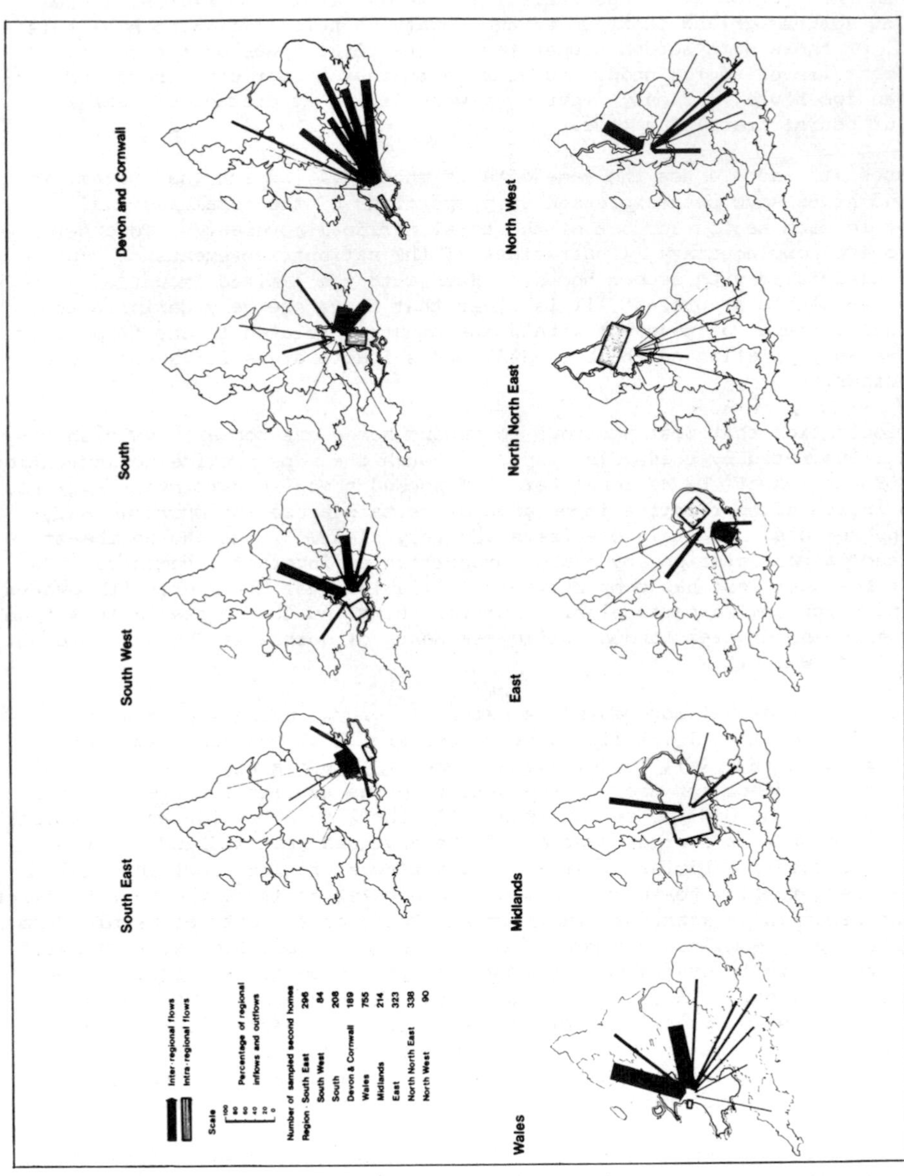

Fig. 7.3 Regional inflows to second homes in England and Wales

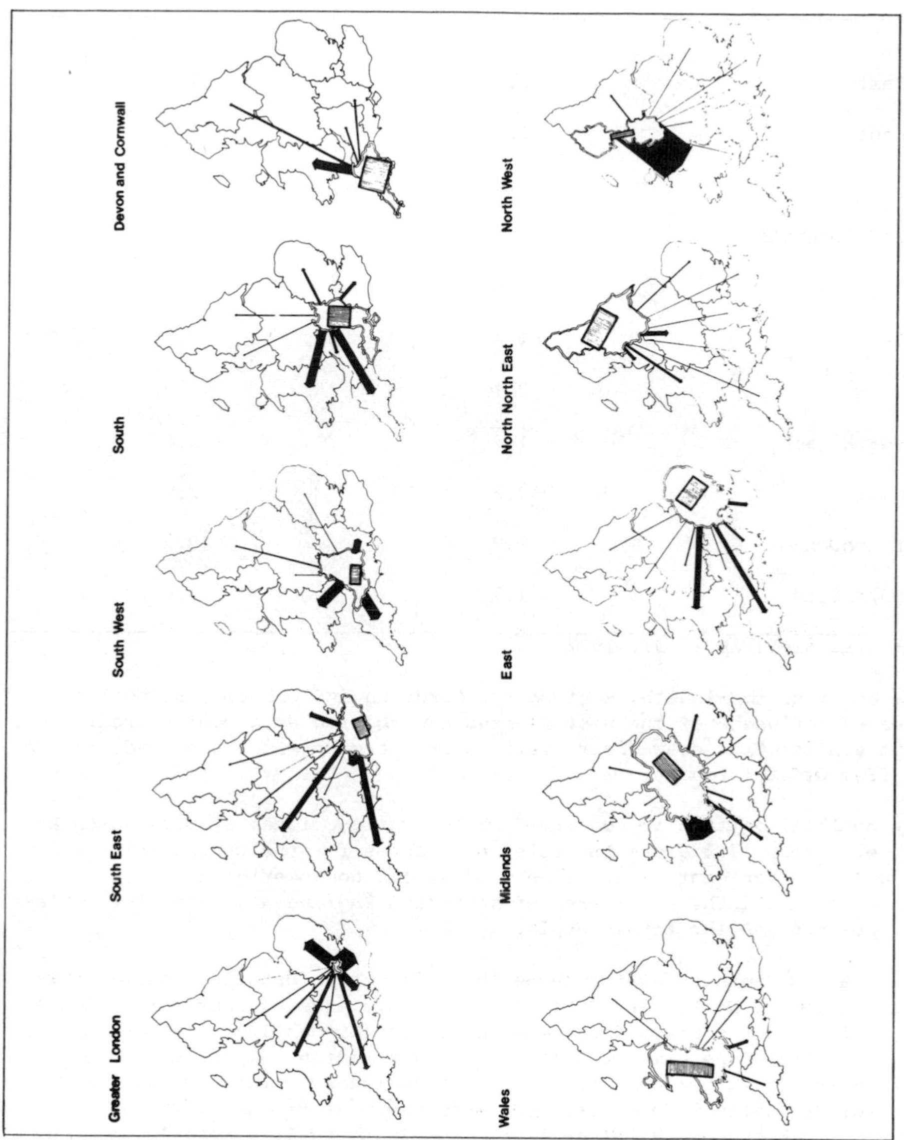

Fig. 7.4 Regional outflows to second homes in England and Wales (key as for Fig. 7.3)

TABLE 7.2. The movement to second homes in west-central Wales and southwest Devon

Origin	West-central Wales	Southwest Devon
	%	%
South East	3.1	14.9
South West	6.5	10.7
South	4.8	11.6
Devon and Cornwall	-	8.3
Wales	8.6	0.8
Midlands	51.4	14.9
East	3.1	14.9
North/North East	1.7	1.6
North West	9.2	2.5
Greater London	9.9	18.2
Scotland/Abroad	1.7	1.6

Source: C.L. Bielckus *et al.* 1972

central counties (Merioneth, Montgomery, Cardigan and probably Radnor) show the greater influence of the west Midland conurbation as a source area, while the southern counties draw their visitors from a much wider area and, increasingly, from Greater London.

This national pattern is confirmed by the various local studies which are available. Table 7.3 gives the relevant figures for the Denbighshire study, where nearly 60 per cent of all owners of second homes originated in the Merseyside area and the wider area of northwest England accounted for no less than 80 per cent of the total sample.

The data for Caernarvonshire (Pyne 1973) is not so detailed, but 37 per cent originated in North West England and the Midlands account for another 26 per cent. In the study for Carmarthenshire (Hughes 1973) 36 per cent of owners of second homes came from the South East region, 31 per cent from the rest of Wales and 15 per cent from the west Midlands. The corresponding figures for Merioneth were 42 per cent from the west Midlands, 20 per cent from the North West and 17 per cent from the South East. Finally, a study by H.D. Clout (1972) of the Clun and Bishop's Castle area of Shropshire also provides a local example of the broad pattern mentioned. Of the owners of about 170 second homes located in the area, approximately two-thirds travelled from the west Midlands, a distance of only about 50 miles (80 km).

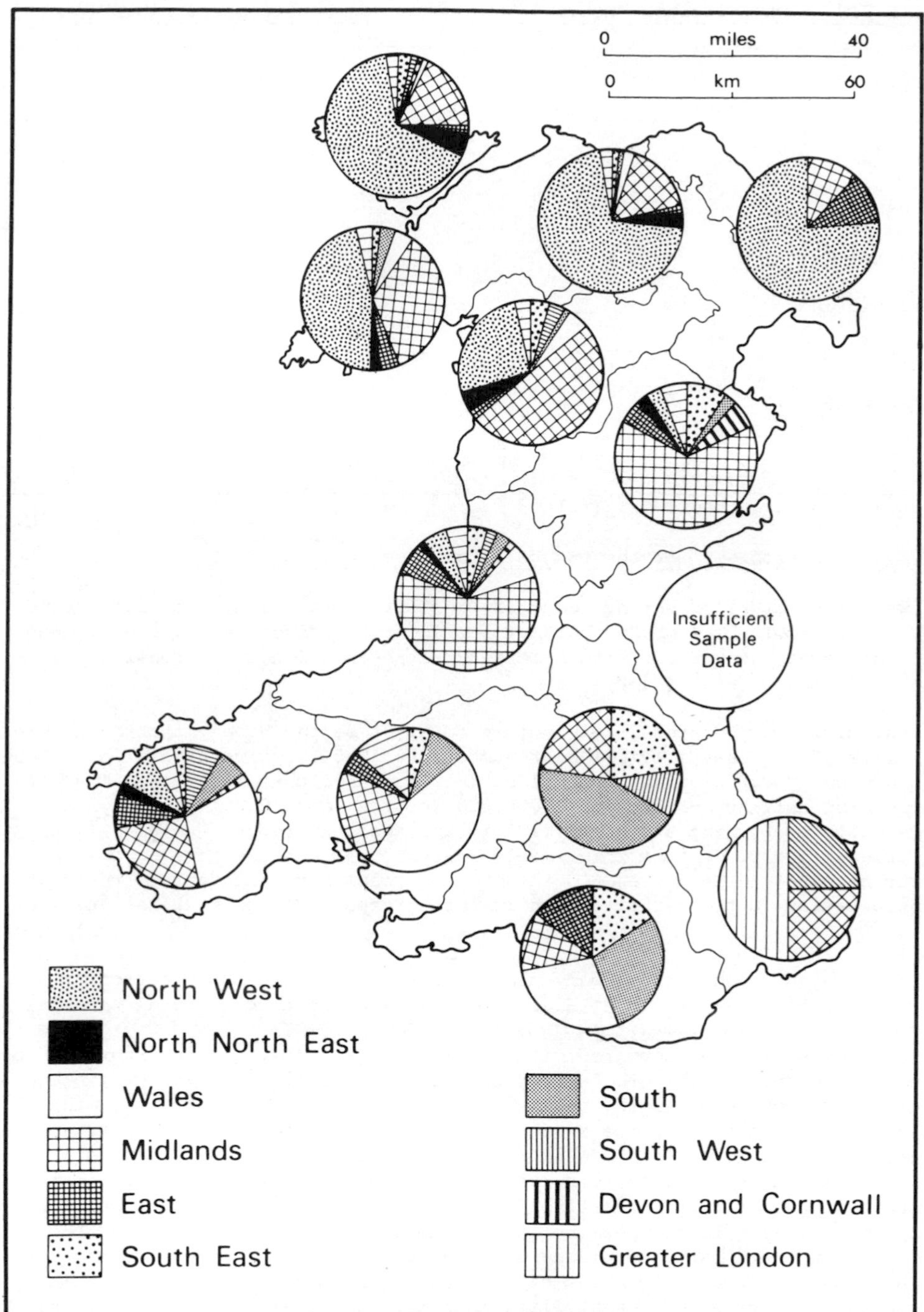

Fig. 7.5 Origins of second-home owners in Wales

TABLE 7.3. The origins of second-home owners in Denbighshire 1969/70

Origin	Percentage
Merseyside	58
Lancashire	10
Cheshire	12
West Midlands	10
North	2
South East	6
Other	2

Source: C.A.J. Jacobs 1972, Table 3

Problems for the future : increased accessibility

When the future of second homes is considered, two important facts stand out: the growth in numbers, both of permanent buildings and caravans, and the increased accessibility to remote rural areas which an increasingly affluent population will enjoy.

Estimates vary on the likely future total of second homes, though the Wye estimate of at least a tripling of numbers by 1985, to give a total of between 600,000 and 750,000 built properties, does not seem unreasonable. The corresponding estimate of perhaps 2,000,000 for the year 2000 is clearly not acceptable to Downing and Dower (1973), and the DART report quotes a figure of around 1,000,000. At this level, however, projections take on the character of a Herman Kahn scenario and it is perhaps more relevant to restrict consideration to the relatively short-term prospect of the next ten years or so.

Motorway developments already planned for this fairly short period will inevitably help in opening up areas which have hitherto been rural backwaters. Even though the increase in the actual length of motorways by 1980 will be relatively small when compared with the major road construction programmes of the last ten years, the growth will be very important in respect of linking routes and access to marginal areas. Even short extensions of, say, the M5 into the southwest or of the M4 further westwards into Wales will have a major impact upon previously isolated rural areas. In this context, the estimates of increased accessibility to certain areas, which foresee increases in the numbers of people within relatively short distances of between two and three times the present level, seem relatively modest. Areas where second homes are important are far more widespread than other recreational resource areas, such as National Parks or Areas of Outstanding Natural Beauty. Accordingly, estimates of increased accessibility made for such areas as National Parks (for example, R.T. Jackson 1970) will have to be modified with this in view.

The traffic problems which arise from this situation have been largely ignored so far. It is true that there has been much discussion of the likely impact of increased accessibility, but this has often been viewed purely in terms of more second homes in the landscape and greater social conflict. Only recently has it been suggested that one result may quite simply be more cars and more road congestion (Hillman, Henderson and Whalley 1973). The economic and environmental impact of some of the flows shown in Figs. 7.3 and 7.4 are obvious even now: the congestion on the M4 westwards out of London on Friday evening is but one example of many which could be given. When there are another 500,000 families travelling to second homes by 1985 the situation will be critical at certain strategic points on the road network.

Problems for the future : implications for the environment and resources

The impact of second homes upon the landscape and upon the rural economy and culture of a region provides another source of conflict. Opponents of second homes see them as a drain upon local resources, particularly in terms of housing for local residents, as a force making for social and cultural disruption within the local area and, as far as caravans and purpose-built properties are concerned, as a blot on the landscape. In recent years this antagonism has been particularly evident in Wales, where nationalist feeling against the invasion of rural areas by second-home owners from England has resulted in direct political action (Welsh Language Society 1972). Protagonists argue that the scanty economic evidence which exists suggests that there is a net benefit to the local area rather than a loss, and that the changing nature of the rural economy and the impact of urbanisation in its other forms contribute far more to the disruption of the social order than do a few second homes. They further contend that aspiring second-home owners and local people compete for different forms of property and, moreover, that the renovation of old and frequently derelict properties has a beneficial rather than a detrimental effect upon the landscape.

Solutions to the adverse effect on landscape may well be comparatively easy. Even though this country lacks the advantages of large areas of dense forest in which second homes can be suitably located, as in Scandinavia, it should be possible with a little ingenuity and common sense to master this problem, which is essentially one of local design. Other problems by contrast are far more wide-ranging in their implications.

The problems of resource allocation, particularly those involving housing, employment and investment in services, have suffered by being considered all too often from this local viewpoint. As with many other elements in the rural economy the mistake of viewing problems of second homes as though they were isolated from the rest of the region has meant that only part of the problem has been appreciated.

The necessity of considering second homes at a regional rather than simply at a local scale has been argued in the American context by Ragatz (1970). The point he makes has equal relevance for this country. The occupier of a second home in Denbighshire also has a first home in Liverpool. His decision to visit his second home for perhaps thirty weekends per year and for three weeks in the summer may indeed result in a total financial gain to the area in respect of food and other services of around £400 annually, but there are also implications in terms of opportunities foregone in the urban area. The ramifications of this more comprehensive approach to the problems presented by second homes are numerous. Leisure time spent in Wales can mean the under-use of resources in Liverpool; a two-home family can mean different housing requirements in the conurbation; the absence of a proportion of the most mobile element of the population from the town can result in less congestion on roads at certain times of the year, even though there may be major traffic problems at others. In short, second homes should not be regarded as isolated rural phenomena with isolated rural problems, but as elements in the economy of the city-region which have substantial spatial and temporal variations.

Conclusion

Earlier in this chapter, when some possible totals for the number of second homes in, say, 1985 were considered, a figure of perhaps 750,000 was tentatively suggested. The problems which such a total might bring to this country have conventionally been considered simply in terms of exaggerated versions of the present situation: more landscape conflicts, more traffic congestion, more social disruption and more service provision. It may well be, however, that such an attitude is far too simplistic and that radical changes in life styles over the next decade or so will make simple extrapolation of numbers of second homes and their consequent problems irrelevant.

The present attitude, which treats the second home solely from the viewpoint of the local area without considering any of its regional implications, has rightly been criticised, but perhaps even this attempt to link first- and second-home areas in one view is too elementary in its conception. Second homes are at present regarded as a new problem of outdoor recreation, involving certain rural areas and certain parts of society; the future for second homes is only conceived as a number, not as a major change in life styles.

Brian Berry, in his classic paper on the United States in the year 2000 (1970), has explored this possible future. He has argued that we are moving into an age of *telemobility* where the functioning of society will be dependent on electronic rather than simple mechanical systems. As such, the distinction between work-place and play-place will disappear, and the journey to work - and the journey to play - will become unnecessary. In his own words: 'Traditionally, we have moved the body to the experience; increasingly we will move the experience to the body and the body can therefore be located where it finds the non-electronic experiences most satisfying' (p.49).

At least in terms of present attitudes, the location where the *non-electronic experiences* are most satisfying for many people is the second home in the isolated rural area. One of the major problems which most occupiers of second homes now face is the mad retreat from the city on Friday evening and the unwilling trek back two days later. If this could be avoided, if work could be carried on at the second home with a minimum of disruption, then the second home, if in fact it could still be termed such, would have reached its apogee.

Even in the very short term, there are bound to be radical changes in areas where second homes are found. It is a short step indeed between a few second homes and the invasion of permanent dwellings and industry, not of a conventional type but of a distinct *post-industrial* kind. If this *invasion,* as Berry calls it, of the city-region takes place, then there will have to be a revolution in our thinking on regional dynamics and on the role of the second home within so-called *rural* and *urban* areas.

REFERENCES

Barr, J. (1967) 'A two-home democracy' New Society 7th September, pp.313-5.

Berry, B.J.L. (1970) 'The geography of the United States in the year 2000' Transactions of the Institute of British Geographers 51, pp.21-53.

Bielckus, C.L., Rogers, A.W. and Wibberley, G.P. (1972) Second Homes in England and Wales Studies in Rural Land Use 11, Wye College, University of London.

British Travel Association/University of Keele (1967) Pilot National Recreation Survey Report No. 1 British Travel Association, London.

Capstick, M. (1972) Some Aspects of the Economic Effects of Tourism in the Westmorland Lake District Department of Economics, University of Lancaster.

Clout, H.D. (1972) Rural Geography Pergamon, Oxford.

Downing, P. and Dower, M. (1973) Second Homes in England and Wales Countryside Commission, HMSO, London.

Hillman, M., Henderson, I. and Whalley, A. (1973) 'Traffic to holiday homes' Built Environment 2 (8), pp.454-5.

Hughes, R.E. (1973) The Planning Implications of Second Homes Unpublished M.Sc. thesis, Department of Town and Country Planning, Edinburgh College of Art/ Heriot-Watt University.

Jackson, R.T. (1970) 'Motorways and National Parks in Britain' Area 2(4) pp.26-9.

Jacobs, C.A.J. (1972) Second Homes in Denbighshire Tourism and Recreation Research Report 3, Denbighshire County Council.

Norfolk County Council (1972) Second Homes in Norfolk: Preliminary Note unpublished report, Structure Plan Studies.

Norrbom, C-E. (1966) 'Outdoor recreation in Sweden' Sociologia Ruralis VI(I) pp.56-73.

Northumberland County Council (1971) Second Homes in Northumberland, Summer 1970: Notes on Survey Report to the County Planning Committee.

Pryce, W.T.R. (1967) 'The location and growth of holiday caravan camps in Wales' Transactions of the Institute of British Geographers 42, pp.127-52.

Pyne, C.B. (1973) Second homes Caernarvonshire County Planning Department.

Ragatz, R.L. (1970) 'Vacation homes in the north-eastern United States: seasonality in population distribution' Annals of the Association of American Geographers 60, pp.447-55.

Tuck, C.J. (1973) Second homes Merioneth Structure Plan, Subject Report No. 17, Merioneth County Council.

Welsh Language Society (1972) Holiday Homes Report No. 3, The Society, Cardiff.

Chapter 8

SELF-CATERING HOLIDAY ACCOMMODATION: THE ROLE OF SUBSTITUTION

R. S. Crofts

The Problem

In recent years caravans have been increasingly regarded as problems in rural planning as a direct result of the predominantly coastal locations of stances and the very high growth rates in numbers of both static and touring units, such that the supply of pitches falls short of demand. These problems have been exacerbated by difficulties in controlling extensions to sites after licences have been granted by the local authority, and particularly by the difficulty of controlling illegalities stemming from the exemptions granted in the first schedule of the Caravan Sites and Control of Development Act of 1960. By contrast, planning problems arising from the transfer of properties from primary residences to second homes, by the conversion of pre-existing properties and increasingly by the development of purpose-built constructions, have as yet been relatively unimportant owing to the more rigorous nature of the legislation. Nevertheless, even here high rates of growth and rapidly increasing demand have resulted in demand far exceeding supply. The reduction in the supply of pre-existing houses, available directly or by conversion for second homes, will thus cause major problems in the provision of housing in rural areas and have increasing social and economic repercussions.

Previous research concerning the various forms of self-catering holiday accommodation has tended to treat the component parts in isolation. Although most studies accept, for the purposes of definition, that static caravans are second homes, touring caravans are rarely if ever treated alongside the wholly static permanent properties. Rather, these studies concentrate upon the social characteristics of the occupiers of second homes (Clout 1970), their locational preferences (Aldskogius 1967), the pattern of journeys from primary residence to second home (Tombaugh 1970) and the economic and social effects of such developments (Jacobs 1972; Pyne 1972). P. Downing (1973, p.1) recognised this tendency in a recent review of second home studies by Welsh local authorities and remarked that '...the deliberate exclusion of caravan second homes is puzzling'. Similarly, caravan studies have been largely concerned with such topics as the locations of units, the supply of and demand for pitches, site planning and traffic generation (Owen and Duffield 1971, 1972; Scottish Countryside Activities Council 1971; Scottish Tourist Board 1969), although a few have included discussions of planning implications and possible solutions to the problems posed by caravans (Jacobs 1971; Pryce 1967). There is apparently no study that covers the whole spectrum of self-catering holiday accommodation.

The aim of this chapter is, therefore, twofold. First, it will discuss the problems arising from the existence of different types of self-catering holiday accommodation, namely touring and static caravans, chalets and built second homes as observed from a case study of sixteen parishes on the mainland of Argyll in western Scotland. Although it is recognised that some of these types of accommodation can be residential (Dower 1974 and Chap. 11) they are regarded here as tourist accommodation. The second, and main objective of this chapter, is to show that the numerous planning problems which have arisen from the development of caravanning and the increasing social and economic problems caused by the development of second homes can be partially resolved, or at least reduced, by increasing the supply of alternative types of self-catering holiday accommodation as substitutes. This argument is by no means original, for it is an extension of suggestions previously made by tourist boards and other groups (see, for example, Countryside Commission for Scotland and Scottish Civic Trust 1972; English Tourist Board 1973; Jacobs 1971; Scottish Tourist Board 1969) that chalets are to be preferred to static caravans on permanent licensed sites. They create fewer environmental and aesthetic problems, increase the profitability of sites and fulfil the increasing demand for self-catering accommodation of higher quality (English Tourist Board 1973; Welsh Tourist Board 1969).

The discussion purposely does not deal with the demand for self-catering holiday accommodation as a whole or its component parts, or with the attitude of users towards the provision of, and direction to, alternative forms of accommodation in place of caravans and built second homes. Such research should be undertaken by, or on behalf of, the national tourist boards.

Definition

There is a great deal of ambiguity in the definitions of second homes as a result of disagreement about the types of structures and accommodation to be included, the nature of use and the constraints imposed by the primary sources of data. Consequently, although most all-purpose definitions embrace caravans (Dower 1974), the latter are always specifically excluded from the subsequent discussion (Downing and Dower 1973; Bielckus *et al.* 1972; Tombaugh 1970). Only in a few studies, where permanent static caravans are recorded in the rating and valuation rolls, are they included in the discussion of second homes (Blackadder 1971; Hornby 1973; Jacobs 1972). Touring caravans and other mobile forms, such as tents and houseboats, are always excluded. The term *second homes* must, therefore, be used with care. For the purposes of this chapter, which deals with a range of accommodation embracing touring and static caravans, chalets and built second homes, the term self-catering holiday accommodation is more appropriate. Even this term is used in a restricted sense, as it would include all mobile forms such as tents, holiday camps and houseboats if the English Tourist Board's definition were adopted (1973). The latter types are omitted from this discussion as they raise somewhat different planning problems and are not controlled by the same legislation. Furthermore, by including accommodation that can be rented, leased or purchased, the definition differs from that used in other studies where only rented accommodation is discussed (Owen and Duffield 1973). The definition adopted in the case study reported in this chapter is: *static, semi-mobile and mobile self-catering accommodation which is owned, leased or rented by a family that lives elsewhere.* Four components are identified and defined as follows:

a *touring caravan* is a mobile unit, not permanently sited and sufficiently short to be legally towed, but including motor caravans (i.e., self-propelled vehicles with sleeping accommodation);

a *static caravan* is permanently placed on a site throughout the summer, is too long to be legally towed by road and may be used either as holiday accommodation or as a permanent residence (though the latter type is of negligible importance in the survey area);

a *chalet* is a purpose-built prefabricated dwelling for holiday accommodation;

a *second home* is defined as a permanent property (other than a chalet) owned or rented on a long lease by a household that lives elsewhere (this is a modified version of Dower's 1974 definition).

All the information was gathered from valuation rolls for Argyll and Bute (Argyll and Bute Joint Valuation Committees 1973) and specifically excludes caravan second homes and all properties where the occupier's address was given as care of an agent. The data on caravans and chalets was collected during a field survey in the summer of 1972.

The case study

The mainland of Argyll consists of the coastal districts of Lorn, Mid-Argyll, Knapdale and Kintyre stretching from Loch Leven to the Mull of Kintyre. It is a traditional holiday area for the residents of the Clydeside conurbation and is based on the resorts of Oban, Lochgilphead, Tarbet and Campbeltown (Pattison 1967). Caravan-based holidays have become dominant during the last two decades in the Firth of Clyde holiday region, of which the southern half of mainland Argyll is a component part. Within the region as a whole, Pattison (1967) identified 14,192 static caravans and 2,072 touring caravans, representing respectively 23 and 3 per cent of all holiday accommodation in 1966; holiday houses (second homes) accounted for a further 5 per cent, holiday huts (dating from pre-1947) and chalets for 0.5 per cent. The dominance of caravans over other forms of self-catering accommodation in the study area is confirmed by the 1972 survey which enumerated 1,021 static caravans, 975 touring caravans, 19 chalets and 653 second homes (Table 8.1). With such a large concentration of caravans (by Scottish standards) in a relatively small area (810 sq. miles or 2,100 sq. km) numerous planning problems inevitably arise. The situation is aggravated by the characteristics of the units and the application of existing legislation. The annual rate of increase in the number of caravans located in the region at the height of the season is extremely high (see below). Touring caravans are highly mobile and have flexibility of location. Furthermore, most caravans are concentrated in the coastal zone which is physically and aesthetically more fragile than elsewhere and already contains the majority of residential, commercial and industrial developments. Equally, loopholes in the existing legislation are frequently exploited and local authorities have insufficient staff to enforce regulations and reduce illegalities. These problems can be exemplified by reference to the comparative distributions and growth rates of the different forms of self-catering holiday accommodation.

Distribution

The parish statistics (Table 8.1) and the spatial pattern (Fig. 8.1) reveal distinct differences in the distributions of caravans, chalets and built second homes.

Caravans have a predominantly coastal location, a feature which is also characteristic in England and Wales (Burton 1966; Pryce 1967). However, the pattern in the study area is largely determined by the restraints which the

TABLE 8.1. Caravans, chalets and built second homes in mainland Argyll, 1972

Parishes	Caravans[a] Touring	Static	Total	Chalets[a]	Second homes[b]
1. Lismore and Appin	21	60	81	0	108
2. Ardchatton and Muckairn	339	178	517	0	58
3. Kilmore and Kilbride	288	136	424	0	37
4. Kilninver and Kilmelford	42	10	52	0	12
5. Kilbrandon and Kilchatton	1	33	34	0	117
6. Craignish	5	11	16	2	16
7. Kilmartin	6	2	8	0	17
8. Kilmichael Glassary	18	19	37	0	60
9. North Knapdale	27	204	231	2	34
10. South Knapdale	15	42	57	8	48
11. Kilcalmonell	68	23	91	1	41
12. Saddell and Skipness	23	11	34	0	57
13. Gigha and Cara	0	0	0	0	3
14. Killean and Kilchenzie	32	122	154	4	13
15. Campbeltown	64	111	175	0	19
16. Southend	26	59	85	2	13
Total	975	1021	1996	19	653

Sources: [a]Field survey 7 - 12 August 1972
[b]Valuation Rolls 1972-3

terrain and historical factors have imposed on the location of roads. Four factors operate to accentuate the concentrations within the coastal zone. The most favoured locations are where the coastal terrain is regular and has a low gradient, particularly where low-level raised rock platforms and shoreline terraces are present. Although these features are well-developed throughout the area, they are used only where they are accessible, as along the shores of the Sound of Kerrera, in Benderloch and along the east and west coasts of Kintyre. In all instances the caravans are visible from a wide area of the surrounding country and the adjacent islands. The gently undul-

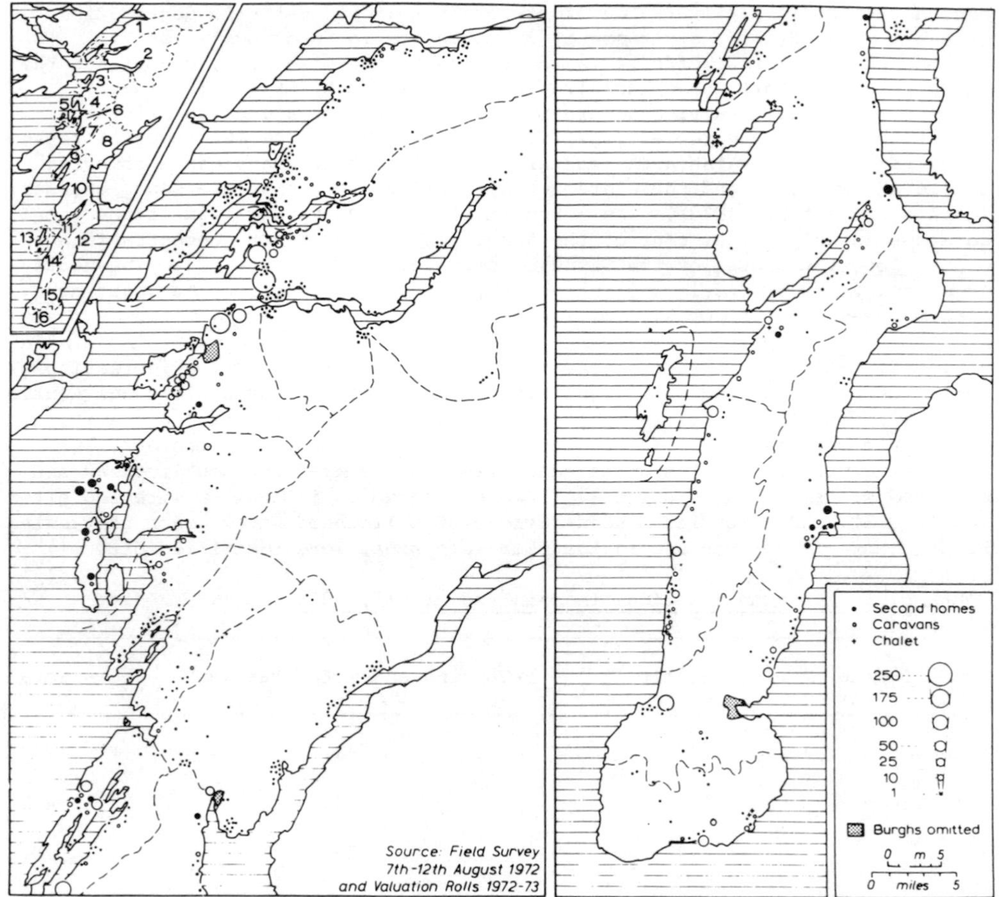

Fig. 8.1 Caravans, chalets and built second homes in mainland Argyll, 1972

ating, well-drained links which commonly occur behind sandy beaches are regarded by tourists and developers alike as ideal sites for caravans. As beaches and links are much less frequent in the districts north of Kintyre, concentrations of caravans in these locations create particular problems with regard to physical damage and reduction of environmental stability, and conflict with daytime recreational uses (Crofts 1973). The attractions of sites near service centres such as Oban, Lochgilphead, Tarbert and Campbeltown, in an area where such centres are infrequent, are self-evident and are partly a reflection of the pattern of traditional resort-based holidays characteristic of the region. As a result there is congestion, and conflicts arise from competition for accommodation between residents and visitors. Finally, locations adjacent to, or accessible from, the main trunk roads in the Scottish Highlands, such as the Lorn district near Oban, are in great demand and there is consequently considerable congestion. Coastal locations in general and coastal concentrations in particular may therefore result in aesthetic degradation, damage to the physical environment, urban congestion and social conflict. In some areas all four effects may occur, as in the Oban area, comprising the parishes of Ardchatton and Muckairn and Kilmore and Kilbride (Table 8.1). Oban is the largest service centre in the area and, as a long-established resort, contains many recreational facilities; one of the main tourist trunk roads passes through the area (Carter 1971), the whole coast has a fringing low-level terrace; and there are few attractive and accessible sandy beaches (Crofts and Ritchie 1973). As a result it contains 52 per cent of the total caravans in only 18 per cent of the area. The three major concentrations occur along the shores of the Sound of Kerrera, at Ganavan, and to the north of Connel Ferry at Ledaig and Tralee Bay, all of which are on the coast and within a few miles of Oban.

The situation is further aggravated in mainland Argyll by the increasing number of units located on illegal sites. Under the Caravan Sites and Control of Development Act (1960), all sites must be licensed with the local authority, apart from certain exemptions listed in the First Schedule of the Act. Sixty-five per cent of the units identified in the area were on licensed and exempted sites, but many units (21%) were located on illegal, unlicensed sites (Table 8.2). Substantial concentrations of unlicensed sites, each containing 50 per cent of the caravans in the immediate area, were identified directly

TABLE 8.2. Caravan locations in mainland Argyll, 1972

Type of Site	Static	Touring and motor caravan	Total
Licensed	610	682	1292
Unlicensed	211	204	415
Farms	171	29	200
Wild	29	60	89

south of Oban, in mid-Argyll and east Kintyre. Farms in the seven Crofting Counties (which include Argyll) are permitted to have up to three caravans at a time on their land for a maximum of twenty eight days a year. Ten per cent of the caravans were so located, but in many instances the statutory number was exceeded and, as they were mainly static units, they were in effect permanent stances. Some units do not occur on any proper site. Such *wild* locations, usually lay-bys and abandoned stretches of road, contain 4 per cent of all caravans, usually touring caravans which stay for only a short time. Although the percentage is small, the total number of caravans in *wild* locations (89) is considerable, especially as such caravans are also localised, particularly along the west Kintyre coast. In the study area, therefore, at least a quarter and possibly a third of the units are on illegal stances.

In contrast, there are few chalets, which comprise only 0.7 per cent of the accommodation surveyed (Table 8.1). They are mostly modern, purpose-built units located on estates, but there are also a few *holiday huts*, dating from the inter-war period when such accommodation was characteristic of the Firth of Clyde holiday area (Pattison 1967). It is true that the number of chalets doubled between 1972 and 1973, but the type, site and size of such developments can be more readily controlled by the local authority than can those of caravan sites, through the provisions of the Town and Country Planning (Scotland) Acts and the Building Standards (Scotland) Regulations.

Built second homes comprised only 24 per cent of the total accommodation surveyed. However, they are of considerable importance when viewed in relation to their contribution to the housing stock, accounting for about 14.5 per cent of all private houses and 10.3 per cent of all houses. These latter percentages are comparable with those noted in parts of North Wales where second homes are thought to be more highly developed (Jacobs 1972; Pyne 1972). There are wide variations within mainland Argyll (Crofts 1974), with proportions reaching 78 per cent of all houses in the villages on the islands of Seil and Luing, concentrations which exceed those found elsewhere in Scotland (Aitken 1974, personal communication). These built second homes are predominantly pre-existing properties, either modernised houses or converted buildings, and are therefore primarily located in villages around the coast. The highest concentrations, in terms of absolute numbers and proportion of the housing stock, occur where there has been a change in the economic status of an area, as with the closure of the slate quarries on the islands of Seil and Luing. The rationalisation of agriculture also releases a small number of isolated properties which have become second homes. As the second homes are largely located in existing settlements, their impact is predominantly social, as is shown by the attitude of the local residents to *incomers* in the Crinan area of Knapdale (Hornby 1973). In the Highlands of Scotland there is increasing conflict between local residents and purchasers of second homes as the supply of the existing properties available for second homes is limited and considerably below the demand for them (Highlands and Islands Development Board 1972; Inverness County Planning Dept. 1974; Ross and Cromarty County Planning Dept. 1972). Pressures for purpose-built holiday homes and for preferential treatment for local residents and incoming workers will inevitably increase and require local authorities to formulate policies to deal with this problem.

Growth rates

The distributions already discussed give a static picture of the situation in the summer of 1972, but it is desirable to ascertain the rates of growth of the different types of accommodation and thereby to assess the desirability of improving the supply or diverting demand towards substitutes. An attempt has therefore been made, by analysing changing patterns and numbers, to identify the growth of different types of demand and the locational preferences of users.

The growth rates for numbers of caravans must be treated with some caution, as the surveys on which they are based are not wholly comparable. However, in the absence of other data they give a general indication of trends in numbers and locational changes. The surveys carried out in 1971 and 1973 by the local planning authority (Argyll County Planning Office 1972, 1973a) and that undertaken in 1972 by the writer are both reliable and comparable, whereas the survey conducted in 1965 by Pattison is less comprehensive. Average annual growth rates of 21 per cent were recorded between 1965 and 1971, of 26 per cent between 1971 and 1972, and of 54 per cent over the two-year period from 1971 to 1973. Furthermore, according to calculations from local authority records there was an average annual increase in numbers of stances on licensed sites of 16.5 per cent between 1961 and 1971 (Argyll County Planning Office 1973b). All these growth rates are considerably higher than those quoted for other areas; for example, the annual increase in the later 1960s in Devon, Cornwall and Broadland averaged between 3 and 5 per cent (English Tourist Board 1973). Although there are fewer caravans than in parts of coastal North Wales (Jacobs 1971; Pryce 1967), the rates of increase recorded in mainland Argyll are higher and all the more alarming as there is no indication that they are slackening. Projections of the likely growth of caravan units throughout Argyll have been made by the local authority (Argyll County Planning Office 1973b), though unfortunately the estimates for annual growth rates between 1973 and 1976 (a minimum of 5 per cent and a maximum of 10 per cent) are based only on statistics for their 1971 survey, and are, therefore, considerably below the observed rate of increase for the period 1961 to 1973. Even if a 5 per cent growth occurred, between 843 and 1,266 new stances would be required above the 1971 total. It is unlikely that the opening of new licensed stances can satisfy even these low estimates of projected demand, and hence the deficiency of pitches on legal sites will increase, with consequent overcrowding on licensed sites and an increase in the number of illegal pitches on unlicensed sites, on farms, and in *wild* locations. Indeed, this pattern is already evident, for the major proportion of the growth of units between 1971 and 1972 occurred on unlicensed sites.

A 68 per cent increase in the number of chalets was also observed between 1972 and 1973. Although this figure must be treated with caution, it is indirectly comparable with rates observed in Devon, Cornwall and Broadland where the growth rate for chalets was four or five times higher than that for caravans. Rapid proportional increases are likely to continue, but it will be many years before the number of chalets equals that of caravans.

No long-term rates of growth were calculated for built second homes. A comparison of the valuation rolls for the years 1971-2 and 1972-3 for all properties with an address in Tayvallich (Knapdale) showed that no additions had occurred, but in the village of Carradale the number of second homes rose from 20 in 1965-6 (Pattison 1967) to 31 in 1972-3, representing an annual growth rate of 7 per cent. These figures, although liable to a large degree of error, can be compared with an estimated annual growth rate of 7 per cent for the whole of Scotland (Aitken 1974, personal communication).

This analysis of distributions and growth rates of self-catering holiday accommodation thus reveals that caravans not only occur in greater numbers and in a highly concentrated manner, often in sensitive and illegal situations, but also have remarkably higher growth rates than chalets and built second homes.

Planning problems and controls

In addition to the issues discussed above there are several planning problems arising from the existing legislation on caravans and housing. There is undoubtedly truth in the English Tourist Board's (1973) suggestion that planning regulations were applied more rigorously towards static caravans than towards chalets, for many local authorities, e.g., in Denbighshire and Argyll, see the conversion of static caravan sites to chalet sites as a partial solution to the problems posed by caravans. However, several important loopholes in the Caravan Act have been exploited and militate against successful planning for caravans. In Argyll many licensed and exempted sites contain more units than their licence permits, whilst there are at least twenty unlicensed sites and many *wild* locations which the local authority cannot police adequately owing to lack of staff. Secondly, the Caravan Act does not contain regulations on design for either caravans or sites, although non-mandatory recommendations had been introduced at various times to improve site planning and location (Ministry of Housing and Local Government 1960, 1962, 1969). Thirdly, the Act contains a series of exemptions which in themselves are reasonable, but have created loopholes which can be exploited. The First Schedule of the Act lists the exemptions, of which five are open to a broad interpretation. Paragraph 2 states that touring caravans may stop anywhere for a maximum of two nights providing that there are no other caravans at that location and that this practice occurs for no longer than twenty eight days a year, conditions which can be interpreted as legalising *wild* caravanning, provided that neither lay-bys nor the grass verge adjacent to roads are used, as such activities would be regarded as highway obstruction and therefore contravene road traffic legislation (Highway Act (1959), Road Traffic Act (1969)). Farm sites are exempted in Paragraph 3, which is reinforced by Statutory Instrument 976 (1965); the statute allows all holdings of two acres or more in the Crofting Counties to have three caravans on their land during the summer half of the year, a provision which is blatantly broken on many farms. Certain organisations such as the Caravan Club of Great Britain are also exempted, provided that no more than five caravans are located on a site for a period of no longer than five days (paragraphs 4 and 5); and while these conditions are usually adhered to, there are certain exceptions. Caravans for the use of agricultural, forestry and construction workers are also exempted (paragraphs 7-9), but this concession is open to broader interpretation and results in the development of long-term residential sites. Although the Caravan Act is undoubtedly a pioneering piece of legislation, the loopholes in the exemptions and the difficulties in enforcing regulations create serious problems for rural planning authorities responsible for large areas.

Control of the development of second homes, on the other hand, can be more closely regulated by applying the appropriate sections of the Town and Country Planning (Scotland) Acts and statutory building regulations, together with any restrictions which the local authority wishes to impose when giving permission for conversion of properties to second homes. Similarly, the siting, design and occupancy of chalets are controlled by the Building Standards Regulations (Scotland) 1963, as amended in 1967, and the Town and Country Planning Acts; furthermore, if chalets are constructed on caravan sites, conditions as to siting, numbers, design and occupancy can be attached to the site licence (Crosbee 1970). There are obvious loopholes in these latter developments owing to the difficulties of applying the relevant sections of the Caravan Act.

The single most important difference in the application of planning controls to second homes/chalets and to caravans is that, whereas, owing to a lack of adequate control, caravans have been allowed to increase to the point of saturation in Argyll and many other areas, the relatively recent demand for, and growth of, second homes/chalets has been recognised by national agencies and local authorities, and steps are being taken to control undesirable developments at the outset. Some considerable time will be required to formulate and implement policies for caravans which will restore a wholly legal system. It is these problems which lead to the suggestion that purpose-built self-catering holiday accommodation (and possibly, in the initial stages, built second homes) be substituted for caravans.

Substitution

In recent years, a change has been recognised in the predominant type of holiday accommodation demanded by tourists in Great Britain, from those in which service is provided (hotels, boarding houses, staying with friends) to self-catering types (camping, caravans, holiday camps and rented accommodation) (Countryside Commission 1970, p.12; Patmore 1972, p.144). More recently a further shift in demand from static caravans to chalets and built second homes has been identified in France, Sweden and the United States of America (Clout 1972), England (English Tourist Board 1973) and Wales (Wales Tourist Board 1969). The former trend is readily identified in Argyll, but the latter is not yet clearly recognisable. Indeed, it is likely that the greatest demand for a considerable time will be for caravans, probably exceeding the supply of stances and hence intensifying physical, aesthetic and associated planning problems. There are three ways of approaching the problem (Fig. 8.2). The most obvious method is to increase the capacity to satisfy the demand by

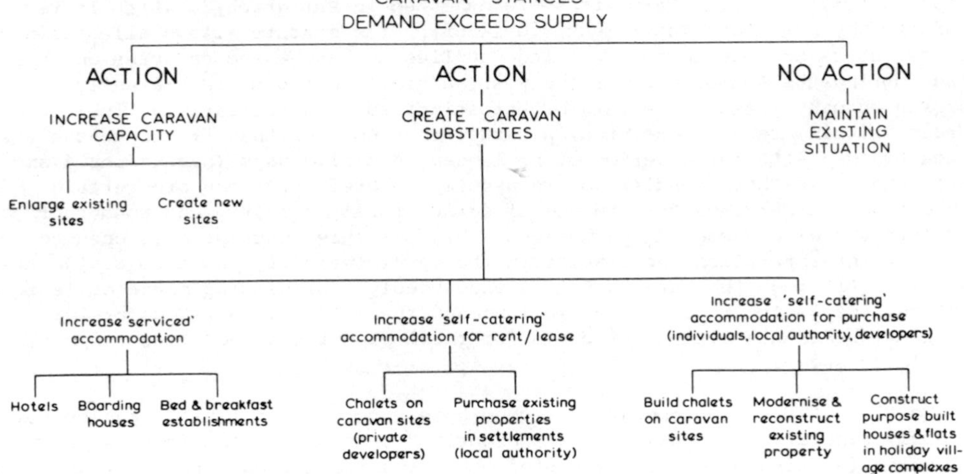

Fig. 8.2 Alternative strategies for meeting demand for caravan stances when demand exceeds supply

enlarging existing caravan sites and creating new sites for both touring and static caravans. Although this is a simple and effective short-term solution, it has a number of unsatisfactory features. The coast and the countryside are becoming increasingly overcrowded with the spread of *semi-urban* developments which cause further aesthetic degradation and reduce environmental stability; furthermore, this strategy intensifies the inadequacies of the Caravan Act. A second and easier solution is to retain the *status quo*, but if this is done the present problems multiply; for, as licensed sites become more overcrowded and health hazards increase, there is further growth in both the number of illegal unlicensed sites and the size of farm sites, and increasing *wild* caravanning, thus accentuating difficulties of planning control, creating further aesthetic problems and more pollution. In the circumstances, therefore, the third solution, the creation of caravan substitutes, is the most plausible. There are three ways of effecting this strategy. The first, to increase *serviced* holiday accommodation, is not practicable in view of the changing demands for holiday accommodation discussed earlier. The most feasible methods are to provide self-catering holiday accommodation either for rental or lease, or for purchase; this could be done either by improving existing properties or by constructing purpose-built types. The precise methods of meeting the demand by creating substitutes will be determined by several factors, including the type, ownership and availability of the existing house stock; the attitude of government bodies, local authorities and the local population to the development of tourist accommodation; the costs of different types of accommodation; and the flexibility of prospective clients.

Of these factors the housing stock has the single most important influence at the present time. The availability of pre-existing houses for use as second homes is controlled by the needs of the local population and by the attitude of property owners, and in part reflects the economic viability of the area. Yet, the change from first-to second-home status is not automatic, as it depends on the condition and ownership of the property. The quality of houses available may not satisfy the demands of prospective purchasers of second homes, although until recently this difficulty could be largely overcome by means of mandatory improvement grants from local authorities and, in some instances, by discretionary grants. Owners may prefer to keep a property empty or lease it, rather than sell it as a second home, a control which is frequently used, as entries in the valuation rolls for Argyll indicate, though some, such as the Forestry Commission, take a different attitude and sell surplus buildings and land by auction or competitive tender: 'The purchasers, especially in parts of Wales and Scotland, often acquire these properties for use as second or holiday homes to which we have no objection' (Forestry Commission Estates Management Division, personal communication 1973).

The limited supply of properties in the area and indeed in the Highlands as a whole, the probable increased demand for permanent residences and the relatively high costs of house building (Highlands and Islands Development Board 1972) suggest that the supply of existing properties for second homes will continue below the level of demand. Furthermore, as the concentration of second homes in settlements increases, social problems will arise and it is therefore desirable for the local authorities to create substitutes for built second homes as well as for caravans. It is in this context that private and grant-aided schemes for constructing purpose-built, self-catering holiday accommodation gain in importance. The impetus for these schemes lies in the earlier suggestions that chalets should replace static caravans. For example, the Scottish Tourist Board '...encourages the development of chalet parks rather than support the continued proliferation of static caravans' (1969, p.26). The latter have an adverse impact on the environment, but chalets generate a higher revenue because they have a longer season, have lower depreciation rates (Scottish Tourist Board 1970) and greater flexibility on sites (Parnell 1969), and contain better sanitary and other services (English Tourist Board 1973). Despite the higher capital outlay for chalets (see Table 8.3), they become better long-term investments than static caravans when grants, loans and rentals are taken into account (Countryside Commission for Scotland and Ross and Cromarty County Council 1973) and hence are supported by central government planners (D. Lyddon in Countryside Commission for Scotland and Scottish Civic Trust 1972, p.8). As a result, the Highlands and Islands Development Board, for example, has been extremely active in promoting the development of purpose-built accommodation. Their Holiday Cottage Scheme,

TABLE 8.3. Differential costs of self-catering accommodation

	Purchase Price (£)	Weekly Rent (£)
Static caravan	860 - 2,400*[a]	8 - 26[b,d]
Touring caravan	300 - 2,000*[b]	14 - 18[b,d]
Motor caravan	1,200 - 2,000*[b]	30 - 50[b]
Tent	150 - 280*[b]	7 - 12[b]
House/flat	8,500 - 25,000[c]	15 - 50[d]
Cottage	5,000 - 15,000[c]	15 - 45[d]
Chalet	3,400 - 6,700*[a,c]	11 - 32[d]

* Fully equipped and furnished

Sources: [a]Willerby Caravan Co. brochure, 1973 (cf.Castle Sween Bay chalets)
[b]AA camping and caravanning handbook 1972
[c]Newspaper advertisements and estate agents
[d]Mid-Argyll, Kintyre and Islay Tourist Association 1973

introduced in May 1972, was suspended ten month later, having attracted 10,000 enquiries. A further scheme, still in operation, permits crofters to construct purpose-built holiday cottages of approved design for summer letting on their land; the Board provides grant aid and supplementary loans are arranged from the Department of Agriculture and Fisheries for Scotland. The Board also offers assistance to local residents working in the crofting counties for the construction of up to five chalets and the extension of crofting houses to provide holiday accommodation, and to external developers for schemes of six or more chalets (HIDB brochure, Assistance to Tourism). In other instances individual landowners, both public and private, have taken the initiative. The Forestry Commission has a pilot project in the Strathyre Forest, Perthshire, to study the feasibility of log cabins, and in Knapdale, Castle Sween Bay Holidays have received planning permission to construct a number of holiday chalets, houses and bungalows at Fearnoch and Kilmory.

The opinions of the local population must also be considered, particularly in view of the opposition generated by the development of second homes in Wales. Control of the change of properties from first to second homes, reduction in the number of caravans, and the substitution of both by chalets offer a more realistic and acceptable alternative, particularly if the chalets are located on existing caravan sites and in discreetly-sited holiday villages.

The second most important factor controlling the viability of such substitution is the attitude of the prospective visitor who wishes to rent, lease or purchase self-catering accommodation for holidays. The most crucial questions are where do they want such accommodation and how willing are they to accept alternative types of accommodation, either by suggestion or by direction? In many instances financial constraints are overwhelming. Consideration of the costs of renting and purchasing different types of accommodation (Table 8.3) reveals that whereas all types have a similar weekly rental, purchase costs differ widely, so that most users are probably unable to buy houses, cottages or even chalets. Nevertheless, the demand for self-catering accommodation remains, and if it is to be met, private developers, and more especially local authorities, should provide such accommodation for rental and/or lease with the help of financial aid from central government. Such developments should be regarded as a better long-term investment than static caravans.

Conclusion

In view of the large and rapidly increasing numbers of caravans, the resulting planning problems in the remoter rural regions, as exemplified by mainland Argyll, and the probable scarcity of built second homes to satisfy the growing demand, the development of purpose-built self-catering holiday accommodation in the form of chalets and other pre-fabricated structures should be regarded as a suitable substitute. In the long term it is not only caravans which will cause planning problems, for '...whilst second homes consist merely of properties no longer wanted as first homes, they cause relatively few problems, but when they grow beyond this, political, social, economic and environmental problems arise' (Downing and Dower 1973, p.32). Only by controlling the number of caravan sites, their size and location, by restricting the number of transfers from first to second home, and more particularly, by providing suitable purpose-built substitutes for caravans and built second homes, can the planning problems be lessened.

Acknowledgements

The assistance of J.E. Crofts and W. Ritchie during the caravan survey is gratefully acknowledged. Thanks are due to R. Aitken and J.E. Crofts for their constructive criticisms. I am indebted to the County Planning Officer for Argyll for permission to use data from the 1971 and 1973 caravan surveys.

REFERENCES

Aldskogius, H. (1967) 'Vacation house settlement in the Siljan region' Geografiska Annaler 49B, pp.69-96.

Argyll County Planning Office (1972) Caravan Survey, 1971 Unpublished maps, Lochgilphead.

Argyll County Planning Office (1973a) Survey of Caravan Sites, 1973, Lochgilphead.

Argyll County Planning Office (1973b) Draft Caravan Policy, Lochgilphead.

Argyll and Bute Joint Valuation Committee (1973) Valuation Roll of the County of Argyll.

Bielckus, C.L., Rogers, A.W. and Wibberley, G.P. (1972) Second Homes in England and Wales Studies in Rural Land Use No. 11, Wye College, University of London.

Blackadder, A. (1971) Second Homes in Scotland Report to Scottish Development Department, Edinburgh.

Burton, T.L. (1966) 'Caravan sites for holiday makers' Town and Country Planning 24, pp.113-19.

Carter, M.R. (1971) 'A method of analysing patterns of tourist activity in a large rural area : the Highlands and Islands of Scotland Regional Studies 5, pp.29-37.

Clout, H.D. (1970) 'Social aspects of second-home occupation in the Auvergne' Planning Outlook 9, pp.33-49.

Clout, H.D. (1972) 'Second homes' in Rural Geography Pergamon, Oxford, pp.69-81.

Countryside Commission (1970) The Planning of the Coastline, HMSO, London.

Countryside Commission for Scotland and Ross and Cromarty County Council (1973) Torridon - Conservation and Economic Opportunity : a Case Study, Countryside Commission for Scotland, Perth.

Countryside Commission for Scotland and Scottish Civic Trust (1972) The Caravan in Scotland : Chaos or Compatibility, Countryside Commission for Scotland, Perth.

Crofts, R.S. (1973) 'The utilisation of sandy coasts in the Scottish Highlands' Paper presented to the Annual Conference of the Institute of British Geographers, Birmingham.

Crofts, R.S. (1974) 'Caravans and second homes : rural planning problems in Argyll' Paper presented to the Annual Conference of the Institute of British Geographers, Norwich.

Crofts, R.S. and Ritchie, W. (1973) Beaches of Mainland Argyll Department of Geography, University of Aberdeen.

Crosbee, E.H. (1970) The Second House Internal Report, Scottish Development Department, Edinburgh.

Dower, M. (1974) 'Second homes in Great Britain : a general introduction' Paper presented to a conference organised by the Town and Country Planning Association, Birmingham.

Downing, P. (1973) 'Second homes' (review) Recreational News 54, pp.1-2.

Downing, P. and Dower, N. (1973) Second Homes in England and Wales Countryside Commission, HMSO, London.

English Tourist Board (1973) Static Holiday Caravans and Chalets Research Unit Report, London.

Highlands and Islands Development Board (1972) Housing in the Highlands and Islands, Inverness.

Hornby, M.R. (1973) A Pilot Study of Second-home Ownership in Two Selected Areas of Argyll : Islay and the Crinan Canal Area M.Sc. Thesis, University of Strathclyde (published in 1973 as a report by the Highlands and Islands Development Board, Inverness).

Inverness County Planning Department (1974) Inverness-shire : Second Homes Inverness.

Jacobs, C.A.J. (1971) Caravanning in Denbighshire Tourism and Recreation Research Report No. 1, County Planning Office, Ruthin.

Jacobs, C.A.J. (1972) Second homes in Denbighshire Tourism and Recreation Research Report No. 3, County Planning Office, Ruthin.

Ministry of Housing and Local Government (1960) Caravan Sites and Control of Development Act (1960) : Model Standards, HMSO, London.

Ministry of Housing and Local Government (1962) Caravan Parks : Location, Layout and Landscape, HMSO, London.

Ministry of Housing and Local Government (1969) Caravan Sites Development Control Policy Notes No. 8, HMSO, London.

Owen, M.L. and Duffield, B.S. (1971) The Touring Caravan in Scotland : a Research Study Scottish Tourist Board, Edinburgh.

Owen, M.L. and Duffield, B.S. (1972) The Touring Caravan in Scotland : a Research Study, Supply-Demand Report Tourism and Recreation Research Unit, University of Edinburgh.

Owen, M.L. and Duffield, B.S. (1973) Pilot Study of Self-Catering Accommodation in Northeast Scotland Tourism and Recreation Research Unit, University of Edinburgh.

Parnell, B.K. (1969) Lochaber and North Argyll Department of Planning, Glasgow School of Art.

Patmore, J.A. (1972) Land and Leisure Pelican, Harmondsworth.

Pattison, D.A. (1965) County of Argyll : Areas of Great Landscape Value and Tourism Development proposals Report to Argyll County Planning Department.

Pattison, D.A. (1967) Tourism in the Firth of Clyde Ph.D. thesis, University of Glasgow.

Pryce, W.T.R. (1967) 'The location and growth of holiday caravan camps in Wales, 1956-65' Transactions Institute of British Geographers 42, pp.127-52.

Pyne, C.B. (1972) Second Homes County Planning Department, Caernarvon.

Ross and Cromarty County Planning Department (1972) Holiday Homes : progress report, Dingwall.

Scottish Countryside Activities Council (1971) Touring Caravan and Camping in Scotland, Edinburgh

Scottish Tourist Board (1969) 'Caravanning and camping in Scotland' Selected Studies 8, Edinburgh.

Scottish Tourist Board (1970) Tourism in Scotland, Edinburgh.

Tombaugh, L.W. (1970) 'Factors influencing vacation home locations' Journal of Leisure Research 2, pp.54-63.

Wales Tourist Board (1969) Tourism in Wales, Cardiff.

Chapter 9

SECOND-HOME DECISIONS: THE AUSTRALIAN CONTEXT

R. W. Robertson

The inhabitants of developed nations now have at their disposal greater amounts of leisure time than ever before and expect to acquire still more - four-day, thirty five-hour working weeks already have been adopted by some companies in Australia, long service leave is common and four weeks' annual leave is almost universal. Paradoxically, complaints are sometimes heard that this modern age provides an ever widening range of choice, especially of leisure opportunities, but sets a pace of life that militates against enjoyment of the options chosen. One result may be the large and increasing numbers of the population who seek out and temporarily inhabit environments entirely dissociated from the day-to-day pressures of the work place and even the home. This is amply illustrated by the weekend and holiday exodus from the city to the countryside and seashore. A significant proportion of this weekly and seasonal migration consists of owners of second homes attempting to *get away from it all*.

A *second home,* for the purpose of this chapter, is defined as a single family dwelling of permanent construction intended primarily for leisure time use on a private personal basis; the owner(s) must have some other form of shelter which is considered their primary place of residence. As well as separation from the work place and the primary home, such second homes usually provide their owners with convenient access to some recreational resource and with a symbol of prestige. Ironically, the owners of these so-called *places to get away from it all* often encounter a considerable amount of *it* when they arrive; trim to paint, lawns to mow, rates to pay and a host of other tasks similar in nature, if not in scale, to those generally associated with their permanent residence. Despite these drawbacks there has been a dramatic increase in ownership of second homes over the past decade. Concentrations of structures ranging from one-room shacks to veritable mansions have become prominent in many areas, but particularly in shoreline landscapes.

What is the scale of this phenomenon in Australia? According to a census of the Bureau of Statistics, there were approximately 200,000 households owning second homes in Australia in 1971 (Table 9.1). This represents about 5.4 per cent of all Australian households for the same year and, judging by the rate of property sales and completion of second homes on the South Coast of New South Wales, is likely to continue growing (Fig. 9.1). It is interesting that a larger proportion of the rural community than of the urban community in Australia owns a second home. Granting the continuing relative affluence of Australian society as a whole, there is no reason why the percentage of households owning second homes should not climb as high as the 18 per cent estimated in France (Clout 1969, p.440) or over 20 per cent, as in Sweden (Aldskogius 1967, p.69).

The average improved value of second-home properties on the South Coast of New South Wales was about $10,000 in 1972, according to property valuations carried out between 1970 and 1972 by the New South Wales Valuer General's Office.

TABLE 9.1. Approximate proportions of rural and urban households owning second homes, for each state, 1971

State	Urban Households	Rural Households	All Households
	Percentage of all households		
New South Wales	4.6	7.19	4.9
Victoria	5.2	6.39	5.3
Queensland	5.5	9.3	6.2
South Australia	4.7	8.6	5.3
Western Australia	5.3	10.5	6.2
Tasmania	7.2	8.1	7.4
Australian Capital Territory	6.4	7.9	6.5
Northern Territory	7.0	4.7	6.3
Australia	5.1	7.9	5.4

NOTE These percentages are derived from data gathered during the 1971 Australian Census. Unfortunately there was some ambiguity in the definition of *second home* used on the survey schedule. This may have resulted in some false statements regarding ownership, but would not have altered the general patterns shown above.

By applying this value to the total number of second homes in Australia we can derive a total improved valuation of approximately $2,000,000,000 (though this is clearly an understatement, since the average sale price for a property with a cottage on the New South Wales Coast in 1975 was close to $20,000). Virtually all of this valuation is located within a narrow coastal strip and a large percentage is close to the major metropolitan areas of the country. Owners of second homes are thus important not only for their number but more for their present, actual and future potential impact on what is rapidly becoming a scarce resource - coastline that is easily accessible, unsullied and of high recreation potential.

Determinism versus probabilism

In order to understand the landscape resulting from the development of second homes, the discussion in this chapter focuses on the decision-making processes of those who choose to invest their leisure time and surplus income in second homes. Rather than attempting to deduce what the second-home decision process might have been from observations of present conditions, an attempt is made to understand the process by setting up a tentative decision framework and then fitting real world data to it. The traditional, and deterministic, approach to this type of problem has been to regard the pattern of second-home development as *revealed site preferences* (Rushton 1969). This

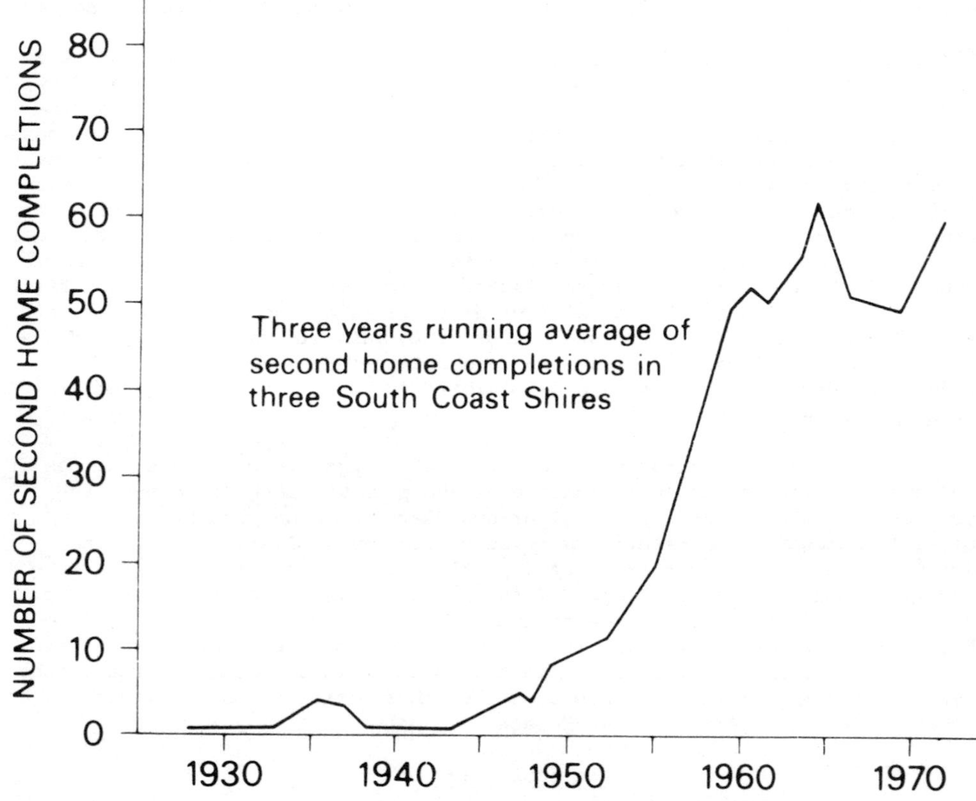

Fig. 9.1 Three-year running average of second-home completions in three coastal shires of New South Wales

suggests an assessment of site characteristics and usually involves some inference about the relative attractiveness of these characteristics, which in turn leads to the proposition that those characteristics are the reason why people chose that location.

In short, the technique involves going to a place where there are second homes, looking at the features of the place, assuming that those features are attractive to the owners and further assuming a causal relationship between those features and the location decision. The role of site attractivity in even the simplest of location decisions has been the subject of much discussion, especially among recreation researchers (see, for example, J.H. Ross, 1973) and is far from resolved, let alone the problem of how to assess the relative attractivity of various segments of, or individual features within, the landscape. To say that most Australian owners of second homes are attracted to the coastline is hardly a revelation. Given the wide variety of location-investment trade-offs faced by most potential buyers of second homes, a deterministic approach is unlikely to yield much information about the steps in the decision process or the critical junctures in making choices.

Such a *geomorphologic* approach to the investigation of decision processes (that is, attempting to deduce *process* by observing existing *structure*) does not allow for the fact that the last buyers in a particular second-home subdivision face a set of site characteristics that is quite different from those faced by the first. A deterministic approach also seems inappropriate because it implies that decision makers, in this case buyers, take inevitable courses of action that are dictated by situations and circumstances beyond their control rather than act as free-agents *choosing* from alternative courses of action one that will probably assist them in satisfying their desires. This latter probabilistic view assumes that the decision maker recognises those incentive (catalytic) and permissive (inhibiting) elements in the decision context which may foster or impede his success. In order to maintain the integrity of the decision maker in this chapter and in recognition of the complexity of the second home decision process, a probabilistic approach has been adopted as far as possible.

Rather than viewing site characteristics as things directing the choices of a potential buyer, buyers are regarded as shoppers who make choices on the basis of what they regard as useful or not useful at a particular time. J. Wolpert's concept of *place utility* is of value here (Wolpert 1965). The individual evaluates the utility of a particular place according to his subjective transformation of the actual environment (his mental map, according to P.R. Gould 1966), that is, he evaluates its utility with respect only to that portion of the environment that he perceives as relevant to his decision making. Two consumers therefore might choose the same location for a second home for entirely different reasons or, for that matter, chose entirely different locations for the same reason.

Previous work

There is a growing body of literature dealing either directly or indirectly with the phenomenon of second homes. Much of the published work has been primarily descriptive, and much is parochial to the point that generalisations are location-dependent and do not lead to a broader level of explanation of either process or spatial form. Progress has been limited, for the most part, to increasing the detail and accuracy of this descriptive work. A few studies carried out in Canada, Sweden, and the United States have probably been the most valuable in terms of predicting as well as describing second-home settlement patterns, although literature on the topic comes from a broad range of other countries, including Czechoslovakia, France, Germany, Great Britain, Australia and New Zealand. A brief critical review of some of this work will indicate the logical and informational gaps that need filling.

Summer cottages were the subject of a pioneering thesis and some subsequent articles by R.I. Wolfe (1951, 1956 and 1965). In his earlier works he described the phenomena in Southern Ontario and attempted to define recreational travel zones for residents of Toronto; in his view, cottages were simply dwellings in a summer city where people seek the illusion but emphatically not the actuality of isolation from their fellow men. The work of I.U. Fine and R.E. Tuttle (1966) in Wisconsin provides a more detailed view of second-home owners, but it was not until 1968 that any substantive analytic work appeared in North America (E.L. David 1968a, 1968b and 1969) provided one of the earliest of such studies, using regression techniques to determine the importance of various site characteristics in predicting values of lake shore properties. She found that property values were negatively related to steep or swampy land and positively related to water quality, proximity to population centres and the pressure of development at other nearby lakes.

Regression analytic techniques using greater and greater numbers of increasingly complex parameters form the backbone of research on second homes in North America. Two centres of interest developed, one around the Great Lakes and the other around reservoirs in the Appalachians. The former group consisted of R.D. Nichols (1968), L.W. Tombaugh (1968 and 1970), and R.L. Ragatz (1969, 1970a and 1970b), each of whom produced doctoral theses on the topic of second homes. All were heavily descriptive and, in terms of the preceding argument, may be classified as strongly deterministic; for example, Tombaugh, using Multiple Classification Analysis, discovered that the age, income, and occupation of a *vacation home* owner, as well as the distance he is willing to travel, were relatively poor predictors of the environmental type he will choose. The latter group comprised R. Burby, T.G. Donnelly and S.F. Weiss, whose work consisted, for the most part, of applications of models of urban residential development to second home situations (Burby and Weiss 1970; Burby 1971; and Burby, Donnelly and Weiss 1972). In the last of these studies Stepwise Regession was used to test the ability of thirty independent variables (including physical, accessibility and institutional characteristics of a site) to predict the location of *vacation homes*. Even though only 20 per cent of the variance was explained, the results were judged to be acceptable for purposes of isolating key variables of site attractiveness to be used in the simulation model that followed. As might have been expected, the ability of the simulation model to predict present development patterns around two large reservoirs in the eastern United States was less than moderately successful.

Aldskogius (1967 and 1969), applying Wolpert's concept of *place utility* to the second-home phenomenon in Sweden, has probably contributed most toward understanding the evolution of settlement patterns of second homes, even though his work also begins with an element of determinism. He assumed that those seeking second homes attempt to maximise *recreational utility* and consult their mental map of the spatial variations in recreational utility when choosing locations. Aldskogius used Stepwise Regression to describe the spatial association between settlement patterns of second homes and site chracteristics, but he recognised two drawbacks in using this analytical technique:

1. settlement patterns of *vacation homes* represent the accumulated result of location decision-making over a long period, whereas some of the behaviouristic assumptions in his model and a few of the independent variables (in their operational form) refer to the situation in only the latter part of that period;

2. linear multiple regression analysis is a deterministic statistical model which may not be appropriate for the analysis of a settlement pattern that is, presumably, strongly influenced by random deviations from the postulated behaviour in choosing locations (Aldskogius 1969, p.76).

He then developed a simulation model that incorporated elements, such as information feedback, that led to clustering of settlement through a process of imitative or risk-minimising behaviour.

Unlike Tombaugh, who allowed only a low level of substitution of sites, on the grounds that people seek specific locations to cater for site-specific recreational activities, Aldskogius recognised that, in making spatial choices, the decision maker will evaluate recreational place utility in terms of such factors as site attractiveness and the time/cost inconveniences associated with increasing length of journey, and that these are probably substitutable and, to a certain extent, are traded off. Using his simulation model, he generated a pattern of settlement that strongly correlated with the observed pattern ($r = 0.8$), his model accounting for about 65 per cent of the variation in the observed pattern of second-home development. Nevertheless he felt that the oversimplification necessary to represent the behavioural factors, which are anything but simple, cast doubt on the ability of the model to explain the *process* of second-home development.

A major shortcoming apparent in much of the work on second homes lies in the assumptions made at the outset about the potential owners. It may be assumed with some degree of assuredness that buyers of second homes seek to maximise *place utility* within the limits of their imperfect knowledge. However, *place utility* is a composite of many real and perceived factors. In this context, *place utility* for any potential buyer is the summation of all the services or benefits that a buyer expects to accrue to himself over his costs. For example, a potential buyer attempting to maximise his returns on a utility function made up of 80 per cent recreation value and 20 per cent investment value will be likely to choose a different location from someone attempting to maximise on a utility function that includes 50 per cent recreation value and 50 per cent retirement value. In order to remedy these shortcomings it was felt that a schema of the second-home decision process might provide a further step towards understanding the development of second homes. The following framework is an attempt to identify those points in the decision process at which potential consumers make judgments about likely returns for investment. This framework may also assist in sorting owners of second homes into groups according to the types of values they wish to see maximised.

The Decision Process

Before the decision process is discussed, it is necessary to outline briefly the several spatial dimensions of place utility that are likely to be considered by a prospective buyer of a second home. Three scales of characteristics - locational, situational and site - become apparent in attempts to classify factors that may influence judgments about utility. The locational characteristics of a place include its location, relative to other places within the prospective buyer's activity space. Of primary concern here is the expenditure of energy necessary to overcome the distance between permanent and second homes, for which the traditional surrogate measures are travel time and distance. The situational characteristics of a place include such factors as its location relative to the various elements that make up the nearby environment of the second home, such as the beach, local golf course, nearest business centre, location of friends and distance from the nearest main road. The site characteristics are those more immediate features of the block and/or second home that might influence the prospective buyer's choice, and might include the aspect of the site, slope, view, tree cover and other factors that are liable to affect the construction and aesthetic value of a cottage.

Aside from the scalar factors, the utility of any consumer durable such as second homes, also has three distinct temporal dimensions; its anticipated utility or service expectations, its actual utility or function once it has been acquired, and its projected utility or future service expectations. In this chapter the decision process is regarded, not as ending once the second home is acquired, but rather as an ongoing process of evaluating utility, the outcome of which results in the retention, alteration or disposal of the property (Fig. 9.2). Anticipated utility might, for instance, include expectations about recreation, investment, retirement or some combination of these. These expectations may be generalised (the prospective buyer having a set of notions about the advantages and disadvantages of ownership of a second home)or function- and even place-specific (the prospective buyer having heard about or used a cottage and recognised the likely capacity of a particular location to meet his particular utility expectations).

Anticipated Utility

These concepts are now considered in the context of a study of owners of second homes in three coastal shires of New South Wales, undertaken by the author. A self administered questionnaire was sent to the home address of 1,900 probable owners of second homes whose names were drawn from the rates records of Eurobodalla and Imlay Shires and Kiama Municipality, three local government areas typical of coastal shires around Australia that contain relatively popular locations for second homes. A total of 1143 (a 76% response) of these questionnaires was returned of which 878 were ultimately used in the analysis.

In this study, it was found that 42 per cent of the sample made their decisions with the intent of maximising second home utility for annual holidays, 30 per cent for weekend use, and 15 per cent for retirement. The owners were asked to rank in order of importance to them five likely reasons for acquisition (Table 9.2) and it was therefore possible to differentiate consumers on their mix of utilities as well as on their first preferences. For instance, a high proportion of those who rated weekend use first listed retirement as their second preference, whereas those whose first preference was annual holiday use, tended to consider use for retirement as a low priority. Not surprisingly, a significantly high proportion of middle-aged coupled indicated that they had purchased their second home for retirement while among young families investment was most often the primary reason for acquiring a second home.

In seeking to maximise their returns on investment, potential buyers of second homes differentiate the product they intend to purchase on a variety of utility parameters. Apparently recreational factors are only one part of a complex set of values associated with the anticipated utility of a second home. Other examples of variation in location and investment choices with variations in anticipated utility can be seen in Tables 9.3 and 9.4. Whilst almost 50 per cent of those who acquired a second home for annual holiday purposes lived further than 150 miles (240 km) away from their cottage, only 11 per cent of those whose primary purpose was weekend use were willing to travel that far. In rating a series of location characteristics according to importance in their location choice, a higher proportion of the weekend cottagers placed *easy travel* first than any of the other types of owner (Table 9.5). Proportionately more second homes that were intended for either weekend use or retirement had a valuation of under $6,000 than did those intended for annual holidays and a significantly greater proportion of investment cottages than of any other type

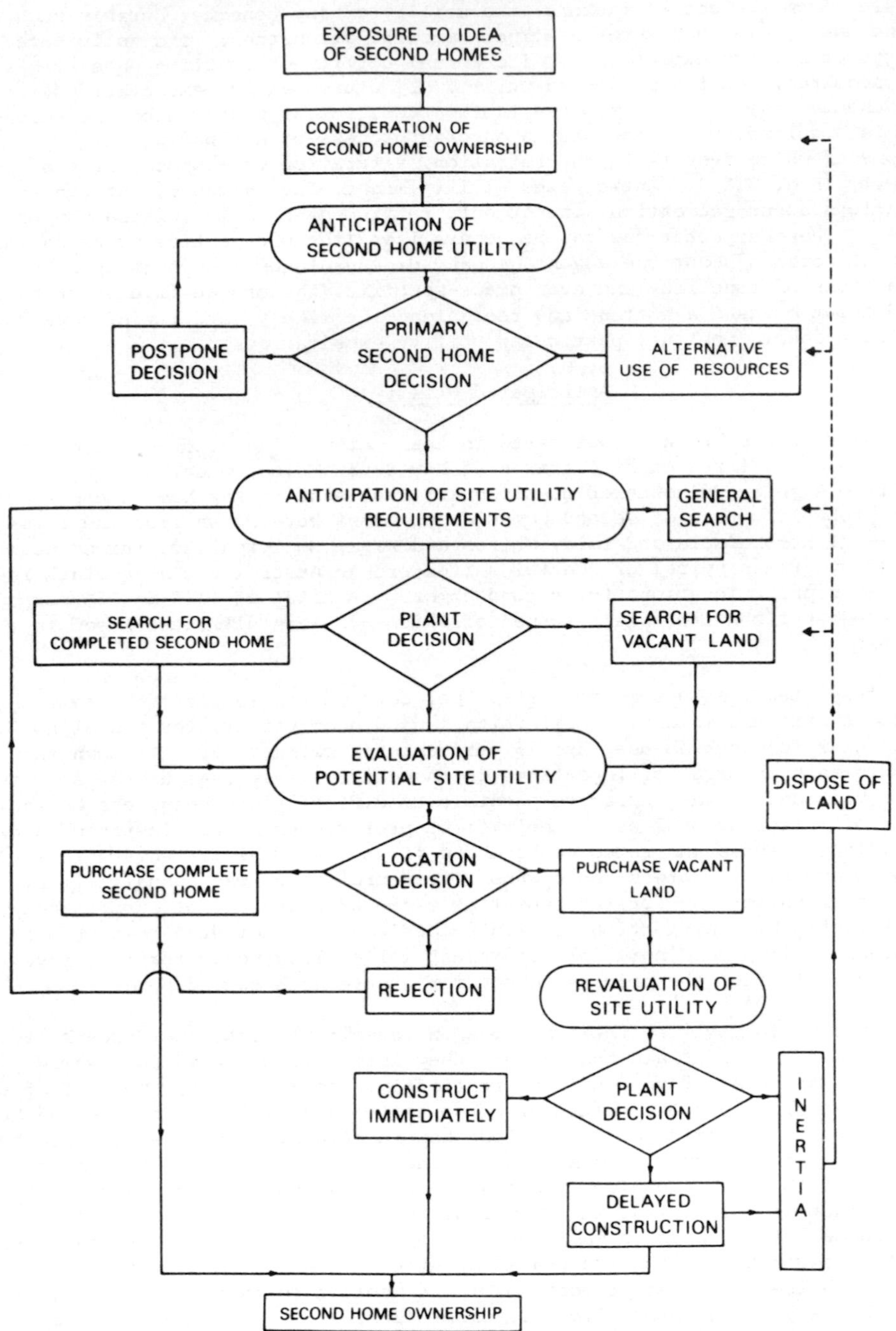

Fig. 9.2 Schema of second home decision process

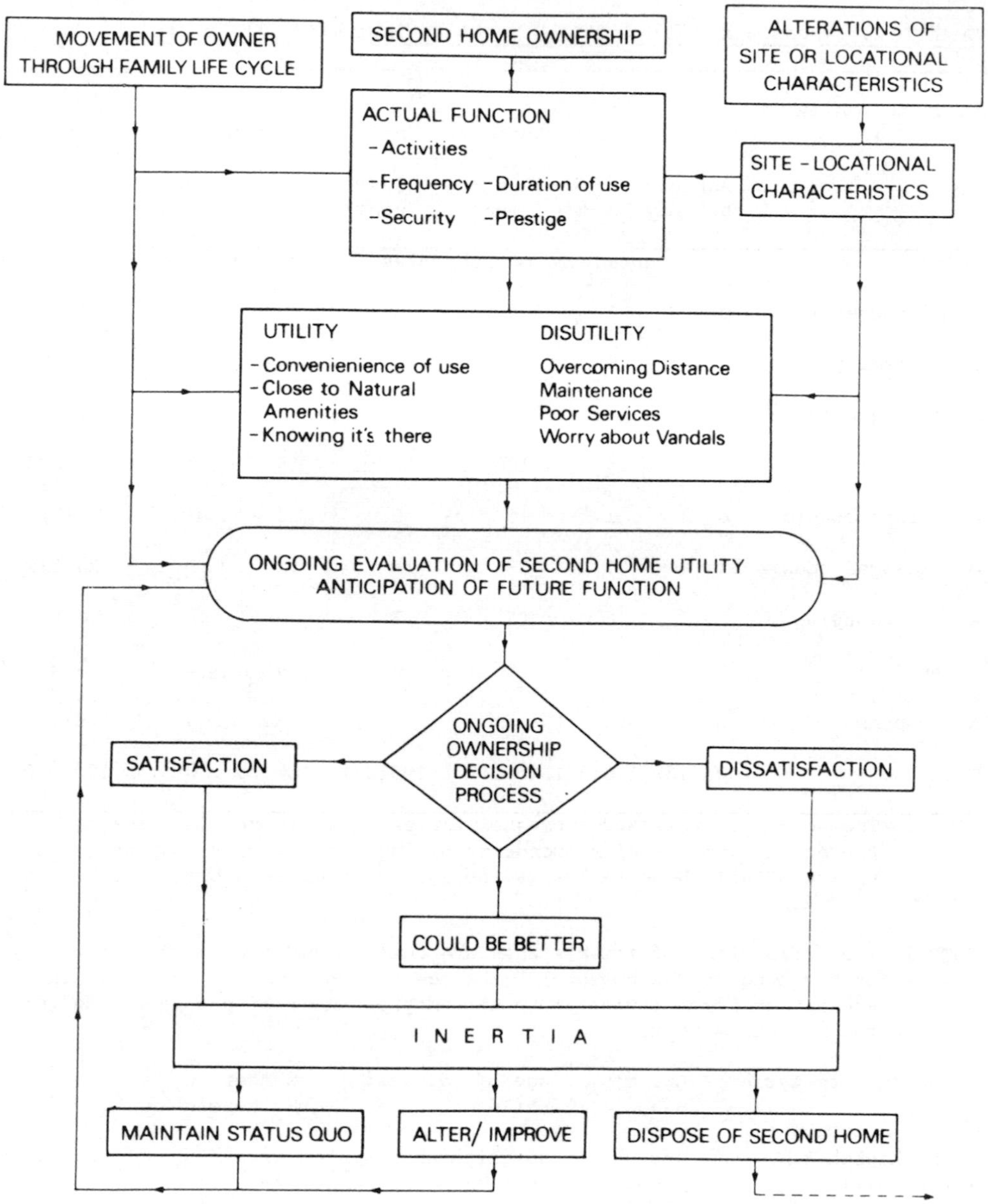

MOVEMENT OF OWNER THROUGH FAMILY LIFE CYCLE

SECOND HOME OWNERSHIP

ALTERATIONS OF SITE OR LOCATIONAL CHARACTERISTICS

ACTUAL FUNCTION
- Activities
- Frequency - Duration of use
- Security - Prestige

SITE - LOCATIONAL CHARACTERISTICS

UTILITY
- Convenienience of use
- Close to Natural Amenities
- Knowing it's there

DISUTILITY
Overcoming Distance
Maintenance
Poor Services
Worry about Vandals

ONGOING EVALUATION OF SECOND HOME UTILITY
ANTICIPATION OF FUTURE FUNCTION

ONGOING OWNERSHIP DECISION PROCESS

SATISFACTION

DISSATISFACTION

COULD BE BETTER

I N E R T I A

MAINTAIN STATUS QUO

ALTER/ IMPROVE

DISPOSE OF SECOND HOME

Fig. 9.3 Schema of second-home decision process

TABLE 9.2. Reason for acquisition, by stage in family life cycle

Stage in family life cycle	First choice reason for acquisition						
	Annual holiday	Week-ends	Retire-ment	Invest-ment	Other	No response	Total
	Percentage of responses in each category						
Young household	0	1	1	3	0	0	1(6)
Young family	8	5	5	23	4	6	7(60)
School-age family	35	32	24	32	46	24	32(283)
Older family	21	25	16	10	15	22	21(183)
Childless couple	0	1	0	0	0	0	1(5)
Middle-aged couple	21	21	38	19	15	33	24(212)
Elderly couple	7	6	5	3	8	6	6(53)
Other	5	5	6	6	4	4	5(46)
No response	3	3	4	3	8	6	3(30)
Total	100(372)	100(271)	100(127)	100(31)	100(26)	100(51)	100(878)

NOTE 1 The source of this and subsequent tables, the figures in brackets are the actual numbers of respondents giving a particular response, the source of all these tables is the survey undertaken by the author in 1971/2.

NOTE 2 The definitions of these stages are complex and are based on the age of the head of the household, the age of the youngest child (if there are any children living at home) and the number of people living in the household, viz:

Stage in Life Cycle	Age of Head	Age of youngest child	Number in Household
Young household	<25	no children	1-2
Young family	18-35	<6	2+
School-age family	25-55	6-17	2+
Older family	35-65	>17	2+
Childless couple	25-45	No children	2
Middle-aged couple	46-65	No children	2
Elderly couple	66+	No children	2

Other : Any household which will not fit into the above categories, including several where the second home was jointly owned by several households.

In households with three or more people the primary control on classification of a household is the age of the youngest child in the household, as this appears to have a stronger influence on the range of choice of alternative actions available to those households than the age of the head.

TABLE 9.3. Reason for acquisition, by distance from permanent home

Distance between permanent and second home	First choice reason for acquisition						
	Annual holiday	Week-ends	Retire-ment	Invest-ment	Other	No response	Total
	Percentage of responses in each category						
Less than 50 miles	1	0	1	0	0	0	0(3)
50 - 99 miles	25	51	38	29	35	40	36(318)
100 - 149 miles	26	36	19	26	19	34	28(251)
150 - 199 miles	17	8	19	16	23	14	15(128)
200 - 249 miles	10	2	6	6	8	6	7(59)
250 - 299 miles	7	1	4	6	8	2	4(38)
300 - 399 miles	10	0	11	10	8	4	7(60)
400 - 499 miles	2	0	2	3	0	0	1(12)
500+ miles	1	0	0	0	0	2	1(5)
Outside Australia	0	1	0	3	0	0	1(4)
Total	100(372)	100(271)	100(127)	100(31)	100(26)	100(51)	100(878)

TABLE 9.4. Reason for acquisition, by improved valuation

Improved valuation	First choice reason for acquisition						
$	Annual holiday	Week-ends	Retire-ment	Invest-ment	Other	No response	Total
	Percentage of responses in each category						
1,000 - 3,000	6	8	14	10	4	13	8(72)
3,001 - 6,000	11	14	12	3	8	15	12(104)
6,001 - 9,000	45	42	32	39	31	37	41(362)
9,001 - 12,000	26	27	27	23	31	19	27(233)
12,001 - 15,000	8	5	7	19	12	9	8(67)
15,001 - 20,000	3	2	4	6	8	4	3(27)
20,001 - 99,998	1	1	4	0	0	4	1(11)
No response	1	0	0	0	0	0	0(2)
Total	100(372)	100(271)	100(127)	100(31)	100(26)	100(51)	100(878)

TABLE 9.5. Reason for acquisition, by locational and situational characteristics

Most important location characteristic	First choice reason for acquisition						
	Annual holiday	Week-end	Retire-ment	Invest-ment	Other	No response	Total
	Percentage of responses in each category						
Low rates	4	1	4	6	4	0	3(25)
Nearby centre	2	2	4	3	0	4	2(19)
Near permanent location of friends and relatives	5	1	3	6	4	4	3(30)
Near second home of friends and relatives	2	2	1	0	0	2	2(18)
Easy travel	27	48	26	26	31	30	34(297)
Good recreational amenities	51	35	48	45	23	32	44(384)
Other	9	9	12	13	38	6	10(91)
No response	1	0	2	0	0	17	2(14)
Total	100(372)	100(271)	100(127)	100(31)	100(26)	100(51)	100(878)
Most important situational characteristic	Percentage of responses in each category						
Boating, fishing	30	24	24	26	23	27	27(234)
Swimming, surfing	40	42	21	39	23	23	36(319)
Other sports	2	1	2	0	0	0	1(11)
Scenic view	18	20	31	19	19	18	21(181)
Community water	4	5	15	3	15	2	6(55)
Sealed roads	1	2	2	3	0	0	1(13)
Other	4	6	6	10	19	2	5(47)
No response	1	0	0	0	0	28	2(18)
Total	100(372)	100(271)	100(127)	100(31)	100(26)	100(51)	100(878)

had a valuation greater than $12,000. It is also of interest that the proportion of owners who considered such things as the availability of a view and an articulated water supply as most important in their location choice was highest among those whose primary intentions were to use their cottage for retirement.

These remarks have dealt with some aspects of the anticipation stages in the decision to acquire a second home. In following a potential owner through the decision process as outlined in Fig. 9.2, we have progressed approximately to the first plant decision and evaluation of potential site utility. It should be noted that these early steps in the process may cover a span of years or may occur all in one afternoon - impulse buying of second homes is not common but has been known to happen. In any case, it may be assumed that at this stage a location has been found in which the various utilities the prospective buyer is seeking are maximised within the range of his limited knowledge. In subsequent steps buyers can be further segregated into those who purchase completed second homes (37% of the sample in this Australian study) and those who purchase vacant land with the intention of constructing a dwelling. Not only can these latter be divided further into those who construct within the same year (45% of purchasers of vacant land) or take longer (2 to 3 years, 28% of such purchasers, 4 to 7 years, 14%, and 8 or more years, 7%) but they may also be separated into those who *do it themselves* and those who have the cottage built by a contractor. It is apparent that second homes are not a homogeneous product and that evaluations of utility at the anticipation stage will vary widely.

Actual utility

At this stage the owner may or may not realise his expectations. Once he has acquired a second home the decision process becomes a continuing cost-benefit analysis, albeit a low-key and often unconscious weighing of utilities and disutilities (Fig. 9.3). The real service provided by the second home can, to some degree, be measured by the use to which it is put, that is, the activities undertaken at the second home (Tables 9.6 and 9.7) and the frequency and duration of visits there (Table 9.8). Some activities, such as swimming, appear to have almost universal appeal while other more sedate activities, such as bowling, appeal more to the elderly. The picture becomes complicated when the activities of adults are separated from those of children and those undertaken as a family unit. For example, a high proportion of boating is undertaken as a group activity while swimming and surfing are more often the sport of children than of adults. Improving the cottage is almost wholly the pastime of adults alone. Responses in all categories (child, adult, and group) were received, even from those who have no children, but often play host to friends and relatives visiting their second home. In fact, many owners indicated that guests were at the cottage on as many days in the year as the owners themselves. The general response in respect of the letting of cottages for rent was consistent with the tabulation of reasons for acquisition, in that some 55 per cent of investors let their second home for rent, compared with only 25 per cent of those who purchased the cottage for reasons other than investment. Most of the remaining types of investors had expectations of speculative gains and presumably intended to sell their cottage at some future date. The frequency and duration of cottage use also reflect original intentions, in that those whose first reason for acquiring a second home was to use it for annual holidays, tended to make far fewer trips than those who acquired their cottage principally for weekend use, even though the total number of days spent per year at the second home was similar in each case.

TABLE 9.6. Stage in family life cycle, by activities undertaken while at the second home

Activity	Young house-hold	Young family	School-age family	Older family	Childless couple	Middle-aged couple	Elderly couple	Other	No response	Total
	Stage in family life cycle									
	Percentage of responses in each category									
Boating	66	47	64	62	60	58	62	41	43	68(516)
Bowling-golf	38	23	31	33	40	36	46	31	17	33(285)
Swimming-surfing	88	98	97	91	100	78	83	81	90	89(785)
Fishing-prawning	33	75	79	70	80	73	80	65	63	74(650)
Clubbing-pubbing	43	28	32	35	40	36	29	26	33	33(291)
Gardening	50	40	44	50	60	46	49	50	50	37(405)
Improving cottage	50	71	73	78	100	75	80	87	63	74(649)
Watching television	38	34	33	29	20	31	36	29	27	31(277)
Other indoor activities	45	51	38	32	40	21	37	22	20	32(299)
Total number	(6)	(60)	(283)	(183)	(5)	(212)	(53)	(46)	(30)	(878)

Note 1. The percentages in each column total more than 100 per cent since households undertake more than one activity while at second home

2. The stages in the family life cycle are defined in Table 9.2.

Inputs to the continuing evaluation of second home utility will vary as the owner moves through the family life cycle and as the area in which the second home is located changes in site, situational and locational characteristics. For example, while an owner has a family with young children the cottage may be used for both holidays and weekends, but, as the children move into their

TABLE 9.7. Reason for acquisition by rental

Rental	Annual holiday	Week-end	Retire-ment	Invest-ment	Other	No response	Total
	First choice reasons for acquisition						
	Percentage of responses in each category						
Rented out	31	21	28	55	50	10	28(244)
Not rented out	65	75	67	39	50	79	68(595)
No response	4	4	5	6	0	11	4(39)
Total	100(372)	100(271)	100 (127)	100(31)	100(26)	100(51)	100(878)

teens and school or other activities occupy more of their time, use of the cottage at weekends may drop. When the children reach their late teens they may have lost interest in going to the cottage with their parents but may begin to use it independently. As the parents move into middle age, relaxation on weekends may once again become a major function of the second home; later it may become a place to entertain grandchildren and even later still a place for retirement. The characteristics of the area may also change in a variety of ways. Among the adverse changes, a once-pristine and secluded site may become popular and crowded, a once well-stocked fishing hole may be depleted or rates and maintenance costs may become prohibitively expensive. On the positive side, the local business centre may come to provide entertainments not formerly available and the expenditure of energy necessary to reach the cottage or the local centre may become much less as a consequence of road improvements and the availability of more reliable and more comfortable cars. The outcome of the cost-benefit analysis or evaluation of actual utility depends on the way in which a range of continually changing factors is perceived and evaluated by the owner. However, even if costs exceed benefits, some inertia must usually be overcome before an owner will attempt to sell his cottage. This inertia comprises a reluctance to give up familiar patterns and is increased by the fact that property is one of the few consumer durables that appreciates in value. There may be some argument about whether potential capital appreciation should be regarded as an inertial factor delaying an attempt to sell or a benefit that keeps the perceived balance of utilities and disutilities tipped in favour of retention of the cottage.

In an attempt to identify the leisure-related utilities of second homes, three major categories became apparent. First, some cottages seem to serve primarily as a shelter that provides both convenient access to various environmental amenities and relatively secure storage space (though the latter is less and less the case as vandalism and theft increasingly affect second homes which, for the most part, are untended during winter weekdays - a trend that may well be reversed as more and more of those owners who intend to retire to their second homes take up residence). In this case the second home may be regarded as the equivalent of an upgraded tent or caravan - the loss of mobility being compensated by increased convenience.

TABLE 9.8. Reason for acquisition by frequency and duration of use

	First choice reason for acquisition						
Trips per year	Annual holiday	Week-end	Retire-ment	Invest-ment	Other	No response	Total
	Percentage of responses in each category						
1 - 5	39	8	29	33	25	22	26(209)
6 - 10	34	24	21	15	42	33	29(227)
11 - 15	14	24	16	22	4	16	18(138)
16 - 20	7	14	14	26	8	9	11(86)
21 - 25	3	8	5	0	0	3	5(37)
26 - 30	2	10	6	0	0	10	5(43)
31 - 40	1	7	2	4	4	2	3(25)
41+	1	3	5	0	14	5	2(19)
Total	100(338)	100(113)	100(244)	100(27)	100(24)	100(46)	100(792)
Days per year	Percentages of responses in each category						
1 - 10	2	1	1	11	0	0	2(13)
11 - 20	5	6	6	7	8	7	6(47)
21 - 30	18	12	16	26	17	14	16(123)
31 - 40	19	16	12	19	21	16	17(132)
41 - 50	20	15	19	11	8	12	17(136)
51 - 60	13	14	15	7	0	18	13(106)
61 - 70	4	7	4	11	8	8	6(48)
71 - 98	12	16	12	0	12	17	13(105)
99 - 199	5	12	11	7	21	11	9(74)
Total	100(338)	100(113)	100(244)	100(27)	100(24)	100(46)	100(792)

Secondly, the cottage itself is sometimes the focus of leisure activities, providing various members of the household with an opportunity to try their hand at plumbing, carpentry or painting without the risk of a major disruption of the household should the attempt fail. With increasing regulation of the construction of dwellings and the availability of prefabricated cottages, the importance of this role is declining although there is still a strong element of *do-it-your-selfism* evident in the ownership of second homes. Thirdly, the cottage may simply be a place in which to relax and do nothing. This is usually the sport of those wealthy and sometimes easily-satisfied owners who can afford to hire local labour to undertake the menial tasks of maintenance. This is a fluid classification in that cottages often serve a multiple function at any one time - providing access to a beach for the children, a place to putter for the father and a place to relax for the mother - as well as varying functions over time.

An indication of the kinds of satisfactions and dissatisfactions among second-home owners was provided by responses to several open-ended questions. While 13 per cent of owners stated that they had no problems, 20 per cent complained about difficulties of maintenance, 16 per cent mentioned the lack of time to use the cottage and the long drive involved, 11 per cent felt that local services such as water supply and sewerage were inadequate, and the remainder were concerned about everything from sand fleas to the difficulties of repelling unwanted guests. Among the virtues of second-home ownership some 42 per cent mentioned either *getting away from it all* or relaxation, and 25 per cent felt that the convenience of having a second home available and ready to use at any time was the best part of ownership. The remainder of the sample had views about benefits ranging from the provision of cheap holidays to the prestige value of a cottage. It might be presumed that the 4 per cent who did not respond could not find anything good about their cottage and would soon join the ranks of those who do not own second homes by disposing of their property.

Projected utility

This last segment of utility evaluation is similar to the anticipation stage before the second home is acquired except that the owner's knowledge is now more complete. He is likely to recognise limitations and advantages that were not apparent to him in the early stages and is probably able to evaluate more realistically the various options open to him. Some re-evaluations are apparent in Table 9.9. Whereas only 14 per cent of the sample

TABLE 9.9. Reason for acquisition for future plans for the second home

	First choice reason for acquisition						
Future plans	Annual holiday	Week-end	Retire-ment	Invest-ment	Other	No response	Total
	Percentage of responses in each category						
Retire	25	30	71	16	27	40	34(299)
Keep it as is	61	55	20	48	46	40	51(447)
Sell it	11	10	7	26	19	14	11(97)
Improve it	1	2	0	3	0	0	1(8)
Give it to children	0	1	0	0	0	2	1(2)
Don't know	2	1	2	3	8	2	2(18)
No response	1	1	0	3	0	2	1(7)
Total	100(372)	100(271)	100(127)	100(31)	100(26)	100(51)	100(878)

indicated that their original intention was to retire to their cottages, some 34 per cent of respondents were considering use on retirement as a primary option and 7 per cent planned to sell their cottage instead.

Recapitulation

Second homes are not a homogeneous product and in order to understand the decision process associated with their purchase they must be disaggregated into their various types. It has been suggested that this might be most effectively accomplished by segmenting the product according to the utilities sought by prospective buyers. These utilities have at least three spatial (site, situational, and locational) and three temporal (anticipated, actual, and projected) dimensions. It is suggested that the schema of the decision process presented in this chapter is an effective way of ordering the various elements of the process so that points of utility evaluation (and thereby points of product differentiation) can be easily recognised. A better understanding of the decision-making process will increase the likelihood of developing successful models of patterns of second-home development.

REFERENCES

Aldskogius, H. (1967) 'Vacation home settlement in the Siljan Region'. Geografiska Annaler 49, pp.169-95.

Aldskogius, H. (1969) 'Modelling the evolution of settlement patterns: two studies of vacation house settlement', Geografiska Regionstudies, 6, Uppsala University.

Burby, R. (1971) 'A quantitative analysis of factors influencing residential location in reservoir recreation areas' Journal of Leisure Research 3, pp.69-80.

Burby, R. and Weiss, S.F. (1970) Public Policy and Landowner Behaviour Water Resources Research Institute, Chapel Hill, North Carolina.

Burby, R., Donnelly, T.G. and Weiss, S.F. (1972) 'Vacation home location: a model for simulating the residential development of rural recreation areas' Regional Studies 6, pp.421-39.

Clout, H.D. (1969) 'Second homes in France' Journal of the Town Planning Institute 55, pp.440-43.

David, E.L. (1968a) 'Lakeshore property values: a guide to public investment in recreation' Water Resources Research 4, pp.697-707.

David, E.L. (1968b) 'The uses of assessed data to approximate sales values of recreational properties' Land Economics, 44, pp.127-29.

David, E.L. (1969) 'The exploding demand for recreational property' Land Economics, 45, pp.206-17.

Fine, I.U. and Tuttle, R.E. (1966) Private Seasonal Housing in Wisconsin, State of Wisconsin.

Gould, P.R. (1966) On Mental Maps Michigan Inter-University Community of Mathematical Geographers, Discussion Paper No. 9, Ann Arbor, Michigan, Mimeographed.

Nichols, R.D. (1968) Lakeshore Leisure Homes in Northwestern Wisconsin: A Geographic Analysis of the Twin Cities Ownership Pattern, University of Minnesota, unpublished Ph.D. dissertation.

Ragatz, R.L. (1969) The Vacation Home Market: An Analysis of the Spatial Distribution of Population on a Seasonal Basis, Cornell University, unpublished Ph.D. dissertation.

Ragatz, R.L. (1970a) 'Vacation homes in the northeastern United States: seasonality in population distribution' Association of American Geographers Annals 60, pp.447-55.

Ragatz, R.L. (1970b) 'Vacation housing: a missing component in urban and regional theory' Land Economics 46, pp.118-26.

Ross, J.H. (1973) A Measure of Site Attractivity, Lands Directorate, Environment Canada, Ottawa.

Rushton, G. (1969) 'Analysis of spatial behaviour by revealed space preferences' Association of American Geographers Annals 59, pp.391-400.

Tombaugh, L.W. (1968) The Location of Vacation Homes in Michigan: A Socio-Economic Study of Environment Preferences, University of Michigan, unpublished Ph.D. dissertation.

Tombaugh, L.W. (1968) 'Factors influencing vacation home locations', Journal of Leisure Research 2, pp.54-63.

Wolfe, R.I. (1951) 'Summer cottages in Ontario', Economic Geography 27, pp.10-32.

Wolfe, R.I. (1956) Recreational Land Use in Ontario, University of Toronto, unpublished Ph.D. dissertation.

Wolfe, R.U. (1965) 'About cottages and cottagers' Landscape 15, pp.6-8.

Wolpert, J. (1965) 'Behavioural aspects of the decision to migrate' Regional Science Association Papers and Proceedings 15, pp.159-69.

Chapter 10

THE IMPACT OF SECOND HOMES

A. SECOND HOMES AND CONSERVATION IN SOUTHERN BELGIUM

G. Albarre

As in other highly populated European countries, where most people live in large towns, Belgium has seen a considerable increase in the number of second homes over the past ten years. So far, however, few comprehensive studies have been made which characterise and quantify this phenomenon. It is estimated that there are some 150,000 country cottages, mobile homes and second homes in Belgium; there are also up to 200,000 illegal chalets, i.e., built in breach of regulations of the Administration de l'Urbanisme and without permission from the competent local authorities (Le Soir, 5 September 1973).

In the French-speaking part of the country, and above all the area south of the Sambre - Meuse valleys, the rural, agricultural and wooded features of the landscape have, in recent years, attracted many nature lovers, town-dwellers seeking peace and quiet, and families in search of inexpensive holidays.

The definition of second homes

It is advisable first to consider the meaning of *second homes*. In Belgium, this notion has an administrative and official interpretation, for reference is made to it on the owner's identity card. The ownership of a second home is, for this purpose, subject to certain conditions, including a minimum length of occupancy and proof of possession of two residences. According to this definition, the majority of second homes are in big towns, as apartments for businessmen, commercial travellers, deputies from rural areas and the like, or apartments used by people who change their place of residence often (J. De Wilde 1968). Unfortunately, the census of population, the only statistical source in this field, groups both official homes and holiday and weekend residences together, and the latest available figures are for 1961. Accordingly, only field surveys can provide information on the dwellings which are the concern of this chapter. These may be defined, according to the French Institut National de la Statistique et des Études Économiques (INSEE), as: *Les résidences secondaires sont des logements que les titulaires n'habitent qu'une faible partie de l'année. Ils comprennent tous les logements de vacances y compris les maisons et les logements meublés loués pour des séjours touristiques (à l'exclusion des hôtels),* though it is better to omit the urban *pieds à terre*, as in the definition of the *maison de campagne* proposed by B. Barbier (1965) and adopted by De Wilde (1968): *Logement appartenant à une personne qui possède déjà une habitation principale, qui réside le plus souvent dans une ville, ou du moins assez loin de sa maison de campagne, et qui s'y rend pour des fins de semaines ou les vacances.*

This definition closely resembles the concept of second homes used by the Countryside Commission: *Occasional residences of households that usually live elsewhere and which are primarily used for recreation purposes, which includes the renovated cottages, new chalets, static caravans, moored houseboats and urban "pieds à terre"* (Clout 1973).

Even field inquiries face certain difficulties, particularly where occupiers of second homes do not wish to disclose their place of residence. This difficulty remains even when documents of the cadastral survey or the records of connections to the public water supply are used (De Wilde 1968).

For these reasons, the only information available until recently has been estimates of varying reliability and completeness. Thus, in the province of Luxembourg, the largest but least populated of the Belgian provinces (230,000 inhabitants), which is particularly well known for its attractiveness to tourists, there are estimated to be more than 7,000 second homes and their number increases by 500 units each year. These homes are often located on the banks of the numerous tributaries of the Meuse which drain the Ardennes. Some plans for housing estates have recently aroused opposition, often active, from supporters of nature conservation, and some local inhabitants resent encroachment by noisy town-dwellers, who have little respect for the environment.

Definitive studies are at present being undertaken by the Fondation Universitaire Luxembourgeoise (FUL) concerning the spatial distribution and the motivations of second-homers and the relationship between the latter and the permanent residents in the province of Luxembourg. In a preliminary paper by L. Goffin (1969) on the province of Namur, three principles of this study had been analysed: (a) the number and localisation of the second homes; (b) typological classification, viz., restored residences, newly-built houses, chalets or static caravans; and (c) origin of the purchaser. For each commune, the ratio of second homes to primary dwellings has been calculated. The survey established that there were at that time (July 1968) 8,090 second homes in the province of Namur, comprising: 2,774 renovated residences (34.3%). 3,285 newly-built residences (40.6%), 2,031 *formes dégradées* (i.e., small chalets, caravans, old static buses and the like, all of which are unauthorised buildings). In certain villages the ratio of second homes to primary dwellings may be as high as 130 per cent because of the presence of housing estates. On average, however, the ratio in the Eau D'Heure valley, where conditions are typical of those in the province of Namur as a whole, and comparable with those in the Sivry region (province of Hainaut), is only 4.1 per cent.

The existence of an increasing number of second homes in a rural environment is shown by the marked changes in the appearance of the surrounding landscape. There may sometimes arise serious problems of coexistence between second-homers and the permanent residents, notably the farmers. For example, M.A. Brier (1970) has studied such questions as: the change in the landscape and the general aspect of the habitat, the rise in price of plots of land and of houses (which some believe may lead to depopulation in the rural regions owing to the departure of residents who seize the opportunity of selling their homes at unprecedented prices); the increase in communal expenditure on the road system, extension of the water supply, modernisation of the electricity supply and the like, and stimulation of local trade. Conflict with farmers is particularly acute in the more populous areas of mixed farming and livestock rearing (Brier 1970). Another source of conflict in recent years relates to various proposals to build pig farms in Wallonia as a result of the legitimate desire of farmers to develop new and profitable enterprises; for permission has been granted in only a few instances owing to opposition from influential residents, who claimed that such farms would constitute a nuisance on account of the smells they would produce.

Fortunately, there are other instances where the same residents are particularly anxious to maintain the charm of the agricultural environment in which they have settled: such is the case in the village of Sivry.

The commune of Sivry

The commune of Sivry is situated near the French border in a grassland and wooded area, lying between the old industrial concentrations in the Sambre valley and those of northern France (Fig. 10.1). It is a large commune covering over 2,300 hectares (5,500 acres), and reached its maximum development in

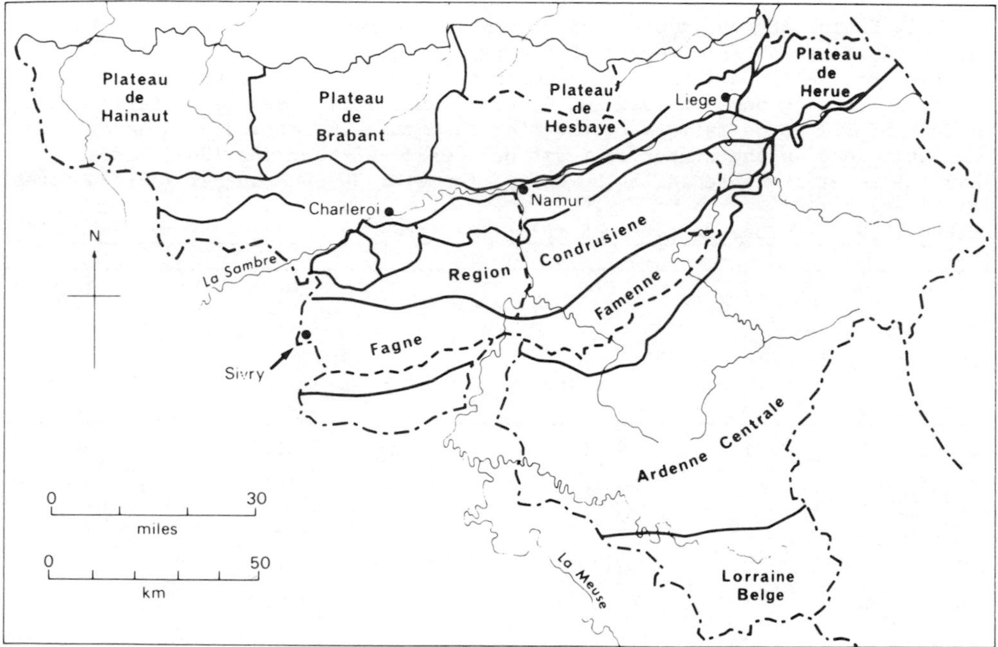

Fig. 10.1 Main agricultural regions of southern Belgium (after C.Christians 1961)

1864, when there were 3,485 inhabitants, compared with 1,411 on 31 December 1972. At that time they were mainly farmers and craftsmen, working in the wool factories or making wooden clogs at home. As a result of the decline in traditional craftsmanship and the concentration of new industries along the Sambre and Meuse valleys, the region experienced a marked but gradual decrease in population, especially from the beginning of this century. At present there is a relative stability and the loss through emigration, which has occurred for more than a century, may cease in the next few years (André 1972).

The relief of the commune, which lies in the large schistose depression of the Fagne, is slightly undulating, and the landscape is essentially one of grassland enclosed in a dense network of quickset hedges, though there is one small block of cereals (Fig. 10.1). The hedges have not been dated, though local historians believe them to be of 17th century origin. They form a true *bocage*, such as one finds more typically in the Pays de Herve, to the northeast of Liège. There are no hedges along the southern boundary of the commune in a zone adjoining the communal woods, for this area was cleared for cultivation in the late 19th century.

Sivry is an area of small farms averaging 10-20 hectares (24-48 acres), and no holding exceeds 50 hectares (120 acres). Each farm is divided into between two and five blocks, each measuring 2-3 hectares (5-7 acres). The landscape is thus of the type identified by H. Uhlig (1967) as *very irregular enclosed small blocks within a pattern of fragmented holdings with isolated farmsteads.*

This field pattern, typical of *bocage* landscape, is however undergoing major modification as a result of the reorganisation of the holdings, as can be seen from a comparison of the number of farms and the cultivated area by different size groups in 1959 and 1970. Table 10.1 shows (a) a fall in the number of full-time farmers cultivating less than 15 hectares (36 acres); (b) no change in the number of farms between 15-20 hectares (36-48 acres); and (c) a net increase in the number of farms of 30-50 hectares (72-120 acres).

TABLE 10.1. Number and area of full-time farms in Sivry, 1959 and 1970

	Full-time farms			
Size of holding	1959		1970	
(ha)	Number	Area (ha)	Number	Area (ha)
1 - 5	19	59.76	6	21.78
5 - 7	10	63.76	6	35.37
7 - 10	8	66.52	8	66.53
10 - 15	31	387.10	13	171.85
15 - 20	14	248.65	14	240.92
20 - 30	4	106.91	7	180.14
30 - 50	2	80.32	7	246.65
Total	88	1013.02	61	963.24

Source: Censuses of Agriculture, Institut National de Statistique, Brussels

Unfortunately, this agricultural rationalisation has led to the rapid disappearance of hedges. Improvements in the layout of fields require the uprooting of the hedges which separate the plots, while the hedges bordering the paths and roads (which total more than 80 km or 50 miles in length) must be maintained by the owners, who find it more convenient to pull them up and replace them with metal and sometimes electric fences. The aspect of the fields and meadows thus changes each year and the mosaic of little plots is progressively replaced by a pattern of large units. At the end of the 19th century, Sivry (which then included the territory of Sautin, separated as a self-governing village in 1914) possessed more than 450 km (280 miles) of hedges, but their length is now estimated at some 200 km (125 miles). From 1950 to 1970, 36 km (22 miles) of hedges were uprooted, a matter of increasing concern to owners of second homes in Sivry who have taken the initiative in an attempt to persuade farmers to maintain the traditional aspect of the landscape.

Second homes and second-home owners in Sivry

About one in eight of the houses in Sivry is a second home (in the wider, non-official sense) and nearly all of them are occupied by their owners. Only one of the second homes is known to have been established before the Se-Second World War and most date from the 1950s and 1960s. In the 1950s, an important period of rural emigration to the surrounding industrial regions, second homes were mainly small farms and other houses bought by town dwellers, but such properties had become scarce by the 1960s and second homes established in this period were either derelict farms which were rebuilt or newly-erected chalets (Fig. 10.2).

According to a sample survey in 1971, which achieved a 35 per cent response rate, owners of second homes follow a wide range of occupations, though one-fifth of those who provided details had retired and more than two-fifths were managerial and professional workers. More than half lived in Charleroi and its environs, a mere 35 km (22 miles) away, and three-quarters came from within a radius of 45 km (28 miles). Most of them sought a way of life different from that which they experienced in the towns. The fact that the majority of second homes had been established in old farmhouses scattered throughout the territory of the commune led to a complete intermixing of second homes and the homes of the permanent residents. Such a distribution can only facilitate contact between the local community and the owners of second homes and help to integrate the latter into their rural surroundings. Those occupiers of second homes who answered questions concerning the reasons for their choice of Sivry showed that its rural character was an important factor, for they listed first: (a) the aesthetic quality of the landscape, fields and woods (43%); (b) the fact that it was a quiet and healthy area (32%); (c) prior knowledge of the area from childhood or from friends or relations (13%); and (d) its proximity to their permanent residence. Eager to maintain a countryside which corresponded with their aspirations in Sivry, and on the initiative of one of their number, they organised a competition among the owners of hedged plots, with assistance from the local authorities and various bodies interested in the conservation of the natural environment.

The hedgerow competition

The competition was designed to identify the best hedges and was judged by a panel of five from among the various organisations sponsoring the competition. A representative of the Administration des Eaux et Forêts was concerned with the variety of species in the hedges and the eventual dominance of important varieties. A member of an educational centre concerned with nature conservation assessed the general aspect of the hedges, the manner in which they were kept, and the knowledge of, and interest shown by, the owners in their ecological role. A representative of an ornithological association was interested in the value of the hedges as a habitat for animal life. A fourth member was made responsible for a quantitative inventory of the hedges (their height, length and thickness), while a geographer was asked to consider the following criteria: (a) the aesthetic aspect; (b) the conservation of the unity of the *bocage* landscape; (c) the proportion of enclosed plots on each farm; (d) the presence of maintained hedges inside the working parcels;

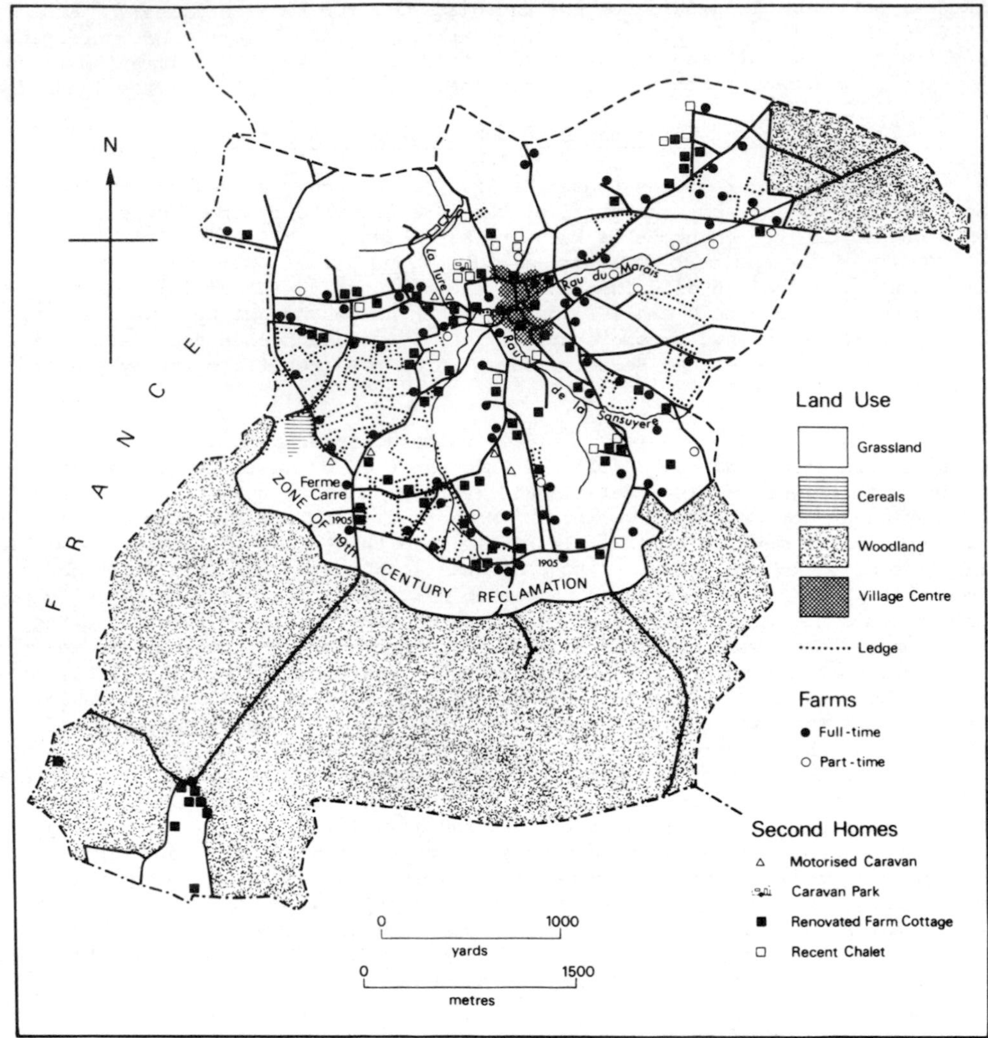

Fig. 10.2 Second homes and land use in Sivry

(e) the presence of camouflaged metal or electric fences; and (f) the location of hedges and their usefulness in providing shelter from strong winds. The importance of the hedges in stock farming was demonstrated to competitors during a visit made by several members of the jury, and in a brochure edited by the organising committee and reproduced in local newspapers (Albarre 1973). It is perhaps disappointing that there were only eleven entrants, since this did not accurately reflect the interest among the farmers. The Committee strictly interpreted its rules and did not accept entries from ten late applicants or from those who returned their forms late. Furthermore, the farming community of Sivry is very conservative and many farmers did not understand either the conditions or the objectives of the competition. Complexities of land tenure were also a factor. Nevertheless, those who participated were among the best and the most enterprising farmers in the commune.

In all, 25 km (16 miles) of hedges were considered in the competition, and monetary rewards were given to the participants on condition that they did not modify the appearance of their parcels during the following three years. While the length entered was little more than a tenth of the total in Sivry, the competition had important repercussions on the inhabitants, whether they were farmers, other permanent residents or owners of second homes. The competition created an awareness of the interest of the second-home owners in the rural environment and brought a call for outside support from the farmers, who will increasingly have to rely on the second-home owners, now equal users with them of the agricultural territory of the commune. In this way numerous obstacles to coexistence between the various social groups have been either eliminated or at least diminished.

Conclusion

The hedge competition in Sivry is a very modest example of the kind of beneficial actions which those new members of the rural community can take in the environment in which they have chosen to spend their free time. It shows that ownership of second homes may be beneficial, not only in a social and economic sense, by providing leadership and by increasing spending in the community, but also by helping to safeguard the rural environment.

After a long period of neglect, the countryside has recently experienced a wealth of interest among the population. Plans for rural development exist in Belgium and neighbouring countries, aimed at supplying agricultural areas with amenities for cultural activities and recreation, and ensuring the promotion of traditional or new products, whether they be craft or agricultural.

A kind of communication has been established between town and country, two very different environments which have too long been opposed. Today there is not a countryman who does not know the town, or who does not take advantage of the concentration of amenities and services which it offers. Increasing numbers of town dwellers are aware of the possibilities for enjoyment in an agricultural environment. It would, however, be unfortunate if countrymen, and above all farmers, came to be considered only as *gardiens de la Nature*. Both groups must learn to live together in harmony in an environment which welcomes some and feeds others.

Geographers, aware of the increasingly complex interpenetration between the urban and rural environments, have encouraged this encounter between farmers and second-homers in order to help communication between them; for without this there would surely be an ineluctable breakdown in the rural environment. This modest competition on quickset hedges in Sivry has been a first step in this direction in Belgium.

REFERENCES

Albarre, G. (1972) 'Conservons nos haies vives' L'Homme et la Nature 6, pp.22-3.

Albarre, G. (1973) 'Les Haies de Sivry' Parcs Nationaux 28(3), pp.140-8.

André, R. (1972) La Démographie du Hainaut (Vol. 2 L'Entre-Sambre-et Meuse hennuyère) Ed. Université de Bruxelles.

Barbier, B. (1965) 'Méthode d'étude des résidences secondaires : l'exemple des Basses Alpes' Méditerranée 2, pp.89-111.

Brier, M.A. (1970) Les résidences secondaires Ed. Dunod Actualités, Paris.

Clout, H. (1973) '350,000 second homes' Geographical Magazine 45(10), p.750.

Christians, C. (1961) 'Contribution à l'étude géographique de la structure agraire dans la partie walloune de la Belgique' Bulletin de la Société belge d'Études géographiques 30(2), pp.257-465.

De Wilde, J. (1968) 'Résidences secondaires et tourisme de week-end en milieu rural' Revue Belge de Géographie 92(3), pp.5-55.

Goffin, L. (1969) 'Les résidences secondaires dans la province de Namur' Annales des Sciences économiques appliquées Louvain 27(3). pp.258-72.

Sol, C. (1971) 'Ceux qu'on appelle les "résidentiels" Le Chevrotin, Sivry, 21, mineographed.

Uhlig, H. (ed) (1967) Basic material for the terminology of the agricultural landscale, (Vol. 1 Type of field patterns), Kommissionsverlag W. Schmitz, Giessen.

B. SOCIAL IMPLICATIONS OF SECOND HOMES IN MID- AND NORTH WALES

J. T. Coppock

Second homes not only have ecological consequences for the environment in which they are located: they also involve interactions between their owners and the local population. Yet, despite the publicity of a general kind which the social implications of second homes has received, there have been little research and few soundly based conclusions. This consideration of second homes in Wales is based partly on published reports by the relevant local authorities and partly on surveys of the Aberystwyth Rural District (Fig. 10.3) undertaken by the Wye College Survey team (Bielckus *et al.* 1972) and by A.R. Pardoe (1973).

During the past decade there has been a rapid growth of ownership of second homes in rural Wales, especially during the late 1960s; in Denbighshire, for example, the annual rate of increase was estimated at 7 per cent between 1957/8 and 1969/70, resulting in a three-fold increase (Jacobs 1972, p.16). While in the 1930s there were small numbers of holiday chalets and probably also other second homes, the great expansion has been in the post-war period; by the end of the 1960s second homes accounted for 7 per cent of all dwellings in Caernarvonshire (Pyne 1973, p.5) and Denbighshire (Jacobs 1972, p.6), and 9 per cent in Anglesey (Archer 1973, p.84), compared with about 1 per cent in England and Wales (Bielckus *et al.*, p.39); locally, proportions were much higher, reaching 49 per cent in Abersoch (Pyne, p.8) and exceeding 20 per cent in half the parishes in Llyn (Pyne, pp.8, 83). These three counties alone had 4,814 second homes in 1970 (Archer, p.84) out of possibly 36,000 built second homes in Wales (Bielckus *et al.* 1972, p.36). A large proportion of these were coastal, as with caravans (Pryce 1967), but they were also scattered throughout the mountainous interior of Wales.

As Fig. 7.5 shows, only 9 per cent of occupiers of second homes in Wales came from Wales and most originated in North West England (35%) and the Midlands (34%) (Bielckus *et al.*, p.58), though a substantial proportion, about two-fifths in Caernarvonshire and Denbighshire, had connections with Wales, having been born there or having Welsh relatives. The county studies indicate that these owners of second homes bring financial benefits, contributing more in rates than they consume in services and making considerable local purchases, in turn creating new employment through the multiplier effect (Archer 1973; Jacobs 1972; Pyne 1973); Jacobs thought that second homes in Denbighshire might create an additional 1,500 jobs in the country (1972, p.50), though Pyne suggested a figure of 990 for Caernarvonshire alone (1973, p.27). There are also environmental benefits through the rehabilitation of derelict or substandard dwellings; many purchasers of second homes have made substantial improvements, a trend encouraged in the 1960s and early 1970s by improvement grants. Nonetheless, second homes are a source of political controversy in Wales (e.g., Denbighshire Free Press 17 July 1971; see also Chap. 14): as elsewhere, fears have been expressed that purchases of second homes drive up house prices and prevent young people acquiring local homes on marriage, thereby contributing to rural depopulation. Fears have also been

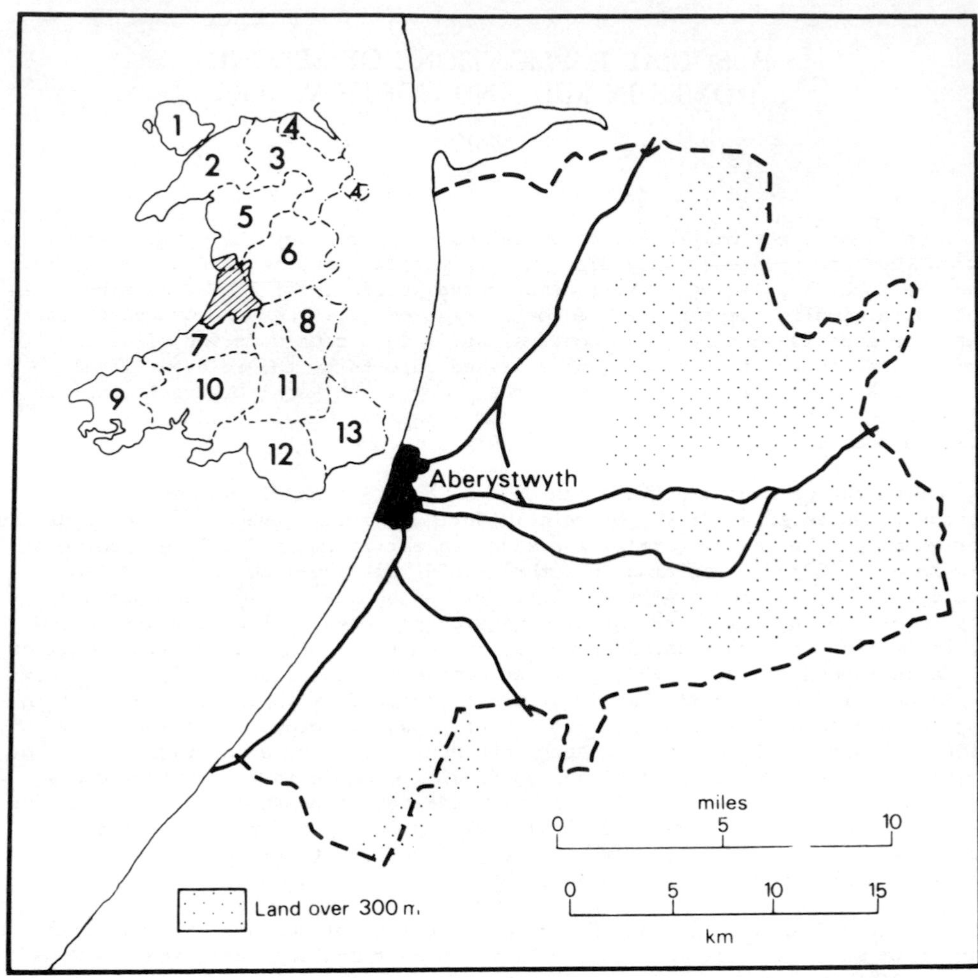

Fig. 10.3 Aberystwyth Rural District

The numbers indicate the former Welsh counties:
1, Anglesey; 2, Caernarvon; 3, Denbigh; 4, Flint;
5, Merioneth; 6, Montgomery; 7, Cardigan; 8, Radnor;
9, Pembroke; 10, Carmarthen; 11, Brecon; 12, Glamorgan;
13, Monmouth

voiced that the incomers are helping to destroy Welsh culture and the Welsh language; the Welsh Language Society has disrupted auction sales in Caernarvonshire, and at least two organisations, Adfer and Cwmdeithas Tai Gwynyedd, have been formed to buy properties and rent them to local people.

It is always difficult to evaluate such claims. Substantial proportions of the properties acquired as second homes were old and unmodernised; in Caernarvonshire, for example, 54 per cent were of this kind. Furthermore, many of these were isolated cottages or in small hamlets, remote from schools and services, and it may be doubted if these would have been attractive to young people in view of the widespread trends towards urban living and rising standards of local authority housing. There is widespread evidence that rural depopulation preceded the growth in numbers of second homes, and the availability of empty or derelict properties has itself clearly been a factor in this expansion: three-quarters of a group of respondents in Denbighshire, chosen for their potential role as *gate-keepers* of local opinion, did not see ownership of second homes as a factor making it difficult for young people to get houses, either because the houses acquired as second homes were not of a type to attract local people or because the young left the area in search of work and the question did not therefore arise (Jacobs, p.37). It may be noted that a survey in the Lake District has also indicated that there were few cases where young people would have stayed if a house had been available at the time of their marriage, chiefly because there was no suitable employment locally (Capstick 1972, p.78). Second homes may thus be a symptom rather than a cause. It is true that there is evidence that prices of houses in such areas have been rising faster than in England and Wales as a whole as a result of the demand for second homes (Jacobs, pp.37, 41), though this may be due largely to competition between potential owners of second homes.

The effects of second homes on community life and Welsh culture are more difficult to evaluate, but some light has been thrown on these questions by sample surveys undertaken in the Aberystwyth Rural District by the Wye team and by A.R. Pardoe. The Wye team undertook field interviews and achieved a response of 60 per cent, giving 292 usable interviews (Bielckus *et. al.*, p.22). Pardoe's survey was a postal one and achieved an effective response of 43 per cent (86 respondents), a comparable figure to that achieved in Caernarvonshire (34%) and Denbighshire (33%) and in other postal surveys. It should be remembered that the results of all these surveys may be biased, though Pardoe found no significant differences between his sample and the total population when checked against rating valuations. Unfortunately, different definitions were adopted in the two surveys, the Wye College team including static caravans, whereas Pardoe used the following: *a static property which is the alternative residence of a household, the principle domicile of which is situated elsewhere and which is used primarily by members of that household for their recreation and leisure*. He excluded static caravans and chalets (included in the Wye sample) as well as the suburbanised parish of Llanbadarn Fawr.

The Aberystwyth Rural District covers some 200 square miles (520 sq. km) of north Cardiganshire (Fig. 10.3). Aberystwyth is the focus of the district and some 80 per cent of the second homes are located in the coastal parishes, especially to the north of Aberystwyth (Bielckus *et al.*, p.75). Other second homes are scattered throughout the hinterland, particularly in the valleys dissecting the moorlands which rise to over 1,000 feet (300 m) and occupy most of the district. According to the Wye survey 43 per cent of the second homes were houses or cottages and 76 per cent of the properties were old (p.79); in 6 per cent electricity had been installed (p.80) and 6 per cent had been reroofed (p.81); it should be noted that the totals from which these percentages are calculated include caravans. At least 38 per cent of the properties were already second homes when they were acquired (p.85). As elsewhere, the occupants were primarily in non-manual employment (68%, p.87) and over half were professional or managerial (p.88). They used their second homes for both holidays and weekends, though nearly half (46%) came for holidays only (p.94); nonetheless, although the low occupancy of second homes is frequently a subject of criticism, owners used their properties on average 73 days in a year (p.98). Pardoe's survey was compatible with this, indicating that half the occupants spent between five and ten weeks at their second homes. Although the figures are not strictly comparable, it is interesting to note that occupancy rates in Caernarvonshire were estimated at 117 days (Pyne, p.16) and those in Denbighshire as 52.5 days (Jacobs, p.19).

The field staff of the Wye survey also interviewed a sample of 462 local residents to obtain their views on the development of second homes (Bielckus *et al.* 1972, p.22). The great majority (87%) were aware of these developments (p.111) and 71 per cent of respondents thought they had not been affected, though the proportion of their contacts who had not been affected was lower (64%). Furthermore, some 70 per cent thought that the trend towards the development of second homes was good and only 15 per cent thought it bad. These figures do not agree with the opinions of the sample of *gate-keepers* in Denbighshire, over half of whom said that the trend was not welcomed and that they would prefer to see the homes occupied by locals, though some recognised that the alternative to second homes was dereliction (Jacobs, p.37). The trend was seen as inevitable, but second homes were usually accepted *with a touch of sadness* (p.40).

Such attitudes did not mean that there was necessarily antagonism between local residents and occupiers of second homes. In Denbighshire two-thirds of respondents thought there was no antagonism (p.40); where conflict occurred it often arose from the application of urban values without thought for local practices, e.g., the use of a chain-saw on Sunday within earshot of a chapel. Individual attitudes vary, at least in part because local residents benefit to varying degrees from the presence of second homes: in general, the Wye survey found that inland rural areas were more likely to consider the development of second homes as bad than were the coastal population (Bielckus *et al.* 1972, p.112), though the Denbighshire report contrasted the coastal areas - where second homes exceeded one-third of all dwellings and housing associations had been formed to safeguard housing for local residents - with the rural areas, unaffected by mass tourism, where reactions have been more diffuse (Jacobs 1972, p.42).

In rural Wales such conflicts, common to all areas where second homes are numerous, are aggravated by differences of language and culture. Nevertheless, though the proportion of occupiers of second homes who were resident in Wales was low, the proportions born in Wales or with Welsh relations were quite high (p.34). Furthermore, a considerable proportion spoke Welsh or were learning Welsh. In Denbighshire a third of respondents claimed to have someone in their families who spoke or was studying Welsh (Jacobs, p.35); in Caernarvonshire a fifth spoke Welsh and a further 18 per cent were learning (Pyne, p.30), and in the Aberystwyth Rural District a third were learning; moreover, in Caernarvonshire, a further 37 per cent would like to learn Welsh (Pyne, p.30). Some indication of this interest is provided by the holding of Welsh language classes in the Midlands and Northwest England (Pardoe).

Language does seem something of a barrier and the Denbighshire local respondents thought there was little contact in social activities, understandable in that many events were in Welsh and were organised through the chapel

(Jacobs, p.38). Respondents were pessimistic that occupiers of second homes would ever become integrated into the local community (p.39). Yet there seems evidence from occupiers of second homes that they have quite considerable contact with the local population and participate in local activities. In Caernarvonshire a third of the owners of second homes were members of at least one organisation (Pyne, p.30), and in the Aberystwyth Rural District 19 per cent belonged to a club or organisation (Bielckus *et al.*, p.113). In Denbighshire, only 11 per cent of occupiers of second homes had not invited any local resident into their home in the previous twelve months, and 47 per cent had invited seven or more, a figure which must be considered against the average occupation of second homes (Jacobs, p.35). Similarly, in Pardoe's survey 85 per cent of owners of second homes had made good contacts or friendship with local residents; and an interaction index, which measured the extent to which local residents visited second-home owners and vice versa, showed a high degree of reciprocal interaction.

Of course, a great deal is likely to depend on the amount of time that occupiers of second homes spend in the locality, and in Denbighshire it was thought that only those who retired to the area had any hope of integration with the local community (Jacobs, p.39). In that county, 45 per cent of respondents intended to retire to their second homes, itself an indication that they did not feel any strong antagonism to their presence (p.33), and in Caernarvonshire the proportion was 59 per cent (Pyne, p.17). In the Aberystwyth Rural District there was a conflict of evidence, for the Wye enquiry found that only 8 per cent acquired their second home with a view to retirement, and only 13 per cent had subsequently decided to retire there irrespective of their initial intention (Bielckus *et al.*, p.95), while Pardoe found that a third of his respondents had acquired their homes with the sole intention of retiring to them, a discrepancy which may in fact be due to the different interpretations of second homes adopted.

Such occupiers of second homes tend to be distinctive and to behave in distinctive ways. In Caernarvonshire, those with links with Wales were more likely to retire to their second homes than those who did not (Pyne, p.18). In Denbighshire, more of those intending to retire to their second homes spent substantial sums on them than those who did not (Jacobs, p.33), and, when they had retired, were more likely to mix with local residents (p.38). Those intending to retire also pose problems, for while they may find isolated cottages attractive on retirement, they may cease to do so as they get older and require medical attention. In 1973 a survey by Cardiganshire County Council showed that the local authority was unable even then to provide the level of socio-medical care it was required by law to do; clearly an increase in the number of elderly people migrating into the area on retirement would aggravate this situation.

Reactions between local residents and occupiers of second homes are, of course, two-way. While there are reports of the misbehaviour of occupiers of second homes (Jacobs, p.40; Pyne, p.31), there are also complaints about local behaviour: a tenth of those responding to Pardoe's survey had been subject to unfriendly remarks and behaviour and a slightly higher proportion were aware of such occurrences to people outside their family. In general, however, those who have acquired second homes appear to be satisfied, and it may even be that they are beginning to share the attitudes of many local residents to further development; it is perhaps significant that 47 per cent of respondents in the Aberystwyth Rural District did not want to see further development of second homes compared with 17 per cent who would (Bielckus *et al.*, p.114). Much more work is needed to establish the attitudes of both residents and incomers but it may not be unduly cynical to suppose that some at least are merely subscribing to the commuters' doxology:

O Lord, we thank Thee that Thy grace
Hath brought us to this lovely place
And now, O Lord, we humbly pray
Thou wilt all others keep away.

Acknowledgment

This contribution is based in part on a paper submitted by A.R. Pardoe, Department of Geography, University College of Wales, Aberystwyth, to a symposium at the annual conference of the Institute of British Geographers in Norwich in January 1974.

REFERENCES

Archer, B. (1973) The Impact of Domestic Tourism Bangor Occasional Papers in Economics 2, University of Wales Press, Bangor.

Bielckus, C.L., Rogers, A.W. and Wibberley, G.P. (1972) Second Homes in England and Wales Studies in Rural Land Use 11, Wye College, University of London.

Capstick, M. (1972) Some Aspects of the Economic Effects of Tourism in the Westmorland Lake District, University of Lancaster, Lancaster, mimeographed.

Cardiganshire County Council (1973) Report, Social Services Department.

Jacobs, C.A.J. (1972) Second Homes in Denbighshire Tourism and Recreation Research Report No. 3, Denbighshire County Planning Department, Ruthin.

Pardoe, A.R. (1973) Personal communication about survey of second homes in the Aberystwyth Rural District.

Pryce, W.T.R. (1967) 'The location and growth of holiday caravan camps in Wales 1956-65' Transactions of the Institute of British Geographers, 42, pp.127-52.

Pyne, C.B. (1973) Second Homes, Caernarvonshire County Planning Department, Caernarvon.

Chapter 11

PLANNING ASPECTS OF SECOND HOMES

M. Dower

Earlier chapters, notably that by Alan Rogers (Chap. 7), have described the post-war growth of second homes in Britain; their apparent number now; their variety and location; and the quickening of public and political interest in them. My purpose here is to look forward to the issues which second homes raise for future planning in Great Britain.

To summarise the present (1972) situation, there appear to be between 300,000 and 350,000 second homes in England and Wales, plus about 40,000 in Scotland (Downing and Dower 1973, Aitken 1974). Of these totals, probably a little over half were *built* second homes - houses, cottages, bungalows, chalets or flats - and the remainder were static caravans (plus a few house-boats). These figures, if correct, imply that *built* second homes represent rather over 1 per cent of the national housing stock; and that somewhere between 2 and 3 per cent of British households own or rent a second home (including both *built* second homes and static caravans). The latter figure compares with estimates of 22 per cent of households in Sweden, 16 per cent in France, 10 per cent in Denmark and 5 per cent in the United States who have regular use of second homes, though it must be mentioned that there seems to be much sharing of second homes in some of these countries, so that the second-home proportion of houses is less than that of households.

As to the growth of numbers of second homes, figures from the sources previously mentioned suggest that, in Great Britain as a whole, built second homes may have increased by up to 20,000 a year, and second-home static caravans by about 12,000 a year, in recent years. Of the *built* second homes, about two-thirds appear to be houses or cottages, a large proportion of which have come into use as second homes by conversion from previous first homes; about a quarter appear to be bungalows or chalets; and the remaining one-tenth or so are flats. As for location, the second homes appear to be widely scattered. About 20 per cent of the national total of second homes appear to lie in south east England, nearly 20 per cent each in Wales and in south west England, 10 per cent in Scotland, and the remainder widely dispersed. Because of the lack of official definitions and of comprehensive information (Chap. 7) we cannot tell how many second homes there are in cities and towns; but we certainly should not assume that the picture is wholly one of country cottages, seaside chalets or rural caravan sites. We should remember, for example, the businessman or politician with a large house in the country and a *pied-à-terre* in the City of Westminster.

Implications of Second Homes

Looking to the future, what are the implications of second homes that should be taken into account by government, local planning authorities and others?

As Alan Rogers records in Chapter 7, second homes appear to arouse strong and conflicting feelings (see also Chap. 14). Some people see them as a flagrant inequity at a time when thousands of people are homeless or in unfit first homes; or as conspicuous consumption of Britain's financial and physical resources; or as a factor in depressing the economy and eroding the social and cultural life of the receiving regions. Others see them as a natural and desirable answer to the demand for recreation and self-fulfilment; as contributing to the national balance of payments and the preservation of the environment; and as a positive help to the economy and social vitality of the receiving regions.

These attitudes are based partly on fact, partly on emotion and on ethical and philosophical principle. They have been most strongly expressed in those more remote regions, such as north Wales, south west England, Norfolk and parts of the Highlands, where dwellings made vacant by economic decline have been bought up by second-home seekers. In such places, where the workforce in the traditional industries, such as farming, fishing and quarrying, has dwindled, the inflow of second-home residents can bring welcome income and employment. It has been calculated, for example, that every six second-home owners in Denbighshire produce (by their expenditure) the equivalent of one local job (Jacobs 1972).

But such income to the receiving area is, by nature, seasonal. It is a useful supplement, but not a complete substitute, for development of primary and secondary industries. Moreover, it has a more pointed impact than some other forms of tourism in that, once the supply of vacant dwellings has been *mopped up*, the second-home seeker may well compete directly with local people for the houses which become available. It is this aspect, together with the distrust of rural people for *incomers* with different cultural ideas, which has caused political emotion in some regions. Local people claim that young local people, wishing to marry or to work nearby, cannot afford to buy houses because the price is pushed up by second-home seekers.

These economic and social effects may be accompanied by impact, for good or ill, on the environment. Where second homes are created by conversion of existing buildings, the impact may be beneficial: the second-home use may justify the preservation, restoration if necessary, and maintenance of existing buildings which usually fit into the character of the local landscape and which may even have architectural and historic interest. A report by Ross and Cromarty County Council in Scotland sees demand for second homes as providing 'valuable opportunities for clearing up ruins and eyesores in many existing settlements' (Ross and Cromarty County Planning Department 1972).

Newly-built second homes, however, are a very different matter. They can have as much impact on the environment as can new housing or new tourist accommodation of other kinds, whether they be isolated cottages in the countryside, groups of chalets, terrace houses round a harbour, or flats in a coastal resort. It therefore rests squarely with the planning authorities to ensure that new second-home development is of such a quality, location, layout and design as to minimise adverse environmental impact and possibly make environmental gain. This applies with equal force to second-home caravans. At present, such caravans are not physically distinguishable from other static caravans and share the same sites or the same types of site. The environmental impact of caravans is well known and most planning authorities have well-established policies relating to them. If the demand for second-home caravans continues, however, it may be necessary to consider how adequate these policies are to cope with the problems which they raise, notably concerning the length of the season of occupancy and the evolution from caravan to chalet or other form of built second home.

In respect of their national implications, second homes are still of minor economic importance. *Built* second homes comprise only about 1 per cent of the nation's housing stock; and the use of second homes only represents about 2 per cent of all expenditure on tourism. However, at a time when there is a severe national shortage of modern housing, any rapid growth in built second homes (particularly if newly constructed) could gain political importance. Already, the Government has decided to stop the payment of improvement grants and the giving of tax concessions on mortgage payments related to second homes. Thus the finance for continued growth in second homes would come almost wholly from private sources. But 10,000 built second homes a year (a conceivable figure) would still absorb, say, 3 per cent of the nation's house-building resources, and the proportion could obviously be far higher in some areas.

Against this cost may be set the benefit, not only to the individual but to the nation, of the recreational and touristic flow which the use of many second homes brings. Like other forms of home tourism, the use of second homes in Great Britain can keep holiday expenditure within this country, or even attract it in from abroad, thus assisting the balance of payments; and it can provide a direct flow of money from first-home region to second-home region, sustaining the economy of the latter. Moreover, it is a flow of singular permanence and strength as compared with other forms of tourism: once he has acquired a second home, the owner may visit it regularly and year after year, spending his holiday money within Great Britain and within the second-home region, without a single word of encouragement or promotion from any tourist board.

Prospects for supply and demand

What, then, are the prospects for future growth in the number of second homes, and what planning issues do they raise?

One can only guess at the impulses - self-expression, escape from daily life, the need for change, the desire to maintain roots in the countryside or in metropolitan culture - which prompt people to acquire and to use second homes. More obvious, perhaps, are the factors which have permitted these impulses to find expression. These include rising personal incomes, car ownership, motorway mobility and, very important, the supply of suitable properties.

The sustained growth in demand for second homes over the last decade or so, together with the growth in related things such as second holidays and car-borne recreation, suggest that the impulses toward second-home ownership are enduring. The future trend in some of the impulse-releasing factors, notably personal income, is uncertain. The present economic depression, the virtual standstill in real incomes, and the high cost of borrowing money, may well mean a slackening of demand for second homes, or at least for those types of second home which demand substantial capital.

As Roger Crofts points out in Chapter 8, we do not know how flexible the demand for second homes may be, e.g., whether the man who wanted an isolated cottage would accept a house in a *holiday village,* or the would-be caravanner would accept a chalet. There are indications that people tend to *move up the market*, e.g., to graduate from a caravan to a chalet, from a chalet to a cottage (Downing and Dower 1973). The past emphasis on isolated cottages has probably been caused as much by the fact of their cheapness and availability as by the desire for seclusion. The holiday cottage scheme of the Highlands and Islands Development Board attracted an enormous response despite the lack of any specific descriptions of site or type of cottage. One can therefore assume, pending further research, that there is a fair degree of flexibility in demand.

But, whatever the demand, it cannot become effective without the supply of suitable property, and that is very much open to doubt, or (more accurately) to public decision. Till now, much of the growth in numbers of second homes has been made possible by conversion of existing dwellings or other buildings, or by the construction and siting of static caravans. Recently, these have been supplemented by a third main source, the construction of new-built second homes, usually houses, chalets or flats. What are the prospects for these three sources of supply?

Most of our present stock of built second homes has been created, sometimes simply by a change of use, sometimes with physical works, by conversion of erstwhile first homes or of barns and other non-residential buildings. Many such properties have become second homes because their earlier function had withered away or did not command a purchasing ability to compete with the second-home buyer. In this sense, second homes are a sequel to change and depression, particularly in the countryside and in remote or coastal or historic towns and villages: for example, the Kentish oasthouse, the farm-worker's cottage in Devon, the quarry-worker's home in Argyll or the fisher-man's house in North Wales.

Change will always be with us, and perhaps depression also, however dynamic our policies of regional development. Farm rationalisation, conversion of hill land from farming to forestry, relaxation of the statutory rules of crofting in the Highlands, further closure of quarries and so on will continue to release property. But the indications are that, with the possible exception of parts of northwest Scotland and the Welsh borders, few areas are likely to have any substantial stock of dwellings surplus to their first-home housing needs. Thus existing buildings may continue to form a major source of new second homes only by dint of direct competition with demands for first homes, or by the conversion to housing use of buildings not now so used, such as Pennine barns. Both have severe implications.

The second possible source of supply is the construction and siting of static caravans, which form nearly half the present stock of second homes. Second-home caravans, of course, form only part of the enormous post-war production of the caravan industry, an industry which certainly seems capable of continuing to produce caravans suited to second-home use at least as fast as the 12,000 a year of the estimated past growth. But the main constraint may well be the shortage of sites with planning permission for static caravans, and the stringency with which planning authorities take enforcement action against the kind of illegal caravan sites which Roger Crofts describes in Chapter 8. The attitude of planning authorities towards caravan sites of any kind varies from friendly to extremely hostile; of those which are ready to contemplate new sites, some are seeking to hasten the transition from caravans to chalets or other forms of built accommodation.

Thus the third main source of supply, the construction of newly built second homes, may become more significant in future. The precedents are already there, in the seaside flats in Torbay and Tenby, the holiday homes beside the harbour at Portmadoc, the Norwegian chalets near Trawsfynydd, the system-built units on the Carmarthen coast and the log cabins in Perthshire. There is a good deal of private-enterprise interest in the second-home market; and the price at which new property can be built is probably still within the pocket of many second-home buyers, although the economic depression and inflation in building costs are bound to influence this.

This brief look at supply and demand suggests that we may be at a most significant turning-point. Until now, built second homes were mostly converted from existing buildings, without the planning authority having much say. From now on, they may be mainly new-built second homes, or newly-sited static caravans or chalets, and the planning authorities may have a significant influence on what is built where, and how many are built.

An Approach to Policy

At present, there is no specific government policy on second homes. The modest fiscal encouragements to second-home ownership are being withdrawn; but the Government has not yet implied that it intends either to discourage second-home ownership or to seek to steer it to particular areas. Such controls as now exist are wholly in the hands of local planning authorities, who can influence the location and the planning standards of any new housing or new tourist accommodation, including second homes. Local authorities can also control the conversion to second-home use of existing buildings *other than* dwellings, for example, old barns or mills. But they have only limited power to prevent physical changes to existing dwellings, and in particular cannot prevent a house becoming a second home, unless the local authority itself chooses to buy the property.

Only in those areas where second homes are numerous and have obvious social and economic effects, for example in North Wales, have local planning authorities already formulated planning policies expressly related to second homes (Jacobs 1972, Pyne 1973, Tuck 1973). The tenor of these policies has been that it is desirable that second homes should not exceed a certain proportion (typically 10 to 20%) of the local housing stock; and that any new second homes should be concentrated in *holiday villages*. Elsewhere, second homes fall within the general zoning and other policies which all local planning authorities in Britain have in relation to housing or tourist development, many such policies being, of course, reinforced by national protective designations such as National Parks.

I believe that now, before the era of purpose-built second homes or of yet more static caravans gets under way, we need a more definite approach to policy. This approach might have four main elements: adoption of a statutory definition of *second homes;* securing of systematic information on the subject; clarification of the basic governmental attitude; and explicit coverage of second homes in the policies of local authorities.

I will consider first the question of *definition*. As others have stated in earlier chapters, there is no official definition of second homes. In their pioneering national study, sponsored by the Countryside Commission, the Wye College team suggested a working definition of a second home as: 'a property which is the occasional residence of a household that usually lives elsewhere and which is primarily used for recreation purposes' (Bielckus *et al.* 1972). This definition, coined for use in England and Wales on a project with deliberately rural emphasis, has a recreational slant which might well exclude significant forms of apparent *second homes* such as the businessman's *pied-à-terre* in town. Moreover, it raises the question of what is meant by *occasional* or *usual*. In their own survey, the Wye College team found some owners who spent as much as 300 days a year in their *second* home!

I believe we need an official definition of second homes, capable of use for all governmental purposes. It must be wider than properties *primarily used for recreation;* and must include those in cities and towns as well as the countryside. For the critical point about second homes, when we come to questions of policy, is that *they are at the point of overlap between housing and tourism* - neither squarely one nor the other, but having the nature and implications of both. The definition must be unequivocal, not dependent on interpretation of such words as usual or occasional; and it must be constant, so that a property is not counted as a first home for some purposes and a second home for others.

I do not claim to have the full answer, but I think the clue is the statutory provision in the Finance Act, now introduced into the Housing Act, whereby exemption from capital gains tax extends only to a man's primary residence. On this basis, a second home might be defined as *a residence which is exclusively or mainly occupied by some one who regards it as other than his primary residence.*

The need for a definition of second homes is matched by the need for systematic *information* on the subject. The population census contains no direct information on them, nor do basic housing statistics. As Alan Rogers describes in Chapter 7, certain major annual surveys provide indicative material on the place of second homes in family expenditure and tourism. The nearest thing to a comprehensive source of information is the rating registers (valuation rolls in Scotland), but they are unclear in many ways and often omit static caravans and houseboats. If it becomes important (as I believe it will) to keep a running check on the number, type and location of second homes, then an improvement of the rating registers is almost certainly the place to start.

A third aspect is the need to clarify the basic governmental attitude. Should the Government encourage, or discourage, the growth of second homes? Should it steer the growth in the most suitable directions? In the present economic climate - and remembering the implications which second homes can have for use of national resources - it seems most unlikely that the Government would deliberately encourage large-scale ownership of second homes. Active discouragement is, indeed, conceivable. It would be quite possible, for example, to proceed from the removal of financial incentives (e.g., exemption from capital gains tax, improvements grants, tax relief on mortgage payments, domestic rate relief) to the imposition of disincentives (such as higher rates on second homes or stamp duty on second-home purchases). The point at which such measures would really *bite* into demand is an open question; and certainly they pre-suppose tighter definition and more certain identification of second homes. Unless the country's economy greatly deteriorates, such discouragement will surely stop well short of any prohibition of the ownership and use of second homes, since this would clearly involve a degree of interference with personal liberties of an order not yet contemplated in Great Britain outside war-time.

Thus the main line of policy is likely to be to *steer* the growth of second homes towards such regions, types of second homes and settings as may be considered desirable. Such steering can be achieved partly by government action, e.g., grants under the Development of Tourism Act, but largely by local authority decisions, with government advice and support.

Second Homes in Local Authority Policy

At regional and local scale, there are three main strands of public action which can be used to steer the incidence of second homes and to soften their impact. These strands are: economic and social development; planning and development control; and housing.

In terms of economic and social development, it must be emphasised that the growth of second homes in some regions (e.g., North Wales) has been a sequel to, or symptom of, economic decline, rather than a *cause* of such decline. In such areas, local authorities may see the inflow of second-home owners as a poor substitute for permanent residents with good local jobs; and they may regret that the economy is so weak that local people cannot compete with second-home buyers on the housing market. The solution to this problem is not to complain about second homes, but rather to boost the local economy. The only answer to social and economic decline is social and economic development.

In such development, tourism can play a significant (though rarely a dominant) part; and second homes, despite their economic and social overtones, may be as valuable as any other form of tourism. The national tourist boards and the Highlands and Islands Development Board are deeply involved in assisting tourist development in depressed regions. The main criterion for that assistance - for example in the *tourist projects* scheme under the Development of Tourism Act - is that the development should sustain or create employment and personal income for people in the region.

If tourism is to benefit the regional economy, it must indeed bring a worthwhile flow of money and employment. This implies that if government bodies and local authorities encourage second-home development, they should seek to secure that the nature of the enterprise is such as to bring such a flow. This might be done in various ways: by encouraging local shareholding in new capital development, as is done by the Shannon Free Airport Company in the *Rent-an-Irish-Cottage* scheme; by giving grants to local people to build one or more units to rent to second-homers, on the lines of the Gaeltacht grants in Ireland; by encouraging the conversion of obsolete farm buildings, or the siting on farms of small groups of chalets or static caravans, so that farmers gain direct income; or by securing, as is done in the holiday cottage scheme of the Highlands and Islands Development Board, that the second home is let to other holidaymakers for a longish season when not in use by the owner.

Local authorities can also do much by their *planning* powers to steer and control second homes so as to minimise their adverse impact and to maximise their environmental and other benefits. As stated earlier, they cannot now prevent a house in *first-home* use from becoming a second home, although the Government could quite easily make such a change of use subject to planning control. But they can control the location, quantity and standard of new-built second homes or of newly-sited caravans. In exercising such control, very clear thinking is needed on the planning principles and standards which should apply to second homes. Are they to be regarded as *housing* or as *tourist accommodation*?

If second homes are seen as housing, with the real-life implication that they could switch overnight to becoming first homes, they should presumably fall within the normal settlement pattern and answer housing standards in space, internal layout, call on public services and so on. If, on the other hand, they are seen as tourist accommodation, should they be subject to the same principles as other such accommodation, in the sense of their location vis-a-vis tourist facilities such as sailing waters and beaches, their density and internal space and their seasonal occupancy? Related to this is the confusion, or at least wide variety of opinion, among local authorities as to the merits of different forms of tourist accommodation - touring caravans, static caravans, chalets, flats, houses (see Chap. 8). There is room for clear thought and hard talk between public authorities and private enterprise here.

Planning authorities can do much to direct second homes into certain settings where their impact is beneficial rather than damaging. For example, they can be used to assist the preservation of historic or other properties which would otherwise fall derelict or be neglected, both in towns and in the countryside: this can be encouraged by such means as the advertisement of vacant historic properties or the purchase, renovation and resale of properties by County Historic Buildings Trusts. Second homes might also bring new life to marginal lands, such as parts of the Welsh hills, the relics of the Industrial Revolution in Pennine valleys, the remains of mineral working or the activities of the armed services in many areas: an existing example is the Norwegian chalets development at Trawsfynydd on the site of the disused army hutment. They can support the recreational use and development of coastal and inland waters: an example is the caravan development beside the Gloucestershire/Wiltshire Water Park. They can bring secondary use and income to private woodlands and State forests, as is already being pioneered by the Forestry Commission at Strathyre in Perthshire. In all such contexts, the planning authority can ensure that the siting and design are such as to prevent damage to the landscape or strain on roads, water supplies or sewerage systems.

Such action in planning may need its counterpart in *housing*, particularly where the demand for second homes is beginning to affect the local housing market. In parts of North Wales and elsewhere, it is already recognised that the adverse effects of second-home demand upon the local housing market cannot be stopped by preventing outsiders from purchasing homes - or even by the direct action of the Welsh Language Society! Local authorities who are concerned to protect housing for local prople or to prevent communities from becoming *dead in winter* may have to act themselves, by purchasing property which comes on the market; by building more homes for local people; by buying land and reselling or letting it to locals for house building; or by encouraging the formation and work of local housing associations. There are real difficulties here in the general pressure on local authority finance, the control by district valuers on the purchase price which may be paid by local authorities and the cost of managing and maintaining isolated properties. But the present Labour Government is moving (August 1974) towards encouragement of municipal purchase of vacant property and of development land, for reasons far wider, of course, than the simple issue of second homes, and one assumes that such difficulties may in time be eased.

In these ways, I believe local authorities in many areas will soon be obliged to take positive action in relation to second homes, and that the Government must help them to do so. Second homes, though still modest in scale from a national viewpoint, are a phenomenon that grows and will not just quietly go away.

Author's footnote:

A deepening economic recession, the removal of fiscal incentives to ownership of second homes and the inflation of transport costs appear to have contributed to a situation in 1976 which is very different from that described above. The numbers of second homes in England and Wales are now (1975 figures) estimated at about 180,000, with another 20,000 in Scotland - a drop of nearly one half. Numbers of *built* second homes have declined by some 60 per cent to form some 38 per cent of the Great Britain total whilst static caravans have decreased by about 30 per cent to form the remaining 62 per cent of this total.

The processes whereby these changes have taken place appear to include outright sales; retirement into the second home (which then becomes the first home); the relinquishment of leases and tenancies which revert to the landlord; and a simple change of use to rented first home or holiday letting. Static caravans may be converted to self-catering holiday accommodation; or taken off a (re-rated and now expensive) site to be kept in the garden of the first home as a *touring* caravan; or simply written off (a 1974 survey by my Trust in selected Scottish areas indicated that about 20% of static caravans there were over ten years old). Our judgment from the available data is that owners who might have been anticipating a retirement home were hit hardest by economic circumstance but the decreased numbers are reflected right across the age and social structure.

However, my view is that the psychological and societal pressures which underpinned the peak demand in 1972 remain unchanged and it is likely that a revived economy will see a revived demand for second homes - although possibly with different emphases. It is not an excuse to stop thinking about future policy related to second homes. Rather, it provides a breathing space for such thinking.

REFERENCES

Aitken, R. (1974) Second Homes in Scotland, unpublished interim report on research project by Dartington Amenity Research Trust for Countryside Commission for Scotland *et al*.

Bielckus, C.L., Rogers, A.W. and Wibberley, G.P. (1972) Second Homes in England and Wales, Studies in Rural Land Use, 11, Wye College (University of London).

Downing, P. and Dower, M. (1973) Second Homes in England and Wales, Countryside Commission, HMSO, London.

Jacobs, C.A.J. (1972) Second Homes in Denbighshire, Tourism and Recreation Research Report 3, Denbighshire County Council, Ruthin.

Pyne, C.B. (1973) Second Homes, Caernarvonshire County Planning Department.

Ross and Cromarty County Planning Department (1972) Holiday Homes : Progress Report, Dingwall.

Tuck, C.J. (1973) Second Homes, Merioneth Structure Plan, Subject Report 17, Merioneth County Council.

Chapter 12

EVALUATING COTTAGE ENVIRONMENTS IN ONTARIO

G. Priddle and R. Kreutzwiser

Introduction

There are now over 250,000 second homes, or cottages, in Ontario and this total is growing at a rate of at least 10,000 per year. Cottaging in Ontario is not only a recreational pastime but almost a way of life for a great many people (cf. Chap. 2). Much of the province, with over 6,000 miles (9,600 km) of Great Lakes shoreline, countless inland lakes and many miles of rivers and streams, provides an excellent physical environment for cottaging (Fig. 12.1).

Although cottaging in Ontario was well established before 1945, it was not until after the Second World War that the real expansion took place. Dramatic increases in mobility, disposable income and leisure time have made it possible for many people to realise the Ontario dream of owning a cottage. Not only has the number of cottages undergone a dramatic increase, but the nature and distribution of cottages have changed markedly, as have the activities and uses associated with cottaging. Many cottages now have electricity, septic tanks, washers, driers and other conveniences. Increasing numbers of cottages are being winterised for use throughout the year. Associated with a large proportion of cottages are one or two boats and often a snowmobile. Activities such as waterskiing, snowmobiling, and now skiing, are changing the nature and use of many Ontario cottages.

The tremendous increase in the number of cottages in the province and the changing patterns of use have, however, created a pressure on cottage environments that has far outstripped managerial ability to cope with it. A lack of understanding of the capacities of lakes and shorelines to accommodate cottaging has contributed to overdevelopment and to the degradation of cottage environments in many areas of the province.

The problems associated with cottage development and overdevelopment are varied. Septic tanks do not function properly under some conditions and water quality has deteriorated. In some areas cottage development has occurred in unique natural environments, and in others, vacation homes have been permitted on hazard land which is subject to flooding or serious erosion. Excessive buildings and docks in some places have created a blighted appearance along the shoreline. Various uses of water bodies may conflict sharply, thereby reducing the quality of the recreational experience in some cottage areas. Several rural municipalities have found it difficult to cope with the rapid development of seasonal homes and with the increased demands for services such as roads, police and fire protection. In some parts of Ontario it is obvious that the physical and social capacity to accommodate this development of vacation homes has been greatly exceeded.

In 1970, an Ontario government interdepartmental task force listed the lack of planning for lake development and of capacity plans as a specific

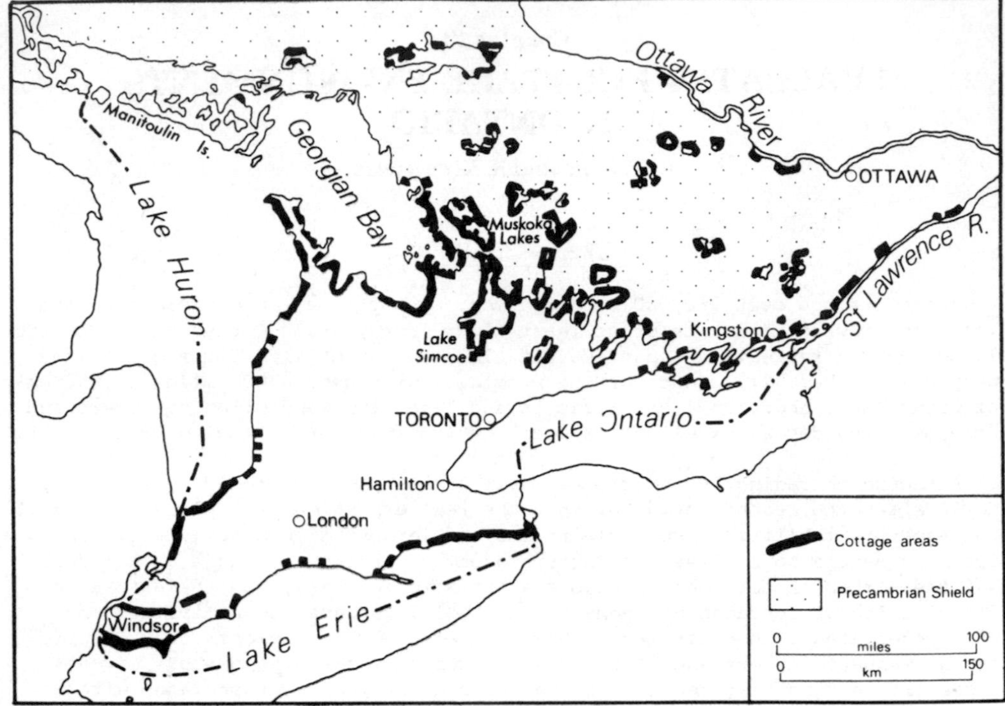

Fig. 12.1 Vacation homes in southern Ontario

problem related to cottaging (Advisory Committee on Pollution Control 1970, p.20). They suggested that, when a proposal for cottage development is submitted to government agencies for approval, only the characteristics of the particular site, such as the capability of the soil for the operation of a septic tank, are considered. Little, if any, attention is paid to the capacity of other elements of the environment to accommodate the proposed development.

This chapter is directed towards a consideration of the physical and social carrying capacity of shoreline areas in Ontario to accommodate cottaging; for while the supply of shorelines in the province is fixed, recreational demand continues to rise. Shorelines accommodate a variety of land uses, urban and industrial, as well as public and private recreation. Methodologies for determining the physical and social limitations of shoreline resources and criteria for determining the capacity of any particular area to accept cottaging are not well developed. In the absence of adequate criteria, however, the development and management of cottage areas can proceed only on a basis of trial and error. Experience has shown that the errors can be ecologically and socially very costly.

Evaluating Cottage Environments

There is a real need within the province to be able to evaluate, monitor, and regulate environments that are primarily occupied by vacation homes as well as those places that are just beginning to experience pressure from the development of seasonal homes or could experience such pressure in the future.

Indeed, it is necessary to proceed on at least two planes: there is a need for immediate and continuing research to evaluate existing and potential cottage settlements, and there is also a need to consider the theoretical value of such studies for the development of meaningful indicators and standards for use in the evaluation of seasonal home communities. Hopefully, such indicators would suggest appropriate standards for maintaining environmental quality.

Another concern of equal or even greater importance is the need to devise a structure of public administration at all levels of government that could effectively legislate and administer existing and proposed standards in places where there are vacation homes. While the importance of both of these concerns is realised, this chapter is restricted, for the most part, to a discussion of the former. It should be said, however, that the provincial government is beginning to pay particular attention to the question of providing an effective administrative structure for seasonal home communities. This attention has developed out of the reform of municipal government that has been taking place in recent years. The real outcome of this reform has been regional government, which should, in the long run, provide a more effective vehicle for the administration of cottage lands. At present the Ontario government is paying particular attention to those counties that are primarily agricultural but in which cottage and recreational development is taking place.

Only in part can the problem of cottage development be cured by an *administrative fix*, which does not provide the meaningful standards and criteria for determining, assessing and maintaining cottage development of high quality. H. Perloff (1969, p.3) has suggested a framework for considering and evaluating the quality of the urban environment and, since the cottage environment is a simplified version of the more complex urban environment, a somewhat simplified and modified version of Perloff's framework suggests itself (Table 12.1). Perloff suggests that the framework involves bringing together the ideas of two concerns which are so far relatively disparate: those dealing with the quality of the so-called natural environment and those dealing with urban matters such as congestion, crowding and noise. He further suggests that his model will allow us to look at the more important elements of the physical environment that directly influence the conditions for living and working of the urban population, particularly where they influence the health, comfort, safety and aesthetic satisfaction of individuals. It is suggested that the urban place can be considered as comprising a series of elements and that what is needed is research into the question of indicators or, if you will, criteria and standards that can be used to evaluate each environmental element, while reorganising that each element may have some effect or interaction with other parts of the system.

This basic approach has utility at two quite different levels, the administrative and management, and the research. At the former level it could be adopted and used by the authorities that evaluate existing and proposed developments of vacation homes. Regulations and standards often do not exist

TABLE 12.1. Framework for evaluating management and research needs for a

Elements of the environment	Existing indicators	Existing standards and regulations	Proposed indicators	Proposed standards or regulations
I. Physical Environment				
(a) Water capability for				
Domestic use				
Swimming				
Boating and fishing				
(b) Soil capability for				
Absorbing wastes				
Sustaining vehicular and pedestrian traffic				
(c) Air				
Climate				
Quality				
(d) Biota				
Vegetation				
Fish and wildlife				
(e) Sensitive or unique environmental areas				
(f) Hazard lands				
Flooding				
Erosion				
Organic soils				

or are inadequate, and in such instances planners and managers could use this framework as a checklist to make sure that, where standards do exist, they are being observed and that, when standards are lacking, such matters are considered or discussed.

At the research level this framework could serve a number of functions: it could suggest where, in fact, research is needed and it would allow the researcher to see the relevance of his work on a particular aspect of vacation home environment to the overall concern. As far as the physical environment is concerned, a good deal has been and is being done or commissioned by the Ontario government that has relevance to this framework. Much less has been done in respect of the social elements identified in this system.

Although it could be postulated that the same indicators of environmental quality would be relevant in any cottage community within the province, adjustments in standards might be appropriate depending on the nature of the environment. A typology of cottage environments for Ontario is suggested (Fig. 12.2).

vacation home environment

Elements of the environment	Existing indicators	Existing standards and regulations	Proposed indicators	Proposed standards or regulations
II. Social Environment				
(a) Functional services				
Sewage facilities				
Solid waste disposal				
Roads				
Electricity supply				
Telephone				
Health services				
Fire protection				
Police protection				
Recreation facilities and services				
(b) Stress				
Density				
Noise				
Smells				
Microclimate				
Design and condition of buildings				
Activity of people				
Flies, snakes, spiders and other pests				
(c) Aesthetics				
Paths				
Edges				
Nodes				
Landmarks				
Districts				

There are several relevant parameters, such as whether a place is: (i) developed or undeveloped; (ii) on or off the Pre-Cambrian Shield; (iii) on the shores of the Great Lakes, an inland lake, a river or a canal. From an administrative point of view one important additional parameter is whether the place in question is on Crown land or private land.

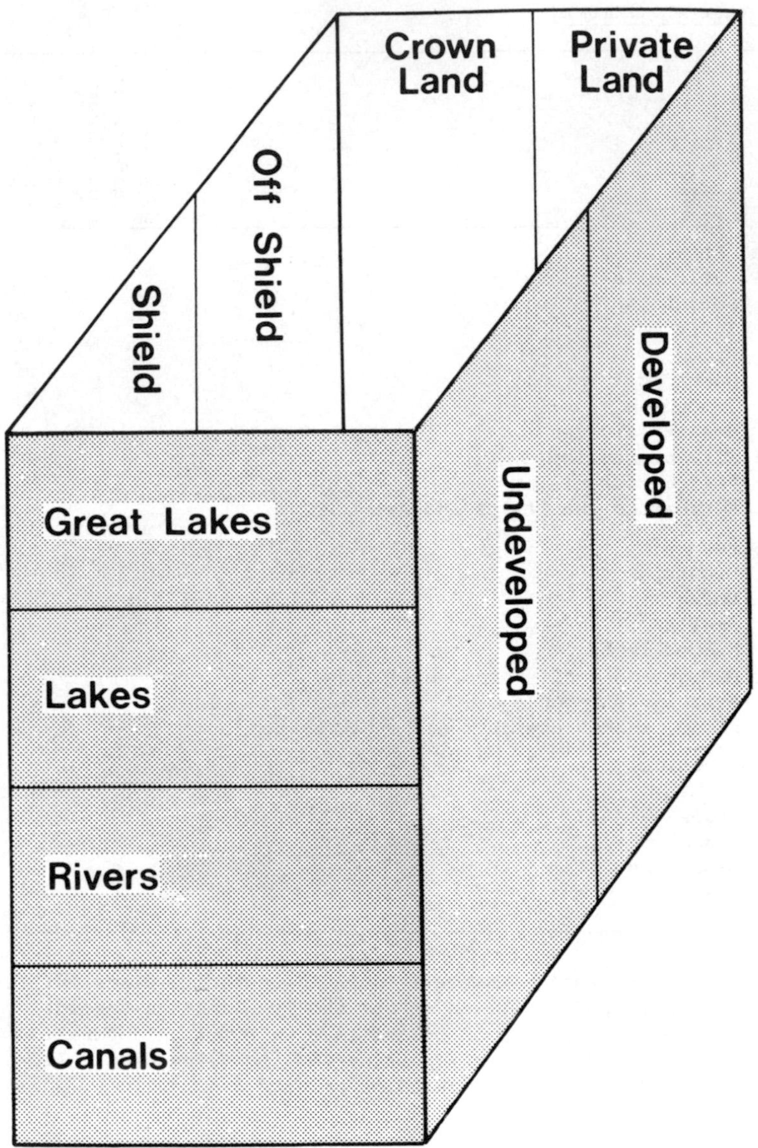

Fig. 12.2 A typology for cottage environments in Ontario

Physical Carrying Capacity

Elements of the physical environment that should be considered in evaluating the quality of cottage environments include water, soil, air, biota, sensitive or unique environmental areas and hazard lands. The Ontario Ministry of Natural Resources (1972, p.8) provides some indicators, standards and regulations regarding the development of Crown land for cottaging.

The policy specifies that a minimum of 25 per cent of the shoreline must be retained by the province for public access and use, and that where there is currently less than 25 per cent public ownership, no further cottage development on Crown land will take place. No cottage development will occur on islands of less than 3 acres (1.2 ha), on lakes of less than 100 acres (40 ha) and on headwater lakes of less than 500 acres (202 ha). Cottage development is also prohibited on streams or narrow channels, known deer yards, fish spawning areas, marshes or wetlands or on special fishing areas, wild river reserves or fish sanctuaries. The policy specifies that land filling will not be permitted to enable areas to meet Ministry of the Environment standards for waste disposal. Design standards are also provided which require buildings to be set back 66 ft (20 m) from the high water line, a minimum lot width of 150 ft (46 m) and a minimum lot depth of 400 ft (122 m). Furthermore, all lots must have a view of the water. While this policy provides minimum guidelines for cottage development, it must be emphasised that it applies only to Crown land.

Some general consideration of an area's capability for cottaging is provided by the Canada Land Inventory's (1967) scheme of classification for implementing an inventory of natural outdoor recreation resources. Land is ranked on the basis of its natural capability to provide opportunities for a variety of recreational activities, including cottaging, based on present popular preferences. The scheme lists moderate backshore slopes, vehicle or boat access, good view, availability of fresh water and satisfactory soil materials for foundations and sewage disposal as important factors in an area's suitability for cottaging. Beach and water conditions affecting capability for swimming, boating and fishing are also important, as these activities are very much associated with cottaging. Nuisance elements such as industrial or traffic noise, air pollution, permanent water pollution or serious infestation by insects, will limit the capability of an area for cottaging.

The Ontario Land Inventory provides a similar but more detailed scheme of classification for assessing the capability of land for cottaging (Ontario Department of Lands and Forests 1968). It suggests that slopes of greater than 15 per cent are too steep for cottaging, and that a deep sand or loam backshore is important.

While the policy for cottage development on Crown land and the schemes of the Canada and Ontario Land Inventories provide some general considerations of the physical carrying capacity for cottaging, more specific guidelines are available for some of the elements of the environment listed in Table 12.1.

Indicators, standards and regulations regarding water quality are reasonably well developed. Indicators of the capability of water for domestic use and swimming include counts of coliforms, fecal coliforms and enterococci. Temperature, turbidity, pH and the presence of aquatic nuisance are additional indicators for swimming. The Ontario Ministry of the Environment (1973a) has established water quality standards for domestic use and for aesthetics and recreation. The Ministry has also adopted guidelines for the protection of fish, other aquatic life and wildlife. In this regard the amount of dissolved oxygen in the water is an important indicator.

Soil permeability is a commonly accepted indicator of the capability of soil to absorb domestic wastes. The Ministry of the Environment specifies tests of soil seepage or percolation for determining the suitability of soil for tile drainage. Requirements for the location of septic tanks and tile beds, such as minimum distances from water bodies, wells and buildings, are also specified (Ontario Department of Health, n.d.).

Although climate, in a general sense, is fairly uniform throughout much of Ontario's cottage country, significant microclimatic differences can exist between shoreline areas even in the same locality. The orientation of a beach with respect to prevailing winds, topography and amount of vegetative cover are some of the factors which may contribute to a climatically more desirable cottage environment. The scheme of capability for outdoor recreation of the Canada Land Inventory, for example, suggests that shelter from winds and exposure to sun are factors to be considered in assessing an area's capability for cottaging.

As previously mentioned, the Canada Land Inventory lists air pollution as a nuisance factor limiting the capability of an area for vacation homes, for it can reduce visibility, injure vegetation and affect human health. The Ontario Ministry of the Environment (1973b) has developed criteria for desirable air quality and established standards for a number of contaminants, including sulphur dioxide and suspended particulate matter, two major pollutants in Ontario.

Previously, inadequate regulations and enforcement have permitted development of cottaging on hazard lands or on lands subject to flooding, erosion, or having certain soil conditions. Problems of flooding and erosion have been especially widespread in the cottage environments of the Great Lakes during periods when lake levels are high. The Ontario Ministry of Natural Resources (1972) has recently proposed a policy relating to hazard lands and sensitive environmental areas for adoption by municipalities in Ontario in their official plans. Hazard lands are defined as all lands having inherent physical or environmental hazards such as poor drainage, organic soils, susceptibility to floods or erosion, steep slopes and other physical limitations to development. Sensitive areas are defined as areas of land or land and water which provide positive values to the public and the environment, including scientific research, education and interpretation, the maintenance of species and the preservation and conservation of unique species of vegetation and wildlife.

Several indicators or identifying criteria are suggested for hazard lands and sensitive areas. Floodplains, for example, are identified by either the 1 in 100 year flood or by the Conservation Authorities Branch of the Ministry of Natural Resources. Hazardous soil conditions are identified as organic or muck soils, shallow depth and poor drainage conditions. Erosion hazard lands are determined by the angle of slope and by the degree of stability. It is suggested that lakeshores with banks susceptible to slumping or to wave or wind erosion, major banks along watercourses, which are actively being eroded or subject to erosion during flooding, and slumping clays associated with slopes should be considered hazardous at all times and should not be developed.

Sensitive areas are identified as having one or more of the following resources: geological or geomorphological features such as eskers or caves, waterfalls and rapids; headwater areas; unique plant communities; deer yards; fish spawning areas; waterfowl nesting areas; cultural features such as burial grounds, battlegrounds, historic buildings, abandoned mining or lumber camps; and representative landscapes and landscape complexes such as the Niagara Escarpment. Specific criteria for identifying sensitive areas have not been developed, but this list indicates generally what is meant by sensitive environmental areas.

For each type of hazard land, floodplain, eroding slope and so on, the Ministry has suggested policies to guide the nature and extent of development, ranging from no development to some limited development under certain conditions. For sensitive areas the suggested policy is that no development should normally occur, but that some limited development might be possible depending on its nature and on the significance of the sensitive area involved. While this policy for hazard lands and sensitive areas is still only a proposal, some municipalities in the province have already adopted the policy relating to hazard lands.

In spite of the existence of some indicators, standards and regulations regarding the physical carrying capacity of shoreline areas for vacation homes, there are serious deficiencies in our understanding of the impact of cottaging on some elements of the physical environment.

Boating is closely associated with cottaging and, while some highly subjective standards have been suggested for determining the number of boats a given area of lake can safely accommodate at any given time, little is known about the effects of exhaust emissions from outboard motors. Both hydrocarbons and lead in exhaust emissions are toxic; moreover, lead accumulates in aquatic plants and animals. Tainting, infection and disease of fish flesh can occur with certain levels of emissions in water (Pollution Probe n.d., pp.25-6). While lead and toxic substance might serve as useful indicators, no guideline or standards exist to suggest what level of boating, and subsequently cottaging, any particular lake can tolerate without adverse ecological effects. Furthermore, there are other nuisance factors associated with boating, including increased turbidity of water, which is due to turbulence from boat motors, and noise.

A second deficiency in our understanding of safe capacities for cottage development concerns some confusion over the most suitable soil types for the absorption of domestic wastes. For some years, sandy soils have been considered a good material for septic tile beds; indeed, sand is a good bacterial remover. However, recent research indicates that sand is a particularly poor phosphate remover, and phosphate is a major contributor to the increased eutrophication of lakes, especially in cottage environments on the Precambrian Shield (Michalski *et al.* 1973, p.2). Some idea of the magnitude of this problem is apparent when it is realised that 30 per cent of the cottages in the Muskoka Lakes region (Fig.. 12.1) have automatic dishwashers which require high-phosphate cleaning products. The problem of phosphate enrichment is further magnified by the use of lawn and garden fertilizers by some cottagers. Clearly, more research is required to determine the most suitable soils for the removal of both bacteria and phosphates.

A serious weakness in our understanding of physical carrying capacity for cottaging concerns the impact of cottage development on vegetation, fish, wildlife and sensitive or unique environmental areas. The Ministry of Natural Resources' policy for cottage development on Crown land specifies that development should not be permitted on known deer yards, fish spawning areas, marshes or wetlands, and should not destroy or impair known unique natural features. A similar policy should also apply to private cottage developments, and indicators, standards and regulations should be developed to suggest what level of cottaging an area can accept without substantially affecting plant and animal communities.

Some research has been undertaken on the impact of outdoor recreation on vegetation (LaPage 1967). Depending on the type of soil and the amount of compaction, changes in soil moisture and amount of plant litter may induce changes in the botanic composition of the vegetation and greatly alter the appearance and character of the area. Some species of plants, such as wild celery and water lilies, do not tolerate much human activity (Threinen 1964, p.353). These and other plants provide food and habitat for ducks, other wildlife and some species of fish. Improvements in shorelines, such as land filling, dredging, construction of docks and removal of plants and weeds to create areas suitable for swimming, which are often associated with cottaging, thus tend to create a sterile environment for aquatic and other wildlife. Further investigations are necessary to develop meaningful indicators, standards and regulations concerning the amount of cottaging that can be accommodated in particular areas without significant disruption of unique or sensitive environments.

Social Carrying Capacity

The concern for the social environment can be considered under three subheadings: functional services, aesthetics and stress. Functional services, be they sewage facilities, roads, electricity, telephone or health services, or fire and police protection, are to a greater or lesser degree provided in cottage communities. Sewage facilities are, for the most part, dependent on septic tanks, and the associated problems have already been mentioned. Road design and standards are determined largely by the level of government represented; township roads are much more primitive than county roads which are in turn of low standard compared to roads designed and maintained by the Ontario government. Electrical supplies and telephone service are available if desired in most centres. Police protection is usually the function of the Ontario Provincial Police, but fire protection is a very real problem for many cottage areas in Ontario; often the only protection is provided by a neighbouring volunteer fire department. Recreational facilities and services in most areas are at best primitive. Certainly the type of standards and criteria that are used in urban municipalities would be of greater relevance.

There is a very great need for a total reconsideration of the functional services used by cottage communities. In many instances the standards that have to be met have evolved in areas of a low population density where agriculture or forestry provided the economic base. It is not implied that the standards applicable to urban subdivisions are necessary; cottage communities must have their own criteria and standards for environmental evaluation. Yet there has at least been some attempt to realise certain basic standards of functional services, even if they are not the most appropriate.

For questions of aesthetics and stress there appears to be an almost total lack of meaningful criteria and standards. In the framework shown in Fig. 12.2 the subheadings under *aesthetics* have been developed from the thinking of K. Lynch, who suggests that our image of the city is composed of identifiable components, namely paths, edges, nodes, landmarks and districts. Paths are channels of movement such as roadways, waterways and walkways. Nodes are points and are generally major intersections or where paths come together. Edges are other linear elements, such as rivers or shorelines, and landmarks are buildings, structures or other features that stand out as entities in the landscape. Districts are identifiable neighbourhoods or parts of a place, such as the waterfront area of a cottage community (Lynch 1960).

As far as stress is concerned there are, as has been suggested, standards for density, and there is now provincial legislation governing levels of noise. The design and condition of buildings is controlled to the extent that building permits must be issued before a structure can be built, while a Medical Officer of Health can condemn a building that he considers unfit to live in.

Cottage areas are amenity environments and certainly both that which creates satisfaction and that which causes dissatisfaction should be identified. Basic research is necessary to establish what people like and dislike about the cottage community in which they are located. D. Tobey's survey of five cottage communities in Maine suggests how such considerations might be identified and rated. Cottagers were given qualitative statements about the community and asked to say whether they agreed or disagreed with them (Table 12.2). This type of research could identify the important parameters of the perceived cottage environment. Once the relevant considerations have been identified, standards and criteria could be established to preserve and enhance the quality of the perceived environment. The method suggested in the Maine study could be used to identify the attractiveness of a place in a manner that would be of direct use to managers.

A methodology has been developed in research into wilderness in the province that can be used to determine people's satisfaction or lack of it with the environment they are using for wilderness travel (Priddle 1973). This research not only identifies the components of satisfaction (aesthetics) or dissatisfaction (stress) but suggests how these considerations can be rated and related to each other (Table 12.3).

A synthesis of these ideas and techniques could be developed not only to tell the manager how residents perceived the quality of their cottage environment, but also to give him an idea of the relative importance of each of their concerns and, hence, how the best return could be achieved from money spent on management.

Conclusion

An attempt has been made in this chapter to suggest the conceptual nature of the problem of environmental quality in cottage development in the province of Ontario. Secondly, an indication has been given of what in fact has been or is being done and what had been neglected. Hopefully, the authors will be given an opportunity to test their methodology and to refine it.

One additional need must be stressed. Each proposed plan of subdivision for cottage development in Ontario is at present considered on its own merit, and little thought is given to neighbouring development. Obviously such an approach is meaningless, particularly in a cottage area where, for example, the body of water may already be used beyond capacity.

TABLE 12.2. Likes and dislikes of cottagers

	I agree Mildly	I agree Strongly	I disagree Mildly	I disagree Strongly
1. I wish there were more space between my home and my neighbours' homes				
2. Taking into account all aspects of this area of the ocean, in general it is not as pleasant for recreation as it was several years ago				
3. There is too much litter and trash evident in the water of this area of the ocean				
4. Most of the seasonal homes in this community are not very attractive				
5. At times there is too much noise from the activities of other people				
6. There are objectionable odours at times from the improper handling of sewage wastes				
7. If I were to purchase a seasonal home, I would be more concerned with the overall quality of the community and less concerned with the quality of the home I was buying				
8. This area of the ocean appears to be as clean as it was a number of years ago				

(8 of 35 questions)

Source: D. Tobey n.d., p.29

TABLE 12.3. Satisfaction and dissatisfaction in wilderness travel

Item	Satisfaction/dis-satisfaction (indicate by no.)	Check column	Rank column
Weather			
Camping			
Insects			
Variety of scenery			
Expanse of open water			
Vegetation type			
Man-made features			
Wildlife			
Quietness			
Boat-beaching			
Viewpoints			
Isolation			
Beaches			
Water quality			
Bathing			
Crowding			
Waterfalls			
Portages			
Garbage			
Behaviour of other people			
Motorboats			
Outfitters			
Fishing			
Shape of lakes			
Park rangers			
Evidence of logging			
Cliffs			
Exposed bedrock			
Rapids			
Dams			

Please check those items that played an important role in your enjoyment or lack of it.
Please rank the ones you have checked in order of their importance.
Please tell me how satisfied you were with each of them.

1. Very satisfied
2. Fairly satisfied
3. Indifferent
4. Fairly dissatisfied
5. Very dissatisfied

It is the belief of the authors that there is an urgent need to take account of both physical and social parameters when considering the environment; traditionally in Canada this has not been done. They hope the framework recommended here will help to make good this shortcoming.

REFERENCES

Advisory Committee on Pollution Control (1970) Environmental Management of Recreational Waters in Cottage Areas of Ontario, Toronto.

Canada Land Inventory (1967) Land Capability Classification for Outdoor Recreation, Ottawa.

LaPage, W. (1967) Some Observations on Campground Trampling and Ground Cover Response, U.S. Forest Service, Research Paper No. 68.

Lynch, K. (1960) The Image of the City, The M.I.T. Press, Cambridge, Mass.

Michalski, M., Johnson, M. and Veal, D. (1973) Muskoka Lakes Water Quality Evaluation, Ontario Ministry of the Environment, Toronto.

Ontario Department of Health (n.d.) Septic Tank System, Toronto.

Ontario Department of Lands and Forests (1968) Methodology for Ontario Recreation Land Inventory, Toronto.

Ontario Ministry of the Environment (1973a) Guidelines and Criteria for Water Quality Management in Ontario, Toronto.

Ontario Ministry of the Environment (1973b) An Introduction to Air Pollution and Its Control in Ontario, Toronto.

Ontario Ministry of Natural Resources (1972) Lake Alert Phase 2, Methodology, Toronto.

Perloff, H. (1969) 'A framework for dealing with the urban environment: introductory statement', in H. Perloff (ed) The Quality of the Urban Environment, Johns Hopkins Press, Baltimore.

Pollution Probe (n.d.) Keep it Clean - A Manual for the Preservation of the Cottage Environment, Toronto.

Priddle, G.B. (1973) 'The behavioural carrying capacity of primitive areas for wilderness travel' Paper presented to American Association of Geographers, Atlanta Ga.

Threinen, C. (1964) 'An analysis of space demands for water and shore' Transactions of the Twenty-Ninth North American Wildlife and Natural Resources Conference, Wildlife Management Institute, Washington, D.C.

Tobey, D. (n.d.) Seasonal Home Residents in Five Maine Communities, Bulletin 700, Life Sciences and Agricultural Experimental Station, University of Maine, Oromo, Maine.

Chapter 13

VACATION HOMES IN RURAL AREAS: TOWARDS A MODEL FOR PREDICTING THEIR DISTRIBUTION AND OCCUPANCY PATTERNS

R. L. Ragatz

The market for vacation homes is becoming a major force in shaping urban and regional development because of the seasonal redistribution of the population. By vacation homes are meant permanently located single-family dwellings used on a private/personal basis for seasonal outdoor recreation; the occupants must have some other form of shelter which is considered their primary place of residence. A study of this seasonal redistribution is important for several reasons.

The first reason concerns the inadequacy of existing urban and regional theory. For the most part, this theory has considered the distribution of population only in terms of permanent place of residence. Most theorists describe a conical distribution with population density dispersing gradually outwards from the centre of an urban mass.

Few studies have considered how this conical distribution varies in terms of seasonal migration or semi-permanent residential occupancy. Studies exist concerning the migration from place of permanent residence to place of employment, usually referred to as the journey-to-work pattern (e.g., D. Carrol 1952; Kain 1962; Oi and Schuldmer 1962). Other studies have been made regarding daytime-nighttime migration or differences in population count during different times of a 24-hour period, one of the earliest and most comprehensive being that by G.L. Breese (1949). Finally, studies have been undertaken concerning the migration from permanent place of residence into the countryside for short overnight periods or for weekend outdoor camping (e.g., Crevo 1962; La Page 1967; Owens 1967).

However, the occupancy of vacation housing implies another type of migration pattern. This is the seasonal or semi-permanent migration from one home to another. The first two types of studies mentioned relate to migration from only one place of residence to the place of either work or entertainment. The third type of study relates to migration of short duration between two places of residence. No one has considered how the population distribution varies among different places of residence for extended periods of time.

The distribution of population in a given locality at different times is a basic factor in regional planning and development. It is essential for sound planning to know not only where people are listed for census counts but where they require services, consume products and so forth. Thus, the patterns of occupancy of vacation homes must be thoroughly investigated and incorporated into urban and regional theory in order to improve the processes of planning and development.

The second reason why occupancy of vacation housing is important relates to patterns of economic development. The location of people always affects the economic activity that is taking place at any given time. Thus, occupancy of vacation housing is directly related to shaping economic activity, especially on a regional basis in the more rural, underdeveloped areas of the country. The exodus of primary industries has caused the present plight of rural areas. Thus, an analysis of a new alternative land use that may be a substitute for traditional, obsolete land uses involves many land areas in the United States. The restoration of land values, the possibility of recapturing sunken capital and vanishing wealth, the creation of a new economic base, and the revitalisation of construction and some service industries are all related to the vacation home market.

A third reason for understanding the occupancy of vacation homes is related to the physical environment. For instance, the United States has been able to achieve high standards of health because large proportions of the population have been concentrated in urban areas. Controls over environmental health could be imposed and medical facilities provided within short distances of a large part of the population. The penetration of thousands of vacation-home families, who for the most part are accustomed to a controlled urban environment, into rural areas, where the sparsity of its population does not warrant such controls and facilities, would only complicate the maintenance of public health. Other potential problems relating to the physical environment include: (i) hazardous driving conditions on rural roads because of probable high speeds and traffic congestion; (ii) invasion of prime agricultural land by vacation homes; and (iii) environmental deterioration if the development of vacation homes takes place in an uncontrolled or unattractive manner.

A final reason relates to social considerations. The occupation of vacation homes has implications for the appropriate integration of urban-oriented vacation-home owners into the local rural community. Each sector of the population must be made aware of the other's values and goals in order to minimise potential forces of disturbance (cf. Chap. 10). Improved channels of communication and understanding must be developed in order to encourage harmonious relationships with as many community decisions as possible made by mutual consent.

Current Extent of the Market

The trend towards vacation-home ownership is strong in the United States. Some three million families own vacation homes, or about 5 per cent of the total number of families in this country. It is also estimated from results of various surveys, articles, and discussions with suppliers of the vacation home market, that somewhere between 100,000 and 200,000 new vacation homes are added annually. When multiplied by the estimated average family size of owners, the figures indicate that between ten and twelve million persons occupy their privately-owned vacation homes sometime during the year. In addition, it is estimated that several million other persons occupy rental units and should be included in the estimate; other types of seasonal shelter also should be considered, such as mobile homes, houseboats and old farmhouses. Studies indicate that the average length of occupancy per vaction home tends to be about three to four months, according to estimates derived from an unpublished nationwide survey by the American Telephone and Telegraph Company (1965) and others. Thus, a considerable depopulation of urban areas and repopulation of rural areas occur during different periods of the year.

The desire to own a vacation home has created a considerable market, although its importance is rarely recognised. Some 5 per cent of the total housing stock in this country can probably be classified as vacation housing. It also appears that more than 1 out of every 10 new homes under construction is now a vacation home. Results from various sources indicate that the average cost of a new vacation home (excluding land) was roughly between $15,000 and $20,000 in 1973, or less than the cost of a permanent home, and it is estimated that from 5 to 7 per cent of the total dollar value in the housing industry, or about $2,250,000,000 annually, is in this submarket.

It also appears that the market will continue to expand. Studies show that roughly 4 per cent of the families (about 4,200,000 in absolute numbers) are seriously considering the purchase of a vacation home in the immediate future (Princeton Research Corporation, personal communication). Another 4 to 5 per cent are considering purchase at some indeterminate date.

If all families hoping to purchase actually fulfil their intention within the next ten years, the annual number of vacation homes under construction could reach over 300,000. Of course, all of these families will not complete their plans. On the other hand, many additional families without present plans will probably enter the market as channels of production are improved and as techniques of marketing and financing are also improved. One way or another, it appears that the market could easily double within the next ten years. This means that some 6 to 8 million vacation homes could be found in rural areas and that some 20 to 25 million people could be commuting between their permanent and vacation homes.

Forces Influencing Demand for Vacation Homes

Urban and regional theorists say that the primary reason for increasing urbanisation throughout the world is to obtain a greater social and economic product through the greater division of labour possible in large cities. A point has been reached in our society where the social product of urbanisation is so great that many families have the *freedom* to own more than one of such expensive items as houses. Thus, through increases in leisure time and income, a sufficient amount of freedom has been achieved so that much of the city population can take advantage of rural pleasures such as space, fresh air and scenery, and at the same time earn a living in an urban centre. The place of work and economic livelihood continues to be where economies of scale and division of labour provide the greatest benefits, but now these benefits are so great that people are free to return to the physical advantages of the country.

A combination of two benefits from this greater social and economic product has provided the basic opportunity for people to purchase a vacation home. The first advantage is having sufficient income to allocate money from the household budget to a non-essential item. The second is adequate time away from the place of employment to spend this income on leisure activities. Without these two factors, a market for an object as costly as a house to be used only for seasonal-recreational purposes would not exist.

While these two advantages may be considered the ones that provide the opportunity for ownership, other factors provide the motive. These include equity appreciation, escape from a busy urban environment, and a chance to participate in outdoor recreation.

Supplementing these factors of motivation are several elements that make participation in the market easier, such as improved accessibility, intensive institutional advertising, and the availability of additional types of vacation homes and sites.

Location of Vacation Homes

Most vacation homes are concentrated in the north-eastern part of the United States (Fig. 13.1). However, data show that they are becoming more evenly distributed around the country. By using the rather poorly defined

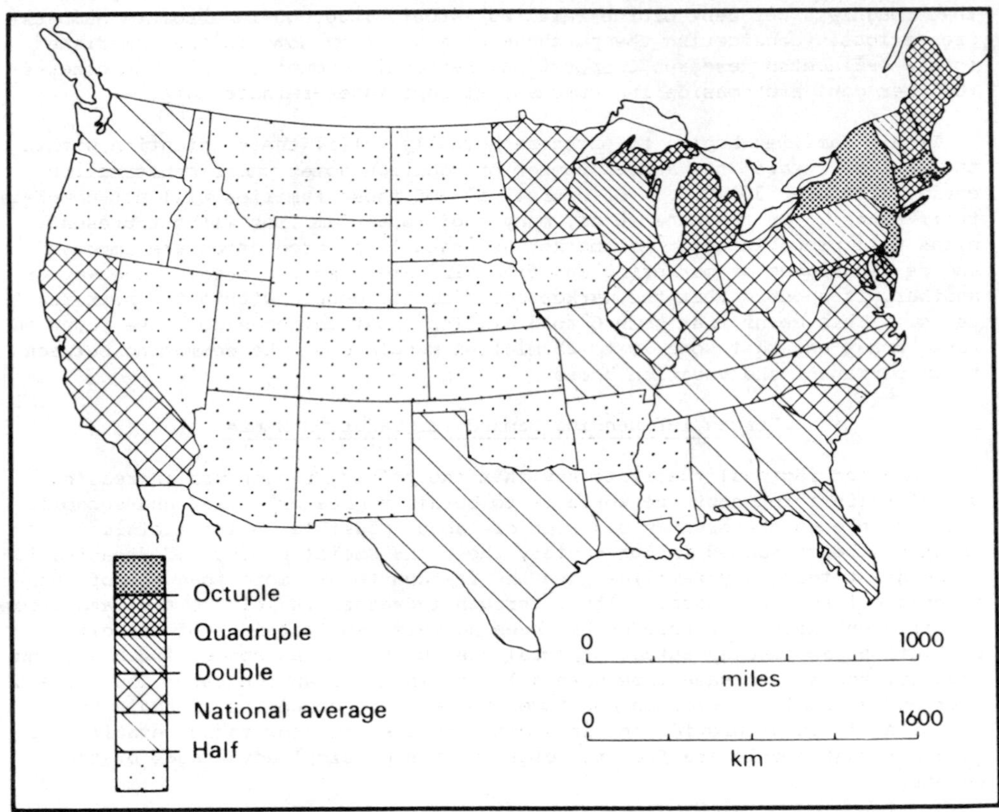

Fig. 13.1 Density of second homes in the United States, 1970

data from the 1950 and 1970 Censuses of Housing, it is found that of the twenty states with the greatest number of vacation homes in 1950, only six (Texas, Virginia, Pennsylvania, South Carolina, North Carolina and Missouri) increased their share of the total by 1970. On the other hand, all but six (Kentucky, Tennesse, Alabama, Lousiana, Oklahoma and West Virginia) of the thirty states with the fewest vacation homes in 1970 showed increases in their share of the total from 1950. Most vacation homes, however, are still concentrated in a few states. In 1970, the five leading states alone had almost one-third (32.9%) of the country's vacation homes and the top ten had over half (50.3%). However, in 1950, the four leading states had 38.1 per cent of the total vacation homes and the top ten states had 62 per cent.

Sites are no longer limited to traditional recreational centres or close proximity to urban centres. Factors such as increasing interest in water and winter sports and improvements in transportation technology have provided an opportunity for greater dispersal. It appears, therefore, that many rural areas with outdoor recreation attractions such as water, mountains or scenery, and in relatively close proximity to urban areas, will be vulnerable to vacation-home development. This vulnerability will tend to increase as nearby recreational land becomes a prime target for developers and speculators.

Although dispersal of vacation homes is occurring, the majority remains concentrated in areas of recreational opportunity within 150 to 200 miles (240-320 km) of major urban centres (a generalisation derived from the surveys by the American Telephone and Telegraph Company, a special US census in 1967, Stanley Works, The Aluminium Company of America, Chautauqua County Planning Board, and McCann-Frickson, Inc.). Vacation homes tend to be found in decreasing numbers in radiating circles from urban clusters. Their density distribution, as shown in Fig. 13.2 can be roughly described as a volcanic cone. The cone has no vertex owing to the location of the central city and

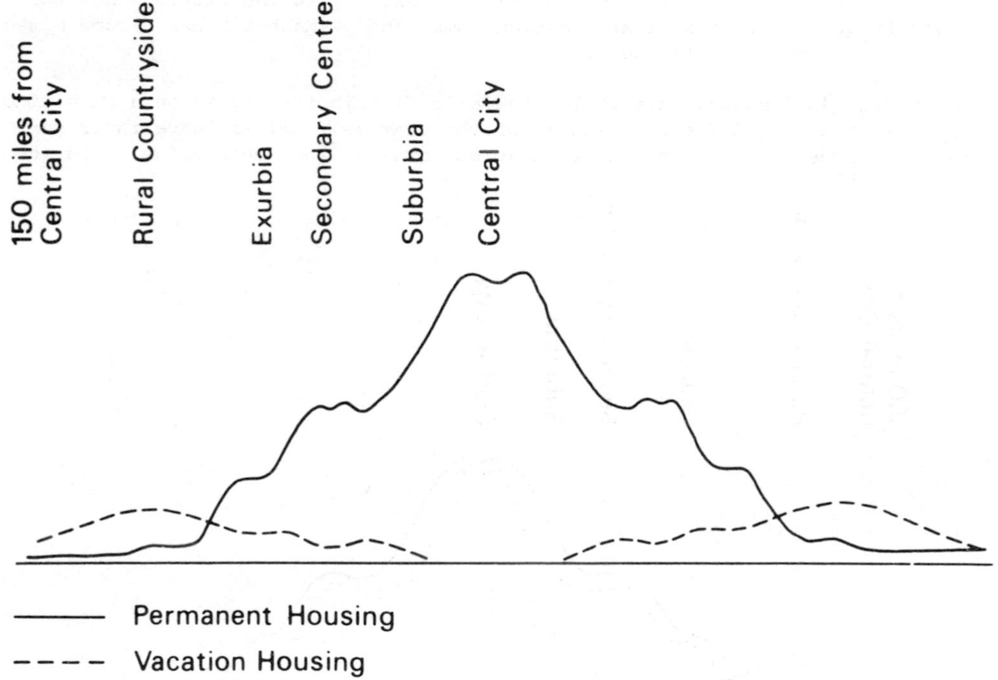

Fig. 13.2 Schematic distribution of vacation and permanent housing

the immediate surrounding suburbs. At some point beyond the central core, a grey area seems to occur where permanent homes in suburbia and exurbia are interspersed with vacation homes. The succeeding rings outward are where most vacation homes are probably located. Density continues to decline outwards to a point about 200 miles (320 km) from the central city where it becomes very low. Unless recreational opportunities are exceedingly good beyond that point, this distance tends to be beyond feasible driving times at weekends.

Rather than being evenly distributed within the individual rings, the units tend to gravitate toward nuclei of various types of recreation, with the degree of gravitation depending upon the attractiveness of the recreation. Primary attracting forces include water, mountains, availability of outdoor sports, scenery or cheap land. Another major factor in the degree of concentration is accessibility from permanent place of residence.

Thus, two series of spatial population peaks and declines can be identified across the country. The first is at the place of permanent residence. Here, the primary peak is the central city, and the gradient outward from the centre slopes downwards. Interspersed throughout this sloping gradient are outlying cities, towns, hamlets and rural farm and non-farm populations of the countryside. A second cone of vacation homes, volcanic in shape, is also present. Specific peaks occur in this cone and represent areas of vacation homes combining recreational attractions and close proximity to the city. The two cones frequently intersect as vacation homes and permanent homes become mixed in areas at the urban fringe.

As Fig. 13.3 shows, this whole schematic distribution takes on a pulsating appearance during different seasons of the year as families leave their permanent residence to occupy their vacation homes in the countryside. During

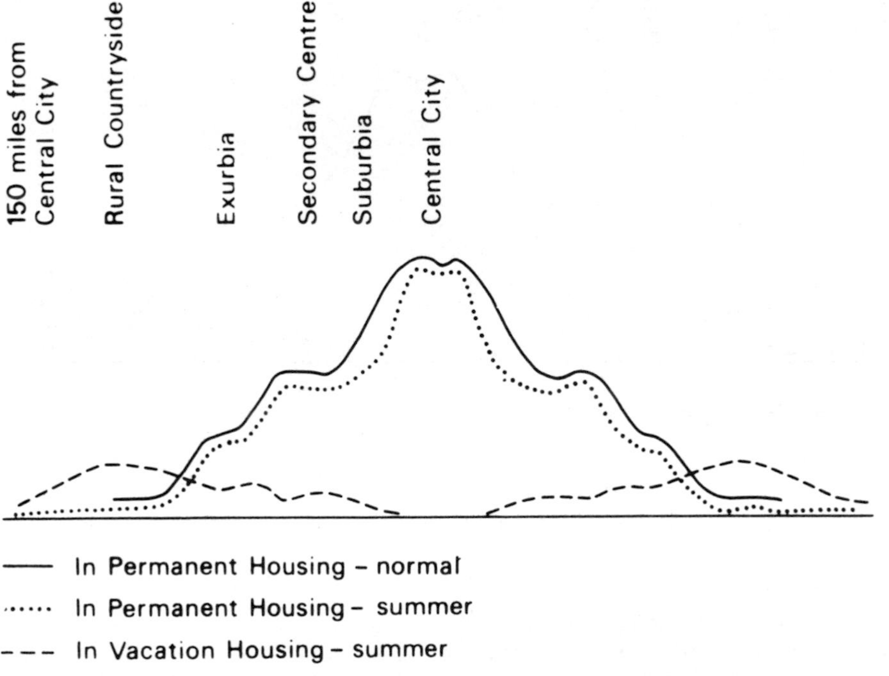

Fig. 13.3 Schematic distribution of population by seasons

the summer, the peak of the major central city slumps and the minor peaks marking the concentration of vacation homes rise. This change will usually be reversed during the winter except in areas excellently suited to winter sports.

Just as various sectors of the entire population have different tendencies for vacation-home ownership, so do vacation-home owners have different tendencies for locating their vacation homes. For example, the head of a younger family with a relatively limited budget may be likely to purchase a small A-frame cabin on a scattered lot in close proximity to his permanent place of residence. As available resources for luxury items increase and as the children demand additional types of outdoor recreation, he may sell the small cabin and buy a more elaborate unit in a complete vacation home community further away from their permanent home.

Thus, different types of vacation-home owners are probably concentrated in unique distributions throughout the schematic cone. These various sectors may be concentrated according to age, income, neighbourhood of permanent home, family size and a series of other variables. Factors such as travel costs (in time and dollars), cost of land, property taxes, availability of certain types of recreational facilities and similarity in family types, all enter into the decision-making patterns of vacation-home buyers and hence into the location of their vacation homes.

A Model for Predicting the Location of Occupancy Patterns of Vacation Homes

The challenge, therefore, is to develop a model which can predict how the vacation-home market operates in redistributing population in rural areas on a seasonal basis. While it is beyond the scope of this chapter to develop a synthetic model in operative terms, enough information is available to indicate the nature of such a model. Although the major variables can be identified and the structural relationships of the model determined, available data are insufficient to provide explicit measurements of these variables and to estimate the parameters specifically.

In developing the model, several components should be incorporated. These include: the propensity of the population for vacation-home ownership; how this propensity differs with various demographic and spatial characteristics of the population; the resultant pattern of vacation-home location and the seasonal distribution of various sectors of the population; and some factors which can change the values of the basic parameters upon which the operations of the model depend.

The first two components, which are concerned with magnitude and variations in propensity for vacation-home ownership, will now be used as a sample for developing more extensively a predictive model. In doing so, present and future demand among various sectors of the population for any given time period might be predicted (Keyfitz 1964a, b; Rogers 1966). The model to follow is adapted from similar models developed in recent years and is described most recently by A. Rogers (1968).

The first step in developing the model is to list some of the characteristics of families which influence vacation-home consumption. These can be shown in the following formula:

D = f (A,E,O,F,Y,V,P,R...m)

where D = demand for vacation homes
A = age of head of household
E = education of head of household
O = occupation of head of household
F = family size
Y = family income
V = family value patterns
P = place of permanent residence
R = past experience with rural living
m = other influencing variables.

Each of these variables could be divided into several subgroups (for example, age: under 30 years, 30-39 years, and so forth). A matrix could then be constructed which would cross-classify these variable subgroupings into a series of individual population classes. Such a matrix is shown in Table 13.1. The horizontal rows represent various classes of the population

TABLE 13.1. Matrix of population classes as determined by variable subgroupings (average of four per variable) which influence vacation home demand

Population classes (i)	Population variables	Age of head of household (A)	Education of head of house hold (E)	Occupation of head of household (O)	Family size (F)	Family income (Y)	Value patterns (V)	Place of permanent residence (P)	Experience with rural living (R)
a		1	1	1	1	1	1	1	1
b		1	2	1	1	1	1	1	1
c		1	1	2	1	1	1	1	1
d		1	1	1	2	1	1	1	1
e		1	1	1	1	2	1	1	1
.		.	.	.	.	.	.	.	.
.		.	.	.	.	.	.	.	.
N (65,792)		4	4	4	4	4	4	4	4

according to subgroups. For instance, population class *a* would include the segment of the total population in age of head of household subgroup *1*, education subgroup *1*, family size subgroup *1*, and so forth. Population class *b* would include the segment of the total population in age of head of household subgroup *1*, education subgroup *2*, family size subgroup *1*, and so forth. Thus, an extensive series of population classes could be listed by cross-classifying all variable subgroups.

Table 13.1 lists only eight variables. If the average number of subgroups for each variable was only four, some 65,000 rows (each representing different classes of population) would have to be completed. However, not all of those population subgroupings would have sufficiently different behavioural characteristics with respect to their activities in the vacation-home market. Therefore, some method should be devised to condense these classes into a relatively small number of groups according to degree of cohesiveness. An alternative to condensing the population classes would be a factor analysis of the variable subgroupings. This would condense the data into a workable number of factors or classes. Perhaps some factors summarising characteristics of status or degree of urbanisation might be more applicable than individual demographic variables.

In summary, the matrix in Table 13.1 thus shows that the total population can be subdivided into a series of individual classes (i) which represents the number of persons (p) having all characteristics unique to that class at a given period of time (t). Thus, p_{it} represents a certain number of persons in population class *i* at time *t*.

The size of the population classes will vary over time as a result of fluctuations in marital status, the national economic situation, social values, and so forth. A useful tool to predict these variations is the cohort-survival method of population projection. Basically, this technique can be used to determine changes in the size of each population class for different time intervals. A certain number of persons in class *a* at time t_1 will remain in class *a* at time t_2. However, a certain number of these households will change to class *b* or class *e* or other classes.

A transition matrix could be developed to show the probability of persons in one class moving into another class by the next time interval. A *death vector* also could be developed to show the probability of persons in each class being eliminated from the population. Finally, a *birth vector* could be developed to show the number of additions to each class. Usually, a cohort-survival projection uses the number of births for this factor. Since this model is concerned only with vacation-home ownership, either the number of new families being formed or the number of new additions to the labour force (that is, potential vacation-home buyers) could be substituted for births.

This cohort-survival projection for each population class can be shown as:

$$P_{it} = P_{i}, t-1 - s_{i} - \overline{d_{i}} + \overline{b_{i}}$$

where P_{it} = population in specific class at a given time period

P_{it} t-1 = population in same class at previous time period

s_i = number of persons leaving this class for another class (from transition matrix)

$\overline{d_i}$ = number of persons eliminated from this class by death (from death vector)

$\overline{b_i}$ = number of persons entering this class from formation of new families or additions to labour force (from birth vector).

The total population at any given time then would be shown as the sum of the individual classes, or:

$$P_i = \sum_{i=1}^{a} P_{it}$$

Each population class will have a different propensity for vacation-home ownership because of variations in such factors as income and family size. Through surveys and research, propensity probabilities can be attached to each class for each time period. Thus, class *a*, which might be composed of high-income families with few children, would probably have a higher propensity probability than, for example, class *x*, which might be composed of lower-income families with more children.

By multiplying the propensity probability of each class by the size of the class, we could predict the number of vacation homes each class will demand at any given time. By adding together the individual classes, we could determine total demand for vacation homes in the entire population. This is shown as:

$$V_i = \sum_{i=1}^{n} v_{it}$$

where V_i = total vacation homes demanded by population

v_{it} = total vacation homes demanded by population class *i*.

We now have a model for predicting the total number of vacation homes owned by the population and its various component classes for any given period of time. This model has limited use, however, as it assumes that demand depends only upon variables of the population. This assumption is invalid, since numerous other variables and factors also influence demand, such as mortgage financing, rationalisation of production and marketing techniques, public policies and availability of recreational land. Therefore, the preceding model can predict the number of vacation homes owned by the population classes only if all other influencing factors remain constant. It is, consequently, incomplete. The following data must be added:

$$V_i = i\,(\sum_{i=1}^{n} v_{it}, F,P,M,I,\ldots m)$$

where V_i = total vacation homes demanded by population

$\sum_{i=1}^{n} v_{it}$ = total vacation homes demanded by individual population classes according to influence of demographic variable subgroupings on ownership propensities

F = influence of mortgage financing on demand

P = influence of production rationalisation

M = influence of marketing rationalisation

I = influence of public policies

m = other influencing factors.

The structural framework of the model is now complete. It permits predictions of the total size of each population class; the change of the size of these classes over periods of time; the propensity of each class of owning a vacation home; the effect of the factors which influence the parameters of the model; and, hence, the total number of vacation homes which will be demanded by various sectors of the population at a given period of time.

Of course, the complexity of the model must not be dismissed. The validity of the above formulae depends upon a multi-variate demand function of a set of complex, interacting factors. These factors include not only those within the building industry, such as the influence of financing, production, marketing, public policies, and so forth, but also those exogenous to the industry, e.g., such factors as the population characteristics of age, income and occupation. These factors, together with many others, operate jointly in the determination of the demand for vacation homes. The problem, therefore, is to represent the interplay of several variables simultaneously.

Several different types of functions are probably assumed by the different variables. In other words, the overall function might range from simple measurement to linear to quadratic and so forth. Also, each of the individual variables would probably require various mathematical transformations in order to satisfy the correct function. Thus, the formula is not orthogonal because, as new variables are added, the effect or influence of the original variables does not remain the same. Not only is it beyond the scope of this chapter to determine the appropriate functions for the formulae, but this determination would require additional data and research findings which are not available at present.

In order to complete the predictive model for the vacation-home market that was suggested at the beginning of this section, the location and product variables also must be considered. These will permit determination not only of the number of vacation homes which will be demanded but also their type of location. The following lists present some characteristics of location and product.

Location characteristics	Product characteristics
Distance from permanent home	Type of construction
Type of lot	Type of unit
Density of development	Intended use
Proximity to recreation	Value and size
Type of recreation available	Tenure
Availability of public utilities and facilities	Intensity of use
Extent of mixture with permanent homes	

The characteristics in each list must be cross-classified with each other, as were the population characteristics. Thus, there would be several classes of location: units on scattered lots, less than 50 miles (80 km) from an urban centre, adjacent to recreation, and others. There would also be several product classes such as conventionally constructed homes of less than 500 square feet (35 sq m) in size, intended for vacation-now, retirement-later use, and so forth.

The next step is to determine the ownership propensities of each of the population classes for each location and product class. Such a process would involve an unmanageable number of calls, so the various classes must be condensed and summarised. As noted, one such tool for this task is factor analysis

Conclusions

The comprehensive model becomes very complex and requires a high degree of quantitative sophistication. The objective here has been merely to describe the components and structural framework of such a model. If completed, the model could predict the number and type of vacation homes and families seasonally distributed in the interstitial areas around and between the metropolitan areas of the country. This predictive power would be useful to public and private-decision makers in establishing development strategies; determining seasonal fluctuations in type and extent of goods and services required on a regional basis; and improving many other operations in community planning and development.

Private decision makers (contractors and other business entrepreneurs), as suppliers of the vacation-home product and related services, would be able to predict the market for their goods and services. The public decision makers (local government units), as suppliers of public facilities and utilities (roads, sewers, water, and so forth), would be able to predict changes in the type and magnitude of public facilities and utilities to be required. Public decision makers in urban centres would also benefit by being able to predict seasonal fluctuations in publicly provided services. The model also has other uses, such as predicting changes in property taxes or patterns of expenditure. It must, however, be admitted that the validity of these predictions frequently depends upon community policy, which can often attract or repel certain types of owners of vacation homes.

REFERENCES

American Telephone and Telegraph Company (1965) A Survey of 9,231 Bell System Telephone Users, New York.

Breese, G.L. (1949) The Daytime Population of the Central Business District of Chicago, University of Chicago Press, Chicago.

Carrol, D. (1952) 'The relation of homes to work places and the spatial pattern of cities' Social Forces 30, pp.271-82.

Carrol, R.L. (1965) A Social Analysis of Southold Town Long Island, Rural Sociology Department, Cornell University, Ithaca.

Chautauqua County Planning Dept (1965) Second Homes and their Impact on the Economy of Chautauqua County, Mayville, New York.

Crevo, C.C. (1962) Characteristics of Summer Weekend Recreational Travel, Yale University Press, New Haven.

Kain, J. (1962) 'The journey to work as a determinant of residential location' Regional Science Association Papers 9, pp.137-60.

Keyfitz, N. (1964a) 'Matrix multiplication as a technique of population analysis' The Millbank Memorial Fund Quarterly 42, pp.75-82.

Keyfitz, N. (1964b) 'The population projection as a matrix operation' Demography 1, pp.56-73.

La Page, W.F. (1967) Successful Private Campgrounds: a Study of the Factors that Influence the Length and Frequency of Camper Visits, U.S. Government Printing Office, Washington, D.C.

Oi, W.Y. and Schuldmer, P.W. (1962) An Analysis of Urban Travel Demands, Northwestern University Press, Evanston.

Owens, G. (1967) Outdoor Recreation : Participation Characteristics of Users, Distance Travelled and Expenditure, Department of Agricultural Economics and Rural Sociology, University of Ohio, Columbus.

Rogers, A. (1966) 'Matrix methods of population analysis' Journal of the American Institute of Planners 32, pp.40-4.

Rogers, A. (1968) Matrix Analysis of Inter-regional Population Growth and Distribution, University of California Press, Berkeley.

Stanmar, Inc. (1962) Market Analysis of Vacation Home Potential in the Boston Area, unpublished study, Sudbury, Mass.

Chapter 14
ISSUES AND CONFLICTS

J. T. Coppock

One of the most striking features of the development of second homes is the variety of interests involved and the extent to which these interests are actually or potentially in conflict. Land owners, land users (particularly farmers and foresters), local residents, conservationists, planners, developers, other recreationists, those who have second homes and those who do not, each have a legitimate interest. On 1 May 1974 the Town and Country Planning Association held a one-day conference in Birmingham to explore the nature of the problems posed by second homes, and invited speakers from these interests to contribute. It is the deliberations of this conference which, in summary form, constitute the bulk of this chapter; for while similar conferences can be (and have been) held elsewhere, the views expressed both provide a sample of reactions in one country and also have a wider relevance.

Neither the speakers nor the other participants represented all the interests involved, though the latter included most of them. The contributions from the platform were heavily biased in respect of political representation and did not include land users, conservationists, owners of second homes, local residents or the public at large (except in so far as their views were expressed by the politicians); despite invitations, they did not include a member of the government. The audience consisted primarily of council members and officials from local government, with a smaller contingent of officials from central government agencies; these groups accounted for over half those present. Others included academic and other researchers and members of amenity and recreational interests; few were land users or (overtly at least) owners or occupiers of second homes. The contributions have been summarised, for they would otherwise have occupied more than one-quarter of this book; the remarks of the principal speakers, intended to be heard by an audience and (with two exceptions) delivered from notes rather than from completed manuscripts, have often been paraphrased and, to that extent, may have been misinterpreted.

The conference was opened by John Cripps, Chairman of the Countryside Commission, who noted that second homes had been very much in the public eye in recent years and had been the subject of one of the first research projects to be sponsored by the Commission after its formation in 1968, when Wye College was asked to undertake the investigation which is the subject of Chapter 6 (Bielckus *et al.* 1972). Michael Dower had then been invited to report on the wider aspects of second-home ownership (Downing and Dower 1973) and, on receiving these two reports, the Commission realised that the subject had implications which went far beyond its own brief. It was hoped that, in the light of the facts and opinions expressed, others (and particularly the Government) would take action.

In his view, there was nothing new about second homes which, to some extent, represented a reversal of a former situation where people living in the country had second homes in the town. Facts were required about second homes -

their number, location, use and the extent to which they satisfied demand; the conference also needed to discuss the social, economic and moral issues raised. To some the term *second home* was almost pejorative, but it was wrong to use it in this way, and he was pleased to note that Shelter, in a recent report, did not dispute the right of an individual to acquire a second home. There were, however, three wider aspects of these reports on which discussion was needed. First, did second homes represent a justifiable call on national resources when four million people were living in substandard or unfit housing? Secondly, what were the effects on the local communities, on their composition and activities; were they being squeezed out and should newly-built second homes be provided as the supply of available houses was exhausted? Thirdly, was assistance in the provision of second homes a justifiable use of public money?

A lead paper by Michael Dower provided a broad view of the various facets of the development of second homes and, in large measure, forms the substance of Chapter 11. He noted the small number of second homes by comparison with many other European countries (though the data might not be strictly comparable); however, the numbers seemed to be growing rapidly and second homes had become the subject of political and public concern over the preceding five years. Because of the recentness of this concern, no official definition of second homes existed and there was a clear need for central government to provide guidance to local authorities.

He discussed the difficulties of definition, regarding that used by Wye College as having (understandably in view of the Countryside Commission's remit) a recreational bias, and preferred *a property owned or rented on a long lease as the occasional residence of the household that usually lives elsewhere,* with the decision of which was first and second home being left to the owner. He also stressed the need for systematic information on second homes, particularly a running check on numbers, type and location. He then reviewed the evidence on number and location, showing that second homes (on the definition used) appeared to be widely scattered but were most numerous within 100 miles (160 km) of their owners' first homes, and were used at weekends as well as on holidays, thus achieving a high average usage of some 90 days a year.

He saw the demand for second homes continuing, despite some uncertainty over future trends in those factors which had facilitated the growth of second homes, such as improved roads and car ownership; supply, on the other hand, was much more likely to be affected by public decision. Few areas appeared to have any substantial stock of existing buildings which, often released by change and depression in the rural economy, had been the principal source of second homes other than static caravans. Although there was no problem in increasing the supply of caravans, there was likely to be a shortage of sites with planning permission; some local authorities were hostile and some of those willing to permit new sites were seeking to encourage the trend from caravans to chalets and other forms of built accommodation. Thus the third possible source of second homes, new-built structures, seemed likely to become the most important. There was clearly a good deal of interest among both developers and potential purchasers, but decisions rested largely with the planning authorities. The present might thus be a significant turning point: whereas second homes had formerly been largely conversions from existing buildings, with the planning authority having little say, *from now on, they may mostly be new-built, with the planning authority saying what is built, where and how many.*

Second homes appeared to arouse strong and often conflicting feelings; some saw them as a flagrant inequality, as conspicuous consumption, or as a factor adversely affecting the economy and the social and cultural life of the receiving regions, others as a natural and desirable answer to the demand for recreation, as contributing to the balance of payments and the preservation of the environment, and as stimulating the economy and social vitality of the receiving regions. Such conflicting attitudes were based partly on fact, partly on emotion and partly on principle, and had been most strongly expressed in the remoter parts of Great Britain, where the work force in traditional industries had declined and where second homes would bring welcome income and employment. But such income was seasonal and no substitute for the development of primary and secondary industry. Moreover, those seeking second homes could compete directly with the local inhabitants once the supply of vacant buildings had been exhausted and this, together with the distrust many rural people felt for *incomers*, had led to political expressions of concern. There might also be an environmental impact, particularly where new second homes had been erected or static caravans sited.

Second homes were still of minor economic importance nationally, but they could gain in political importance at a time of severe shortage of housing. Yet many second homes represented properties which had been redeemed from dereliction; they assisted the balance of payments and could help the economy of regions by a direct flow of money which, compared with other forms of tourism, had a *singular permanence and strength*.

At present there was no specific government policy on second homes, though fiscal concessions had recently been withdrawn. Control was solely in the hands of local authorities, though they had only limited powers to prevent changes to existing buildings and could not prevent a house becoming a second home unless they were prepared to purchase the property in question. Only when second homes were numerous and had obvious social and economic effects had local authorities formulated specific policies, generally to the effect that there should be a limit on the proportion of second homes and that new second homes should be accommodated in holiday villages; elsewhere they fell under general policies for housing or tourism. Before the purpose-built second home became a major element, clear guidance was needed from central government on the principles and standards which should be applied by local authorities. While governments might further discourage second homes, they were unlikely to prohibit them, and the main line of policy was therefore to steer growth towards such regions, types of second home and settings as seemed desirable; such steering might well make the impact of second homes beneficial rather than damaging. Central government and local authorities would have to decide whether they regarded second homes as housing or as tourist accommodation, for different planning principles and standards would apply depending on the choice. Planning authorities might also need to adjust their housing policies to protect housing for local people. In many areas local authorities would soon be obliged to take positive action and must be helped to do so by central government.

The first of the six contributions from the platform was made by William Craig, General Manager of the housing division of Kinch Leisure Homes Ltd. He thought that planners had no right to contemplate the problems of second homes till they had solved those of first homes; for every member of the community must have the opportunity of a first home. He contrasted the life of the towns with the fuller life of the country, which the townsman now sought to enjoy; but this must not bring suburbia into the countryside or deprive the rural areas of their housing stock, despite the greater purchasing power of the town dweller (though it should be noted that to the country dweller, especially the young, it was the towns which appealed). There was some merit in the thought that second homes might be necessary because of the failure of urban planning to achieve the quality of life that people had come to expect. If further inroads were made into housing stock, or further infilling or grant-aided rehabilitation allowed, then it would be our fault if the village died.

His company believed that, to a large extent, the destruction of the village and its life could be avoided, as elsewhere in Europe, by the creation of small second-home communities for relaxation, leisure and recreation; for the purpose of a second home was rediscovery of oneself. Such second-home villages could have, on a small scale, all the amenities which the more affluent societies of the cities enjoyed. If this was done in a far more sophisticated way than hitherto, something could be added to the village instead of destroying it.

Many sites for such second-home villages could be found amongst the abandoned legacies of industrialisation - small sites formerly used for the working of minerals, such as coal, iron ore and slate, all adjacent to existing communities and, just as important, to the countryside, and never too far from the sea; derelict land suitable for second-home development would even be found in inner London in, for example, the disused dockyards near Woolwich. Derelict land, not the village community, must be the site of second homes. He envisaged water-sport villages around old quarries and gravel pits, not around natural lakes, equestrian villages on sites adjacent to forests and rolling hills, and villages around small disused harbours for those interested in the sea. The main need was for *laze-about villages* on derelict land on the urban fringe where much land of this kind was to be found. All these villages, whether *laze-about* or for specific activities, would have a small recreation centre, including a heated pool, children's pools and play areas, squash and tennis courts, sauna bath, restaurant and perhaps (for the larger centres) a small theatre which could be adapted for film or lecture. None would be of any great size, with perhaps the largest not exceeding 20 acres (8 ha), but they might well bring back life to the countryside as well as bringing back people without destroying what they had come to enjoy.

As an example he cited a development near Redruth around the only complete and working tin-streaming industry, where his company was assembling the necessary permission to develop an occupational holiday village on what was a monumental industrial scar. The site was an established attraction to visitors and would eventually provide facilities, not only for the occupiers of second homes, but also for the community of Redruth, for whom expenditure by central government on the sophisticated recreational equipment to be provided could never be justified.

While the first priority must be to provide first homes, second homes would be required in increasing numbers. Those who wanted them must be allowed to have them and to enjoy them, but they must also pay the commercial rates, both for the second homes themselves and for the centralised facilities. There was nothing wrong in having and enjoying a second home, nor was it wrong for private enterprise to provide them; but it was wrong for the owner or occupier of second homes to walk over others and destroy their first homes.

Colin Jacobs, County Planning Officer of Clwyd and formerly County Planning Officer of Denbighshire, provided the viewpoint of a planner. He recalled that the introduction to the Denbighshire Report on second homes (Jacobs 1972) had been subtitled *The Quiet Revolution,* and pointed out that the amalgamation of farms and the decline in employment on the farms had made many cottages in the remoter areas redundant; these were then acquired and re-used as second homes.

His surveys provided an estimate of annual expenditure of £480 per second home, in addition to the purchase price. Socially, it was noteworthy that over half the respondents claimed to have one or more close ties with Wales. He believed that second homes were not especially a Welsh problem, but represented a widespread rural/urban clash. Other findings in the report have been summarised in Chapters 7 and 10.

A major charge levelled against second homes was that they accentuated rural depopulation by putting up house prices, though since Wales was a grossly over-crowded country by world standards, depopulation itself might not be wholly undesirable. The steep rise in prices of cottages had little effect on the housing sought by local residents, for young people today required a council house or a mortgage on a modern house. It is true that government aids, now phased out, had been available on second homes, but the rise in the rateable value attributable to a second home repaid the local element in the sum advanced in less than three years; and, although it took twenty-nine years for the central government component to be repaid, it had also to be recognised that such properties might otherwise have been vacant or derelict and so produce no income. On the other hand, it must also be recognised that once capital assets had been realised by members of the local community through the sale of a second home, subsequent sales bypassed the local economy completely.

The pace of second-home development had been set by migration in search of employment, higher living standards and better social facilities, and dereliction would represent a waste of valuable resources in a period when recreation and leisure were of growing importance. Local authorities accepted a limited increase in second homes, but these were only one of the influences affecting rural areas; a report by Jacobs on first homes in rural areas had shown that just adding to the existing housing stock could have a devastating effect on the Welsh way of life. Houses were built only if they provided a profit to the seller of the land, the developer and the builder. Their coincidence in a village through a planning permission on two or three acres might well mean the addition of twenty or thirty families, probably without local connections but keen to have a house in a rural area and prepared to put up with any inconvenience; such people were likely to be largely out of sympathy with the local community. Until rural workers and entrepreneurs got rewards comparable with those enjoyed by their urban counterparts there could be no return to rural prosperity, though an agricultural industry enjoying comparable rewards would be a step in this direction.

The third speaker was Dafydd Williams, General Secretary of the Welsh National Party, Plaid Cymru. He believed that the second-home problem in Wales was of growing political importance. It was first brought to public attention by the disruption of an auction in Caernarvon by members of the Welsh Language Society, but the problem had been causing concern for the better part of a decade. Second homes were concentrated in the rural areas, particularly in the west from Carmarthenshire to Anglesey, in areas which not only had some of the lowest incomes per head in the whole of Great Britain but were also the stronghold of the Welsh language, two facts which must be taken together. Without a proper solution there would be increasing friction in the Welsh countryside.

The second-home problem had two aspects, social and national or cultural, though these were very closely interwoven. The social problems were very similar to those in Scandinavia or in parts of rural England, but the second was linked, through the survival of the Welsh language, to the very national identity of the Welsh people. Plaid Cymru recognised that the expansion of second homes was the result of economic stagnation and depopulation, and that the only real solution was to provide a level of economic activity which would sustain a permanent, living population in these areas. The acquisition of second homes was in part a reflection of a worldwide drift to the towns, through the decline of jobs in agriculture and the lack of well-paid employment in rural areas. This trend had provided the two principal requirements for the spread of second-home ownership, low levels of income per head and a supply of houses for sale (often admittedly quite derelict properties), though it had also been encouraged by standard and discretionary grants. Nationalist opinion in Wales was aware of the complexity and subtlety of the second-home problem and for this reason had been calling for an economic plan for Wales and a rural development agency responsible to a Welsh parliament.

There were myths among both nationalists and second-home owners. Among the former there was the myth that second homes and the whole tourist industry were an unmitigated disaster for the Welsh, and among the latter, the myth that second-home owners benefited the community to which they came and improved deserted relics that had been sold to them at a handsome profit. The truth lay somewhere between. Occupiers of second homes did contribute something to the local economy, though Plaid Cymru disputed the picture painted by the Denbighshire report, which was based upon subjective answers of second-home owners themselves, who might be expected, quite naturally, to want to show that they were in sympathy with the community and were concerned for its economic interests.

But, while there was a contribution, the extent to which ownership of second homes had grown had created other problems. The social aspect of second homes in Wales could no longer be considered simply as the passive product of economic and social change, for it had acquired a dynamic of its own. Second homes were no longer confined to isolated dwellings without electricity or water; there were now whole villages given over to them. Among the areas of the former rural district councils (RDCs) second homes represented 31.5 per cent of all houses in Teifiside RDC, 20 per cent in Llyn RDC and 15.1 per cent in Cenmaes RDC, and in individual villages the proportion was even higher; the figure for Denbighshire was rather low, reflecting its location in respect of the coast. These were not exceptional figures, and the people of Wales were well aware that a considerable portion of the housing stock was used as second homes. It was no longer correct to suggest that first and second homes could be separated into two quite different parts of the housing stock or that the intrusion of owners of second homes into an area no longer affected house prices. Second homes were raising the prices of houses in rural areas to levels that young people could no longer afford. It was difficult enough for such people to buy a home anywhere, but it was socially unjust when those in west Wales, earning much less than £1,500 a year, were asked to compete with people earning £8,000 a year who already had a home worth more than £20,000 in the more prosperous suburbs of Birmingham, Liverpool or Manchester.

Although the answer was the provision of well-paid jobs in Wales, the intrusion of second-home owners into the market was a contributory factor, forcing up the rate of emigration by increasing the price of housing. Once acquired as second homes, such properties might be advertised as such in England, but not in Wales; large parts of the housing stock thus never appeared on the local market.

This social problem had been aggravated by the availability of grants. Plaid Cymru had welcomed the Conservative government's intention of ending these grants and hoped that the succeeding Labour government would do so; a failure to abolish grants would result in a major confrontation between central and local government. Plaid Cymru found itself in a very difficult position over the national aspect of second homes, for while the party was not chauvinistic, its aim was to win self-government for Wales and to restore the national civilisation of Wales. These aims were shared by many English people who came to Wales, some as owners of second homes, but more often to live and work there; many such people played an active role in Plaid Cymru.

The expansion of second homes was not only socially unjust; it was also a serious threat to the Welsh language and to the sense of national identity which that language helped to maintain. The situation in respect of the Welsh language was critical; between 1961 and 1971 the number of Welsh speakers fell by over 100,000 or from 26 per cent of the population to 20 per cent. There was selective emigration from the rural areas, very often by the most active and best qualified. English language television, the lack of Welsh education for all but a small minority and the lack of Welsh institutions were major factors. Those buying second homes came from a dominant culture which had all the advantages of mass communication, and this and English education were sufficient to bring about a shift in the linguistic balance in the very strongholds of the Welsh language.

In Plaid Cymru's view, the ownership of second homes had gone too far and should be prohibited in Wales and brought within reasonable balance. Where the proportion of second homes exceeded 10 per cent, measures should be taken to reduce that proportion, through differential rating, with a 50 per cent levy on rates on second homes. If this was not sufficient, the sale of a house to another second-home owner should be subject to a levy of 20 per cent of the difference between the purchase price and the true market price as assessed by the district valuer, such a levy being transferred to the local authority's housing account to pay for houses for those who needed them. For Plaid Cymru agreed that there was too great a concentration of people in council houses, especially in the towns, so the villages were being lost to the Welsh way of life. Ownership of second homes in Wales should be restricted in the interest of social justice and to enable the communities of rural Wales to retain their own language and culture.

The three succeeding contributors were politicians, back-benchers from the Labour, Conservative and Liberal parties. Arthur Blenkinsop, Labour MP for South Shields, who had long connections with planning and conservation and was the author of a book on National Parks, declared his interest as the owner of a static caravan in Northumberland within a forty five minute drive of his home in Newcastle.

He thought that, while the Government had been criticised for its lack of policy, the role of government intervention was difficult, and governments ought not to take unplanned or incautious action, especially when it was uncertain where the line should be drawn. Second homes were not occupied exclusively by the wealthier members of the community. Many people in Northumberland had a place on the Northumbrian coast, which provided a cheap holiday and a summer home; such second homes were often unsatisfactory from a planning viewpoint, especially where they had been built by the owners or developed from a caravan. Definition was vital for any form of government action, and a satisfactory definition posed an immediate problem in giving an effect to the decision to withdraw the fiscal privileges of second-home ownership.

Earlier discussion had rightly brought out the fact that second homes could not be treated in isolation; they were both part of the provision for holidays and tourism and part of the economy of the area. Policies and approaches might well have to be quite different even in various parts of the same county.

In his view, there was, in fact, a range of issues. First, there was the need for more accurate information, though this should not inhibit other action. It was particularly important to get information on demand from as wide a section of the community as possible. Secondly, there were economic and social aspects. It was unacceptable that local people in Wales, the Lake District and elsewhere should be denied the opportunity of getting accommodation within the range of their income by pressures from outside. The problems were neither new nor peculiar to Wales (though the survival of the Welsh language did present special problems). They were also part of the wider consideration of the kind of industry that was urgently needed in such areas and the variety of employment, of which tourism was part. The greater willingness of the farming community to accept the need to see how farming could be reconciled with tourism, recreation and other demands particularly in the hills and areas of marginal farming, was very welcome.

He strongly supported the view that local authorities should use the powers they already had, strengthened as necessary, to acquire suitable property where there was a danger of its being denied to local people. While there would have to be more thought about purpose-built holiday accommodation, the fact that it could be used for only a short period of the year was disturbing. Capital expenditure of this sort was socially unacceptable when resources were scarce. Possibly, as was suggested by one of the tourist boards, such accommodation could be re-let when it was not required. In the changed circumstances, it could no longer be assumed that there would automatically be a rising standard of living, both because of the financial difficulties in the United Kingdom and because of problems of world resources. The price of transport had also increased quite considerably. Such factors might restrict development and provide an opportunity to devise a more rational approach.

Yet the desire for second homes was perfectly proper and, while priority must be given to the local community, ways must also be found of satisfying this natural desire for second homes in some quite simple ways which were not socially offensive and would also help to meet the needs of the local community, perhaps in the way suggested earlier by William Craig.

Two other aspects should be borne in mind. There was the question of environmental standards in such matters as siting, density of development and the provision of facilities. All this must be brought within the planning field to ensure that the natural beauty of an area was not harmed, in the interests both of the inhabitants and of those who came to enjoy it. Such problems might appropriately have been considered by the rural development boards which have now been abolished.

The possibilities for recreation and even second homes should also be examined in some of the areas which were discarded in the process of industrialisation and which could now be restored. He had previously regarded National Parks as places to which one escaped because such a mess had been made of the towns, and which had to have some degree of exclusion to preserve them for the future. In the postwar years it had been recognised that this was too narrow a view and that we should attempt to make both urban and rural areas liveable. A negative and exclusive view of National Parks was no longer justified, for they were special in a positive sort of way and were linked to all our needs, whether urban or rural. If industrial areas, such as his constituency, were looked at in this way, they could serve both an industrial purpose and a recreational purpose, perhaps including even second homes.

Graham Page, formerly Minister for Local Government and Development in the Department of the Environment, gave a Conservative view. He thought that many people had an ambition to own a country cottage or a caravan on the coast and that it would be wrong to sneer at this as a status symbol. It was a very great factor for family happiness, providing a sense of togetherness in the family which could be achieved in no other way and thus serving a real social purpose provided it did not harm others. Because it was a very personal ambition, no government should take special measures either to encourage it, by grants or tax concessions, or to obstruct it (though it would, of course, be affected by policies of general application). In his constituency on Merseyside the second home was not the prerogative of the wealthy, but extended to the docker and the car worker. It was only quite recently that it had been hinted that there was something anti-social about second homes and that it would be better if we were all packed together in a Pontins at Lytham St. Annes or bottled up in a Butlins in Wales. The main reason why this attitude had developed was the greater pressure for second homes arising from easier travel by road, and there was reasonable justification for the complaints from some areas against the inflow of second-home owners, not directed at them individually (for there had been very good integration of the second-home owner and the local population), but generally.

Such complaints had been made on environmental grounds (by which he meant planning) and the mis-use of resources. Problems arose not so much when an existing cottage was acquired as when there were new developments. Planning had often been inadequate and there were many instances where the results of planning decisions had been disastrous. There were positive actions which could be taken to lessen the difficulties caused by the influx of second-home owners into villages and also to satisfy the ambition to own a second home. A major problem was that the infrastructure might be inadequate. It was a long-established practice in urban developments for the developer to put in roads (or at least pay for them) and that practice might be extended to all infrastructure, including that for second-home development, and even perhaps to the community buildings. Such a contribution would certainly lessen resistance by local communities. Of course, the developer might object that he was already contributing by increasing rateable value, but this was a falacious argument, for the local authority had to invest in the infrastructure before receiving any return from the increased rateable value and had to bear interest charges on the investment. He advocated abolishing rates on households by transferring commitments such as education to the national exchequer and by replacing domestic rates with a local income tax. In this way the second-home owner would pay according to his income, rather than on the rateable value of his cottage.

The problem of resources was more difficult to resolve. There was no doubt that in many areas, such as the Lake District, those who wanted second homes often deprived the local population of the opportunity of getting their first homes built by using the available resources of the building industry. Better use of these resources should follow from comprehensive planning, from strategic plans, through structure plans to local plans. The economy of such areas was vital in any consideration of the problem of second homes; but with local revenue and the development of full planning, the resources of an area would be more judiciously used.

The last politician to speak from the platform was Mr. Paul Tyler, Liberal MP for Bodmin. He felt that no other part of Great Britain outside Scotland or Wales was as deeply affected as his constituency, and believed that the second-home problem had effects at two different levels, on housing on the one hand and on social, economic and environmental factors on the other.

The significance of the explosion of second homes on local housing had been changed markedly over the preceding two years, since the Wye survey, by the extraordinary shortage of accommodation which had occurred in the rural areas of Great Britain. Until then, housing shortages had been almost synonymous with the slums of great cities, but this was no longer so; in his constituency there was a problem of homelessness as pressing as in any part of the country. In these circumstances, taxpayers and ratepayers had resented subsidising those making a second home at the expense of people who could not find a first.

In addition to the removal of tax relief on mortgages and improvement grants, domestic rate relief should also go, as Liberals had long advocated; the former had been accepted by the other two parties, but the last should be a top priority for government.

Within the new housing authorities, now bigger and better able to tackle housing problems, it was important to see second homes as part of the housing problem instead of merely as a part of the tourist industry and thus of little significance for housing policy. There were two questions for the audience to consider. If, as was likely with a new government, the question of tied cottages was to be reconsidered, was it not likely that such accommodation would enter the market for second homes rather than the permanent housing stock? To take out of permanent occupation a number of such dwellings would clearly be a step backward. Secondly, what were the effects of the Farm Amalgamation Scheme on buildings and their obsolescence and therefore on their prospective dereliction? He would prefer to see a group of good farm buildings being converted sensitively into a small colony of second homes or managed by the local authority on short let, rather than that they should fall down or be converted into permanent dwellings and so put extraordinary strains on other local services because of their isolation (which might even be an attraction to holidaymakers). In this way, too, pressure on the centres of population, the villages and hamlets, might be relieved.

In the wider sense, what had previously been a passive process, the acquisition of what people did not otherwise want, had acquired an active dynamic of its own. In his constituency this change had taken place some years ago, and he did not think the energy crisis would lead to any levelling off in the demand for second homes. As the motorway programme developed, it would become quite feasible for those living in Birmingham to spend weekends in Dartmoor National Park, and this must surely affect the second-home problem. Indeed, the city *pied-à-terre* might actually be encouraged by the rising costs of transport; for instead of commuting daily from Gloucestershire to London, as some people did, they might prefer to acquire a *pied-à-terre* in London, whilst still retaining their country base. The same might apply to a lesser degree in other cities.

It also seemed likely that the impact of second homes had been over-estimated in the reports. Membership of organisations might not be a good guide to social interaction, for joining a local golf club would probably not make much contribution to the local community. The evidence of the contribution to the local community was also suspect. Respondents might tend to suggest that they spent more than they did, and, in any case, expenditure from the same dwelling in permanent occupation would be very much greater. Even more serious was the old myth that those who rehabilitated second homes made a great contribution to the local environment and saved buildings from dereliction, for the Wye report showed that such improvements were of minor importance.

One very serious aspect was the correlation between second homes and retirement. The effects on the local economy and on the provision of local authority services of second homes developing into a massive concentration of retired people could not be ignored and were a very major problem indeed in Cornwall. By contrast, there were also ghost villages in Cornwall which were deserted in winter. There was a need for some protection against those who were voracious consumers of housing and to some extent of roads and other services, but who made a comparatively small contribution to the local economy. The first requirement was definition and the second control. Definition was a problem for the academics and Michael Dower did not think it was insuperable. If it become politically necessary, a definition would be found which would be satisfactory for legislation. The first requirement for control would be to make the change from first home to second home and vice versa a change of use (as it was in fact) within the meaning of the General Development Order.

Other points were made in discussion in which a wider range of interests was expressed. Sam Edwards, a planner, speaking in his personal capacity on the basis of surveys in southwest England, agreed with Michael Dower that no statutory definition was possible and that only the owner could say what he regarded as his second home. He also had reservations about the inclusion of static caravans, which were not regarded as part of a housing stock; indeed, most touring caravans were static in front gardens for the greater part of the year. He was also unhappy about Michael Dower's replacement of an emphasis on recreation by one on tourism and wondered how much of the expenditure by owners of second homes in Denbighshire provided local income; in any case, the estimate of the number of jobs which second homes provided in Wales was very small compared with employment in tourism in southwest England.

William Foster, of the National Caravan Council, understandably took a different view about static caravans, some of which were accepted by the Government as residential developments. He wondered whether caravans were politically more acceptable as second homes than the use of the existing stock of housing (a point which Dafydd Williams later confirmed, though Plaid Cymru would not like to see development of any kind). He doubted whether holiday villages would provide the peace and quiet many people sought. Small-scale development could be provided by farmers without any great loss of amenity. He accepted that there were some terrible caravans and a working party was examining the design of static caravans.

The importance of regarding second homes as part of the housing stock, subject to the same dynamics and the same forces as the remainder, was emphasised by Professor Anthony Travis, Director of the Centre for Urban and Regional Studies at Birmingham University. He noted that the scale of the second-home problem was only about one-third as large as retirement to the coast, and there was an important link in the extent to which second homes became, through retirement, first homes. Another aspect about which information was needed was the extent to which second homes were rented to other people, thereby appreciably increasing the stock of tourist accommodation. He also asked, in the context of demands in a number of European countries (such as Denmark) for the identification of areas of coast and countryside for retirement and recreational use, whether such areas, where development was environmentally, economically and socially acceptable, could be identified in Great Britain.

David Hellard, of the Land Use Department of the National Farmers Union, agreed that second homes were part of the wider question of rural development. It had to be accepted that tourism was bringing or could bring revenue to rural areas and, if such revenue was lacking, some thought should be given to ensuring that it came. He wondered whether a distinction between second homes and tourist accommodation was valid, and whether the farming community might not be able to help in a situation where there appeared to be a limited supply of second homes but a strong demand for a rural retreat. Could not more extended use be made of such retreats by sharing, by club membership and in other ways?

The multi-faceted nature of the second-home problem and the consequent need for multi-faceted solutions were noted by David Bailey, of the Farrell/Grimshaw Partnership. Individuals acting on their own behalf led to the growth of what had come to be quite sizeable commercial enterprises, which in turn led to a loss of revenue from the area. Some investigations should be made of the ability of local communities to increase their control over second-home developments; such investigations could consider the *Rent an Irish cottage* scheme, where government loans were combined with local shareholding to involve local people in second homes, and the development of commercial enterprises to provide professional services to local landowners over the conversion or development of their own estates.

A tourist viewpoint was presented by John Brown, of the Heart of England Tourist Board, who thought second homes were a management problem. He saw the large investment by the public as providing an opportunity in terms of recreation and tourism, for second homes could house other visitors when they were not in use by their owners, and the sale of second homes could help to finance recreational projects on a larger scale, such as sports complexes and recreational developments in relation to new reservoirs. These opportunities had to be taken, for second homes were competing with other outlets for discretionary expenditure, such as a second car or a swimming pool in the first home, though these did not benefit the community to the same degree. Such investments should not compete for local resources, but should be used for the benefit of the local community. The question of occupancy rates was also important, and the tourist boards had identified a huge and increasing demand for short-stay self-catering accommodation, which represented a great social need and a pressure which would have to be relieved. This demand was a potential source of finance for the building of second homes of a socially beneficial kind, which would result in better use of the accommodation built and reduce the amount of land required. The tourist boards could act as letting agencies for such accommodation.

E.R. Heaton, of Greenfield Homes Ltd., thought there was a wider range of incomes within regions than between regions. Low incomes were largely a consequence of the predominance of agriculture and forestry, and the provision of employment in services and manufacture could do much to improve the situation. Because of differences in land prices, adequate housing could be provided at appreciably lower cost than near the conurbations, and such building would itself provide substantial income to the local community.

To Pat Rust, Chief Executive of Wychavon District Council, discussion had not sufficiently differentiated between holiday and leisure accommodation on the one hand and someone's home on the other. The real issue concerned properties suitable for permanent occupation but used for leisure, possibly to the detriment of the local population. The definitions adopted had aggravated the apparent importance of this problem, and he wondered whether there was, in fact, a national problem. In Wychavon District the pressures on rural communities did not come from owners of second homes but from those coming into the District to settle who were prepared to commute long distances and could similarly outbid local people. If tied cottages were released onto the housing market, they would certainly become first, not second, homes.

It was the purchase of second homes with a view to retirement which worried Henry Jones, Deputy Planning Officer of Gwynedd. In the Caernarvonshire study (Pyne 1973), 65 per cent of respondents had expressed their intention of retiring to their second homes in rural areas and villages. The county already had difficulty in providing sufficient money for support services and the demand would greatly increase in the future; planning permission had already been given for an additional 3,000 second homes in the old county. There would have to be greater control over second homes. Second homes, built for personal use and for letting to others, were putting pressure on the resources of the county; they were adding to the stock of housing accommodation but not providing any great economic benefit to local workers. The county was reaching saturation point, but they were still adding to the stock of second homes. District councils would have to look at the total problem and secure houses for local needs, but it was doubtful whether they had adequate finance to deal with the problem or sufficient control over planning. It was difficult to refuse planning permission on environmental grounds, and a justification for such refusals might well have to be that the proposed development was to provide a second home.

These points were reiterated by R.L. Powell, a planner with the Isle of Anglesey District Council, for in Anglesey the land allocated for housing for the local population and essential immigration had been acquired by the more affluent members of the British population. If the district planning authorities were given more finance to purchase land for the provision of housing for those living in the area, they would be in the position to control all housing. If finance was not available, some kind of mini-nationalisation would be necessary. Something had to be done if the Welsh language and the cultural identity of Wales were to be preserved. Mr. Page had criticised the planners, but much of the blame lay on central government. Dwellings could be increased by up to 49 cu.m (1,750 cu.ft) without planning permission and these developments often marred the character of villages. All concerned were slaves to building regulations which must be applied with discretion if effective planning was to take place. The Secretary of State did not help by his lack of support for planners over appeals on design.

In Derbyshire, by contrast, according to Neil Forrest of the County Planning Department, there had been some controversy arising from the kind of social problem associated with second homes, with outsiders bidding-up prices for properties beyond the range of young people, but a survey by the Department and the Peak Park Planning Board had shown surprisingly low levels of second-home ownership, below 0.5 per cent for the whole county. The problems here were due to commuters to the nearby conurbations.

In the Highlands and Islands Development Board's territory, J.G.L. Adams, reported similar social and economic problems, with local people being priced out of the housing market. A pattern was emerging where the local people would end up in local authority housing and the private properties would be occupied by incomers, whether retired or owners of second homes. The problems were aggravated by the high cost of building in the Highlands, which had been further accentuated by the discovery of oil in the North Sea. An additional factor was that many of the homes owned by local people fell below tolerable standards, and the government had decided to discontinue the improvement grants given by the Highland Board.

In reply to these comments, Arthur Blenkinsop doubted if one group of second homes could be isolated from another; there were multiple interactions and it was necessary to take account of all factors. Graham Page similarly thought it was impossible to separate provision for housing and leisure; he also believed that the problems arising from second homes should not be tackled by planning conditions. Design, too, was so much a personal matter. Paul Tyler emphasised that housing stock had become an increasingly precious asset and large resources could not justifiably be used to convert existing properties to second homes or to build new homes.

Professor G.P. Wibberley, Ernest Cook Professor of Countryside Planning at Wye College and University College, London, summed up the conference. He recalled that the Wye College investigation of second homes which he directed was one in which, as the subject unfolded, he began to lose his objectivity and become emotionally and aesthetically involved. The members of the team believed they were studying a fairly simple problem which was part of tourism and outdoor recreation, but the subject was changing while they investigated it. At the beginning they thought they were examining a scatter of isolated cottages which were surplus to the needs of agriculture and the rural community; by the end they found they were in a very difficult sector of the wider field of housing, with the second home changing and becoming a direct competitor with the village house and the country town house (for every country town of quality was being combed for potential second homes). He felt personally involved, too, because he had been born and bred on the Welsh Border, where he was surrounded by young people trying to get out of the kind of properties which were now second homes; so he accepted at the beginning that these were properties from which any decent person would want to get away, even if they were now being sought by the social isolates who were a product of urbanisation. At the same time, he had himself become the owner of a second home on that same Welsh Border for the kind of reasons that Michael Dower had already indicated - ties with his background and with relatives, the desire to let his children have the experience, and a hobby interest in restoring old properties. When he heard criticisms of the owners of second homes, he thought of the very strong ties that developed in a property that was surplus to one's needs and yet seemed to become an important part of one's own development.

As the research developed it become quite clear that the supply of suitable properties fell far short of the demand for them. It could not plausibly be argued that the British were different in their behaviour from the French, the Swedes or the Americans and it had to be accepted that there was a very big potential demand for second homes,for whatever the actual percentage and however second homes were defined, the rates of second-home ownership were very much lower than in many other countries. While such a large unsatisfied demand presented a problem, it would not be a problem if it was anticipated and if ways were developed of handling it.

Should the British do what other countries have done - let existing properties, permit custom-built housing, allow owners of first homes to fight against owners of second homes, and accept the situation found in southeast England where places within 40-50 miles (64-80 km) of London were full of second-home owners? Or should we regard this as just one more manifestation of a very great neglect by planners and others of the real nature of rural development in the United Kingdom? We had to stop thinking that all problems in planning and land use were basically urban, that the countryside would look after itself, that agriculture was a tremendous force for conservation, that the forester would maintain amenity and that the innate character of the villages would ensure a balanced community. This was rubbish and full of the myths strongly held by the English, though less so by the Welsh and the Scots. If things were left alone, practically every village, whether close to the conurbations or far away in Wales and Scotland, would become full of second-home owners, of retired people, and of both long- and short-distance commuters; the local inhabitants would end up living in council houses and all the existing properties and new homes would be occupied by new people. The second home was just one part of the rural continuum; there was a planning problem for all rural communities and no planning authority worth its salt could continue to treat each matter on its merits and thus, in practice, leave the rural areas alone. In the discussion it had been accepted that villages had to be planned to achieve something which would not happen by itself. There was a widespread feeling, perhaps a London approach, that these matters were of minor importance and should be left alone, and that the rural community would not be exploited. The development of second homes in the West Indies had shown clearly what happened when free-for-all development of second homes took place, in an area where the structure of both local and central government was weak and people could do exactly what they wanted. The development of second homes, the use of someone else's environment, was a very exploitive situation, and one which was clearly seen where there were no controls. Mr. Williams of Plaid Cymru was quite right to regard the situation as potentially very exploitative and to demand much more evidence that it was beneficial. Not enough was known about the effects of second-home developments on rural communities, for such information was difficult to get, and it had not been possible in the Wye study to explore this topic adequately. A particular matter of concern was the small size of the multiplier in all studies which had sought to measure it. There had been some gross exaggerations by consultants in the West Indies, for example, and all figures should be regarded with suspicion. It seemed that, while a considerable quantity of money might be spent by owners of second homes (and by tourists), the money left the area very quickly; this was particularly a problem of the remoter parts of the country. Thus it was necessary to examine all the suggestions made by Mr. Page and others for erecting some kind of obstacle which would impede this flow and retain some of the beneficial effects in the locality. In this context, the experience of the Ozarks in the 1930s was particularly relevant. This was an area of poor land and poor agriculture from which large numbers of farmers were leaving because they could not make an acceptable income. Since the Second World War the Ozarks had become a tourist area of considerable wealth, much of it derived from second homes. The basic reason was that local taxes had made it possible to retain in the area much of the money that came to the Ozarks. The Welsh Nationalists were quite right to ask for this kind of solution.

The conference had generally supported the idea that there should be continued monitoring of changes in second homes, though there were difficulties because many people hid the fact that they had second homes and the use they made of them. There was not only a problem of definition but there was also a difficulty of getting information generally. Secondly, a strong case had been made for much more positive planning, as part of rural structure planning. So many villages were becoming one-class villages of one kind or another. What Mr. Williams was rightly saying was that if many Welsh villages became very full of middle-class owners of second homes, the Welsh local authorities would have very great difficulty in getting industry into those areas. Many second-home owners, retired people and commuters in English villages were becoming very obstructive and difficult about industries that made a little noise or created a little dust. In one village, a local housing association which would have brought much needed accommodation to lower-income groups was very effectively prevented. The middle class was a very great danger in many villages.

Lastly, it was necessary to consider alternative ways of improving the situation. In this context, attempts to increase farm-based recreation were particularly to be welcomed, for there were many farmers, especially in the poorer and more isolated areas, who needed supplementary income. It would be very helpful if this strong need to associate oneself with both urban and rural areas could be linked to an existing farm. Of course, if this approach was to be successful, planning authorities would have to think much more flexibly about the changes to farm buildings that could be permitted.

A further need was a Department of the Environment which would take more notice of the rural environment and appreciate that it was changing in all kinds of sophisticated and unusual ways; it was also necessary for the department to monitor the rural environment as carefully as the urban. It should become concerned with the rural economy and not look upon the countryside merely as a place to which people went from time to time and where they occasionally worried about the hills and about one or two pretty villages. The whole basis of the rural community was changing and something very unsatisfactory would result unless the countryside was as consciously planned as were new residential areas.

It is not surprising that many of the points made at this conference have also been made in the preceding chapters of this book, although on this occasion the actors themselves spoke at first hand. The contributions confirm Michael Dower's dictum that attitudes were based partly on fact, partly on emotion and partly on principle. Little can be done to alter emotions or principles (though hopefully they are, to some degree, amenable to reason), but there is a considerable scope for improving the information available, a point which was generally conceded. It must be admitted that information is often difficult to obtain, partly because of administrative weaknesses, but also because it is in the nature of second-home ownership that owners should often wish to conceal both the existence and location of their second homes and the use they make of them; it is also possible that, as was asserted, they do exaggerate the contribution which they make to the local economy, the quality of their interactions with local communities, or the degree of their affinity with them. The fact that second homes have become a political plaything makes it likely that these tendencies will be strengthened. Nevertheless, without adequate information, adequate policies can hardly be expected. A greal deal depends on solutions to the problem of definition and these, too, will not be easy; for it is also of the nature of second homes that they form part of a continuum, whether this is seen as an urban/rural continuum, a housing/tourism continuum, a work/leisure continuum or a work/retirement continuum. Similar and equally great difficulties arise in trying to differentiate between various kinds of second homes, and there will always be arbitrary lines to be drawn.

Despite the strong feelings often expressed about second homes and their owners, there was a fairly general recognition that second homes did fulfil a real need, and Gerald Wibberley emphasised, from personal experience, the strength of the bond that developed with a home which was surplus to one's needs and yet seemed to become an essential part of one's own development. This need seems to be primarily urban, for there appear to be few owners or occupiers of second homes among the rural community, although this may be an illusion arising from lack of evidence; in any case, the changing character of farming (as with the suitcase farmer of the North American wheat belt) and of the rural population (with an increasing proportion of those who live in the countryside from choice and work elsewhere) may well be altering this situation. What is clear is the paucity of soundly based studies of the motivations of second-home owners in respect of both the decision to acquire a second home and the choice of locality, and of the attitudes of local communities. Such motivations need to be explored in depth, for there seem to be discrepancies between what people say and what they do; while there appears to be a general desire to get away from it all, there is also an unwillingness, among a large majority, to choose remote locations (which may be a function of accessibility) and to forego the amenities of civilisation. As Roy Wolfe has shown, the ideal is the illusion of isolation, with neighbours just round the corner (1965, p.7). Similarly, it is necessary to establish what members of a community feel about second homes, and while there have been valuable pioneer inquiries, there are grounds for doubting whether the opinions expressed by politicians, gatekeepers or special interest groups are truly representative. Both kinds of investigation thus need a sound statistical base.

There is an equally urgent need for studies of the impact of second homes, to settle the disputes about the benefits or otherwise they bring and to resolve the question, posed by Gerald Wibberley, whether the income accruing locally stays long in that locality. Of course, a great deal will depend on the frame of reference chosen, since the smaller the area, the smaller the multiplier is likely to be: Gwynedd is likely to benefit proportionately more than Abersoch, and Wales more than Gwynedd. Levels of use need a firmer base; the employment of estimates of visitor-days will give a more accurate indication of occupancy by comparison with other forms of accommodation for leisure and recreation. More objective measures are also needed of levels of expenditure, which need to be matched by complementary information on sales. The same is true of other interactions, most of which remain at the level of assertion, e.g., the additional rate revenue resulting from second homes, the level of expenditure on the provision of additional services and, though more difficult, the costs of congestion and loss of amenity where these occur. How far do purchasers of second homes actually deprive local residents of the kind of accommodation that they both want and could afford? How far is the differential rise in house prices, if substantiated, a consequence of competition between prospective second-home owners for accommodation that members of the local community do not want to purchase? How far do occupiers of second homes bring food from home and purchase little locally? How common is competition between them and local inhabitants, such as that for scarce supplies of water, which Hugh Clout (1974, pp.119-20) describes in the Paris Basin? There is similarly a need for more objective assessments of the social interaction, including the views of representative samples of both incomers and local residents (who must themselves not be incomers at one remove). It must also be asked how many of the alleged adverse effects of second homes belong to the realm of mythology, or are little more than a rationalisation of the dislike felt by at least some members of one community for at least some members of another, such as Welsh for English, or even members of a rural community for incomers of any kind. Again it is probable that the answers will vary from country to country, and even from region to region. Thus, while in Great Britain it appears to be the inhabitants of the remoter areas who are most vocal about second homes, in France the loudest protests appear to come from the Paris Basin and the mayors of the Auvergne spoke favourable of the effects of second homes (Clout 1970, pp.43-8).

The identification of solutions depends in part on better information in all these respects. The first requirement must be an appraisal of the potential supply, and the situation in this respect is vastly different in the various countries of Europe, let alone on either side of the Atlantic. Thus, whereas there is still potentially a very considerable supply of surplus farm accommodation in some European countries (even if it is not necessarily in the right place), as farm reorganisation proceeds, as rural emigration continues and as older people remaining in the rural areas die, this does not generally appear to be the case in Great Britain. It is an interesting contrast that, while the main component of the supply of second homes in North America has long been the purpose-built home, Roy Wolfe has noted, in the postwar period, the increasing importance of abandoned farmsteads in Ontario. Even within Great Britain, there are likely to be considerable regional differences, depending partly on the character of the countryside and its nearness to the sea or other water, partly on location in respect of the main centres of population (and here changing accessibility resulting from developments in the trunk-road and motorway networks must be borne in mind) and partly on the type of accommodation and the attitudes of landowners; empty rural dwellings certainly exist in Fife and Berwickshire, where the traditional farm dwellings, in blocks of four, six, or eight cottages adjoining the steading, are not particularly attractive to prospective owners of second homes and may remain empty; there are also large landowners who do not wish to see the fragmentation of their estates through sales of individual properties.

A second requirement is realistic assessments of demand, and this must be related to the motivations of prospective second-home owners and the degree to which one kind of accommodation is a substitute for another; it is not possible to make such assessments on a local basis, given the nature of travellers to second homes and the flexibility which the motor car provides. Estimates of future demands must always be difficult, especially in a field which is wholly dependent on discretionary expenditure and subject to change of fashion.

Thirdly, there is the need for clear guidelines from central government, though these too must partly wait on a better understanding of what exists, how it is changing and what its implications are. Above all, it is necessary to see second homes as part of the rural economy and not something in isolation. It has been variously suggested that governments should neither encourage nor discourage second homes, or that they should actively discourage them in areas of congestion or where the local community is being adversely affected, the last point being one on which there was universal agreement at the conference; avoiding local conflicts may require some contribution to the cost of an adequate infrastructure. If it is accepted that the demand for second homes is something which must be satisfied in some way (and it is difficult to see how any policy could suppress it in all its forms or avoid, because of its multi-faceted nature, unintended side effects, such as the intolerable congestion which would probably arise through a vast increase in mobile caravans), then the need is to provide solutions which both satisfy the aspirations of potential owners of second homes and the reasonable needs of local communities. The solution which increasingly seems to commend itself to planners is the concentration of second homes in holiday villages, whether on the relatively small scale envisaged by William Craig, or the much larger schemes which are characteristic of the United States at the present time (Ragatz 1969), in serviced (and in America fenced and guarded) estates in the countryside (Parsons 1972), or in concrete blocks of flats, as in La Motte, to the west of the Rhône Delta (Hall 1973, p.215). Such developments represent a widespread trend in many countries and may well reflect the tendency to *move up the market* (Chap. 8). There is no doubt that this approach offers many advantages in servicing second homes, in protecting the environment and possibly in saving land; it permits the construction of recreational facilities (such as golf courses and lakes) which cannot readily be provided for scattered second homes; and it may possibly reduce adverse interactions with the local community; but is this what prospective owners of second homes want?

An alternative solution is the provision of accommodation to let for short periods, or the granting of permission to construct second homes on condition that they should be made available to others when not required by the owner; but this may conflict with the desire to own a place of one's own and the likelihood of greater use as the amount of leisure time increases. The clearest need seems to be some kind of national recreational strategy, as in Denmark and Sweden, in which certain areas are identified as vulnerable and inappropriate for the development of second homes or other recreational developments, while other areas of countryside and coast are seen as suitable. Planners must not only look at the whole range of housing stock; they must also look at all the motivations which lead people to acquire both first and second homes. As the discussion suggested, some of the complaints that are levelled against second homes are more properly levelled against incomers of any kind, whether they wish to retire there or to commute to work places elsewhere, and discriminating against different kinds of purchasers of first homes will be much more difficult. There is clearly a trend towards retirement in areas which attract second homes, and policies which ignored these situations by trying to solve only the second-home problem would not pop the genie back into the bottle. It is also important that the areal frame be widened. It is curious that the acquisition of second homes in other countries received only passing mention at the conference, yet the development of the European Economic Community, with the prospect of unfettered transfer of capital, may accentuate the trends which already exist for the British, the Dutch, the Germans, the Scandinavians and others to acquire second homes on the Mediterranean Coast and elsewhere, while the acquisition by Americans of second homes in Canada or the West Indies are already controversial issues.

The more distant future is much more difficult to foresee. If the scenario sketched by Brian Berry (1970) and others materialises, the distinction, already far from clear, between first and second homes will be further attenuated as the lengthening of available leisure time and the changing character of work enable a steadily increasing proportion of the population to live where they choose, rather than close to their work, and so place a premium on locations which are attractive but remote. A prolonged period of inflation may accentuate the trend towards the purchase of land as an end in itself, which seems to be a major component in the recreational land market in the United States, and, to a lesser extent, in Australia. Perhaps the electronic age and the wonders of holography will obviate the need for second homes and make it a matter of indifference where we live, since we may be able to simulate our ideal environment (or in fact a whole family of environments) in our own first home.

REFERENCES

Berry, B.J.L. (1970) 'The geography of the United States in the year 2000', Transactions of the Institute of British Geographers, 51, pp.21-54.

Bielckus, C.L., Rogers, A.W. and Wibberley, G.P. (1972) Second Homes in England and Wales, Studies in Rural Land Use, No. 11, Wye College (University of London).

Clout, H.D. (1970) 'Social aspects of second home occupation in the Auvergne', Planning Outlook 9, pp.33-49.

Clout, H.D. (1974) 'The growth of second-home ownership: an example of personal suburbanisation', in J.H. Johnson (ed) Suburban Growth, Wiley, London.

Downing, P. and Dower, M. (1973) Second Homes in England and Wales, Countryside Commission, HMSO, London.

Hall, J.M. (1973) 'Europe's seaside: a landscape of leisure', Built Environment 2, pp.215-18.

Jacobs, C.A.J. (1972) Second Homes in Denbighshire, Tourism and Recreation Research Report No. 3, Denbighshire County Council, Ruthin.

Parsons, J.J. (1972) 'Slicing up the open space: subdivisions without homes in northern California', Erdkunde, 26, pp.1-8.

Pyne, C.B. (1973) Second Homes, Caernarvonshire County Planning Department, Caernarvon.

Ragatz, R.L. (1969) The Vacation Home Market: an Unrecognised Factor in Outdoor Recreation and Rural Development, Bulletin No. 4, New York State College of Human Ecology, Cornell University, Ithaca.

Wolfe, R.I. (1965) 'About cottages and cottagers', Landscape, 15, pp.6-8.

INDEX

It is the nature of second homes that they should be related to a wide range of interests; to simplify this index, an asterisk has been placed after all entries that require the words and/or second homes (summer cottage, vacation home, etc.) to be understood. Since most of the chapters have a direct geographical frame, the entries have not been subdivided by countries. It can generally be assumed that entries on pages covered by each of these chapters refers to that area, viz., Canada (esp. Ontario), pp.17-32; Scandinavia (esp. Sweden); pp.35-44; France, pp.47-60; Czechoslavakia, pp.63-73; Caribbean (esp. Montserrat), pp.75-83; England and Wales, pp.85-100; Argyll, pp.103-15; Australia (esp. New South Wales), pp.119-34; Belgium, pp.139-45; Wales, pp.147-52; Ontario, pp.165-78; and United States, pp.181-92.

Other Titles of Interest *(cont.)*

FALUDI, A.
Planning Theory

FRIEND, J. K. & JESSOP, W. N.
Local Government and Strategic Choice, 2nd Edition

GOODALL, B.
The Economics of Urban Areas

HART, D. A.
Strategic Planning in London: The Rise and Fall of the Primary Road Network

LEE, C.
Models in Planning

LICHFIELD, N. et al.
Evaluation in the Planning Process

MOSELEY, M. J.
Growth Centres in Spatial Planning

SANT, M. E. C.
Industrial Movement and Regional Development: The British Case

SOLESBURY, W.
Policy in Urban Planning

STARKIE, D. N. M.
Transportation Planning, Policy and Analysis